I
TASTE
RED

THE SCIENCE
OF TASTING WINE

JAMIE GOODE

UNIVERSITY OF
CALIFORNIA PRESS

A Fine Wine Editions book

University of California Press, one of the most distinguished university presses
in the United States, enriches lives around the world by advancing scholarship in
the humanities, social sciences, and natural sciences. Its activities are supported
by the UC Press Foundation and by philanthropic contributions from individuals
and institutions. For more information, visit www.ucpress.edu.

University of California Press
Oakland, California

Library of Congress Control Number: 2016939465

ISBN: 978-0-520-29224-6

This book was produced by
Fine Wine Editions Ltd.
The Old Brewery
6 Blundell Street
London N7 9BH

Project Editor	Sophie Blackman
Editor	Frank Ritter
Designer	Josse Pickard
Illustrations	Alice Potter
Proofreader	Joanne Murray
Indexer	Ruth Ellis
Production Manager	Anna Pauletti
Editorial Director	Ruth Patrick
Publisher	Philip Cooper

Color reproduction by Bright Arts, Hong Kong.
Printed in China by C&C Offset Printing Co., LTD.

25 24 23 22 21 20 19 18 17 16
10 9 8 7 6 5 4 3 2 1

Contents

Introduction

Take a bottle of wine. Open it. Pour a glass. Take a sip. Think about the experience, and then try to jot down a few notes on what you are experiencing. This is the process of tasting wine, and it forms a large part of what I do for a living. Most people do this simply for pleasure, and drinking wine is usually a pleasurable process. But what is really going on here? On the surface, it is all quite simple. We have a tongue that tastes and a nose that smells, and as we drink wine these two sensory systems detect molecules in the wine that our brain interprets as various smells and tastes. We are also affected by the alcohol that wine contains. But that is an incredibly simplistic view of what is really taking place.

This is a book about wine tasting. But it is a very different treatment of the topic to one you might find in textbooks and wine education courses. And while the focus is on wine, it is actually more broad ranging than that: I am attempting to use wine as a way of exploring the way in which we perceive the world around us. This requires the combination of several disciplines, each of which provides a different lens for us to explore this intellectually stimulating subject. We will be dipping into the worlds of physiology, psychology, neuroscience, and philosophy.

The wine is a whole, and we experience it as a whole. While it is convenient to break down wine into its component parts in order to understand it better—just as it suits scientists to split our conscious perception into discrete sensory systems—this division is somewhat arbitrary. I prefer to take a more holistic approach. After all, as we drink wine we experience it as a unitary sensation; inputs from several senses are combined without us realizing it.

The research process for this book began a few years ago, but as it has intensified over the last few months, I have been amazed by what I have learned. The story of how we experience wine is a wonderfully complicated and rich one. What I have learned has also made me pose questions about the nature of experience itself.

There is an unspoken assumption in the wine trade that tasting is a skill that can be learned, and that as you become more proficient in it you will get closer and closer to understanding, or "getting," the wine you are tasting. It is believed that there is a "true" interpretation of the wine, and the best tasters will get pretty close to achieving it. If you study for specialized wine qualifications, such as Master Sommelier or Master of Wine, you are taught and examined by people who are more experienced than you. Implicit in this practice is an understanding that these people, further down the road in terms of experience and expertise, are right about the wines, and that if you perform well and grow in competence you will grow ever closer to the position they hold in relation to any particular wine.

I do not dispute that some people are gifted tasters, and that these and others may have extensive wine experience, but I am not convinced that there is always a single true or valid interpretation of any particular wine. For a start, we all differ in terms of our biology: we each have a different suite of olfactory receptors, and there are well-documented inter-individual differences in taste perception. Also, wine tasting is an aesthetic process, and we all bring different experiences, expectations, and context to the wine when we come to sample it.

The tasting process of a highly regarded magazine and website, *The World of Fine Wine*, demonstrates this issue perfectly. For each tasting, three individuals take part. There is usually one person with specific expertise in the region, and two experienced generalists; in some cases there may be more than one specialist. Their individual scores and notes are recorded, alongside a group score that combines them. But when it comes to fine, interesting wine, it is rare to see much agreement between the scores. What are we to conclude? Are these tasters incompetent and performing poorly? We would like to think not, because they are experienced professionals. Do they have different preferences? Yes, that could be a partial explanation, because as much as we tasters try to set aside our preferences, we cannot. To distinguish a liking from an appreciation of quality is tough for most of us, although it would be nice to think that it is possible to do so.

None of this suggests that all wine tasting is completely subjective and that anything goes, or that notions of wine quality are entirely arbitrary and personal. The issue of subjectivity versus objectivity in wine tasting is an interesting and important one, and later in this book I will discuss it at length.

I am also going to be arguing that it is time the wine trade adapted and modernized its model for wine tasting. The practice of experiencing wine is richer and more complex than we previously thought, and the growing research on the multimodal perception of flavor is highly relevant to what we do almost every day: taste wine and share our perceptions with others.

As with any text that draws heavily on academic studies, there is a danger that the reader might find this book stodgy and hard to read, worthy but dull. I am aware of this potential problem and so have deliberately kept a brighter tone and introduced a narrative thread through the chapters. Also, for this reason I have decided not to reference the research studies and scientific papers that I have drawn on. While I have tried to give the authors credit, I feel that such references make books seem overly scientific, and that is likely to put people off. However, I have included a bibliography and reference section at the end of the book for those who would like to delve deeper.

On another level, I have been wary of the tendency of popular science books to use a sort of confirmation bias, where exciting, sexy research gets special emphasis, and huge leaps are made ahead of the data in the name of a good story. The publication of a paper in a scientific journal does not always mean that it is true; sometimes peer review (where scientists assess the work of other scientists) will fail, and sometimes scientists extrapolate beyond what their data actually show. I have tried to be careful in this regard, and I hope that what I have written is balanced and, as far as possible, has a sense of perspective.

I was recently discussing the perception of wine with a well-known wine writer of the old school. We were talking about the familiar subject of sweet wines tasting less sweet as they age; the French call this "eating the sugar." The phenomenon has defied explanation for a long time because, as far as we know, the sugar level stays the same as sweet wines age. I suggested an explanation based on the way our brains process taste and smell information, and the way in which these inputs are combined even before we are aware of them. In young, sweet wines, the aromas are very bright and fruity. We use this information from our noses to interpret what we are experiencing on our palates: as the tongue tastes the sugar, the fruity aromas make us think that this really is a very sweet wine. Research has shown that "sweet smells" make people rate a sugar solution as more sweet; indeed, simply imagining a sweet smell can cause people to increase their sweetness ratings.

As the wine ages, its fruity aromas diminish and the savory aromas of mature wine take over. The sugar detected by our tongues is the same, but we interpret the wine as less sweet because of the information received by our noses. We are quite unconscious of how our opinion is being influenced. The writer's response was one of incredulity. "You are having us all as fools," he said. I did not respond but, in truth, when it comes to our perceptions, we often *are* fools. Our brains are tricking us, but we trust what we perceive to be reality. How the brain processes sensory information is one of the main themes of this book.

So, with wine tasting as the test case, this book is a wide-ranging exploration of the nature of perception itself. And while this book is about tasting wine, much of what is discussed is broadly relevant to the perception of flavor in general. It is no accident that people who really like wine are often very interested in other flavor experiences, too. We will begin our journey by looking at synesthesia, a phenomenon in which data from the senses is jumbled up. While it is quite rare to have synesthetic experiences, which might include perceiving sounds in terms of colors, or indeed colors in terms of sounds, it seems that even those of us who are not synesthetes (people who experience synesthesias, often from birth onward) commonly experience the world in ways that combine the evidence of our different senses. It follows that the senses are not as separate as we have been led to believe.

What Does Red Taste Of?

Synesthesia is the remarkable phenomenon in which stimulation of one sensory modality is registered as the perception of another sense. This seems strange—almost inexplicable—but it reveals something about how our sensory systems work. It busts the myth that we are operating like measuring devices. And it is a great place to begin in our exploration of the flavor of wine.

Merging of the Senses

In his book, *The Man Who Tasted Shapes* (1993), neurologist Richard Cytowic describes the case of Michael Watson, one of his patients. The neurologist, who was also Watson's neighbor, had been invited around for dinner. Watson revealed his synesthesia to Cytowic by stating, "there aren't enough points on the chicken," as he was preparing the meal. For Watson, flavors have distinct shapes, and he wanted his chicken to have pointed shapes; instead it was coming out round. His world was very different to that of most people, because for him flavor was associated with shapes, which in some cases he could physically feel. This extended to wine. "The whole vocabulary of wine sounds silly, you know, because most people have to describe one thing in terms of another," said Watson. "Describing some wine as earthy is not poetic to me because it can literally be like holding a clod of dirt in my hand."

Sean Day is another synesthete, as well as being president of the American Association of Synesthesia. Day has what is known as congenital multiple synesthesia. He has three types that have been with him since birth. He experiences music, flavor, and smell along with a concurrent experience of shapes, movements, and colors. Day reports that dairy products produce shades of blue, and he is more likely to consider coffee if it is in dark green packaging, beef in dark blue packaging, or chicken in sky blue.

Day, who writes widely on the topic, also reports a very interesting case of synesthesia in relation to flavor. An English friend of his, James Wannerton, has phoneme-to-flavor synesthesia. For him, some speech sounds produce corresponding flavors. For example, the hard "g" sound in the words "argue" and

"begin" produces the flavor of yoghurt; the combination of the "s" and "p" sounds in the words "super" or "peace" results in him tasting tomato soup. Because Wannerton's synesthesia began when he was a child, the flavors that he tastes in response to words are those of the foods he ate when he was young.

In 2005, researcher Lutz Jäncke and his colleagues from the University of Zurich published their findings on a synesthete called Elizabeth Sulston, a twenty-seven-year-old professional musician. As she began to learn music formally, she noted that particular tone intervals caused characteristic taste sensations on her tongue. Interestingly, beside this highly unusual intervals-to-taste synesthesia, she also has tone-to-color synesthesia, which is more common.

It is hard for the majority of us who do not experience synesthesia to imagine what these sorts of experiences must be like. They are more than just the associations we might make across senses. For synesthetes, the mixing of the senses is involuntary and concurrent. This means that they have no control over it, and the extra sensation occurs alongside the "real"

Banana Trees
Road Goat
Hat Strawberry

The Mixing of Colors and Words

The most common form of synesthesia is known as lexical synesthesia. In this condition, a word (the inducing stimulus) confers a color experience (the concurrent perception). For people with lexical synesthesia, specific words will automatically have a matching color. However, individuals vary in the colors that they experience when they hear the same word spoken.

sensation, with no delay. This is so different from the experience of "normal" people that synesthetes have commonly kept their unusual ability secret. For them, the blending of senses is very real.

Why are we talking about this topic in a book about wine tasting? Because as a window to how we perceive the outside world, synesthesia offers highly relevant insights into the subject.

Synesthesia was not taken seriously by scientists until there arrived a way to test individuals' self-reporting of their experience. The "Test of Genuineness" devised by Simon Baron-Cohen and his colleagues legitimized this field for study. The key aspect of synesthesia that makes it different from the sort of crossmodal experiences normal to all is the fact that the sensory stimulus (the inducer) reliably elicits not only the normal sensory experience, but also an inappropriate sensation (the concurrent). Overall, there are thought to be some sixty different types of synesthesia, but the most common form is when the sensation of particular colors is associated with written or spoken letters, digits, or words. This is known as lexical synesthesia, where words (the inducing stimulus) confer color experiences (the concurrent perception) on an individual in a reliable, reproducible fashion. This is quite different from the way the word "red" might cause us to "see" in our mind's eye objects that are red, or the color red itself. In this synesthesia the subject will actually see (that is, experience) a particular color given a particular verbal cue.

How Common Is Synesthesia?

The most frequently cited figure for synesthetes is one per 2,000 people, but that is considered by many to be an underestimate. Day, who maintains an electronic mailing list for some 850 synesthetes, claims that 3.7 percent of the population exhibit some form of the phenomenon. Other researchers suggest that the frequency of letter-to-color synesthesia is one in 200.

Modern brain-imaging techniques have been used to investigate potential mechanisms underlying synesthesia. The work has recently been reviewed by Jean-Michel Hupé and Michel Dojat, who found that searches for the neural correlates of this subjective experience and structural brain differences related to synesthesia have been unsuccessful, and that no neural correlate of the synesthetic experience has yet been established. Their suggestion

While it used to be thought that synesthesia was more common in women than men, that assumption was probably based on under-reporting of the phenomenon by men.

is that, rather than being a neurological condition, synesthesia might well be special kind of childhood memory.

This is a conclusion supported by Watson and colleagues in a review from 2014. They show that the development of synesthesia is influenced by learning. The stimuli that evoke synesthetic experiences often involve the perception of complex properties learned in early childhood, and the associations synesthetes make with these learned inducers are not arbitrary. Synesthesia can be helpful in learning, too. They argue that, to a degree, synesthesia arises because of the cognitive demands of learning in childhood. Children use it to help in their perception and understanding of a variety of learned categories. "Our thesis is that the structural similarities between synesthetic triggering stimuli and synesthetic experiences are the remnants, the fossilized traces, of past learning challenges for which synesthesia was helpful," say the authors.

Can We Learn Synesthesia?

Synesthesia has a genetic component, but it has been suggested that some sorts of synesthesia can be learned, although this is a controversial ideal. Research by Olympia Colizoli at the University of Amsterdam showed that it is possible to acquire synesthesia in which people experience letters or numbers in color through training. Seven volunteers were asked to read a novel in which certain letters were always written in red, green, blue, or orange. After this training, they performed better than a control group on a test of synesthesia. This suggests that experience can be a contributing factor to the childhood development of synesthesia.

In 2014, Daniel Bor and colleagues started an intensive training program to see whether nonsynesthetic adults could gain some synesthetic abilities through associative learning. Adaptive memory and reading tasks were used to reinforce thirteen specific letter-color associations. Following training, the subjects showed a range of standard behavioral and physiological markers for grapheme-color synesthesia. Reading black text, they even began to see certain letters in color. Such experiences are usually considered the hallmark of genuine synesthetes.

Psychologists are fascinated by synesthesia, not just because it is interesting in its own right, but also because it is a tool that helps to answer difficult questions about perception. One of these issues is called the "binding problem." Within the brain, different aspects of sensory experience are represented in widely distributed areas. Even for a particular sense, different features may be represented in separate areas. In vision, for example, shape, motion, color, and size are all registered initially in separate areas of the brain. Yet we experience these widely spread bits of sensory information as a seamless, unitary perception. The question of how they are brought together is the so-called binding problem.

Addressing how synesthesia relates to "normal" crossmodal experience, philosopher Jonathan Cohen argues that synesthetic perception is actually continuous with normal perception. His argument is based on the nature of "feature extractors," the means used by our sensory systems to pull out features from the overall sensory input that the brain receives. In normal perception, there is integration of information by feature extractors that crosses the boundaries of the different senses. For example, when we listen to someone speak, we extract features of hearing and also vision (we watch their lips) to interpret their speech. Cohen argues that

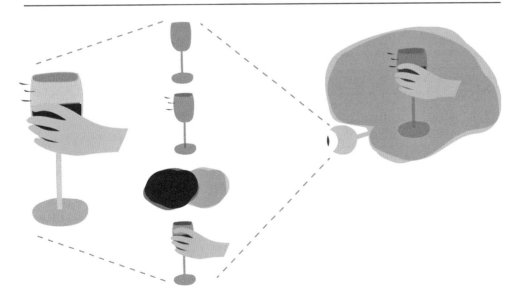

The Binding Problem
Different aspects of the same perception are represented in different areas of the brain. But how are these aspects brought together into one seamless perception? Synesthesia may help to explain how, for example, shape, motion, color, and size are brought together in vision.

if we view normal perception as using what he terms a "dedicated feature extraction view," this exaggerates the difference between it and synesthesia. His view is that we should not think about normal perception in this way. Instead, he suggests that normal perception involves informational integration occurring within and between modalities, which then allows us to see synesthetic perception as more similar in nature to normal perception.

However, other commentators, such as Charles Spence and Ophelia Deroy, argue that there is no correspondence between crossmodal perception and synesthesia. In their view, synesthesia is a pathology; it is faulty wiring that yields clues about how the normal system works. Indeed, this is a recurring theme in biology: disease or malfunction reveals useful information about how the system is assembled. Synesthesia may seem very strange, but it reinforces the fact that we experience a highly edited version of the world around us; in effect, our sensory systems "model" the reality out there, extracting the useful bits of information and presenting them to us in the most efficient way.

Synesthesia and Wine Tasting

The synesthetic phenomenon reveals that many events take place between the sensing of external stimuli and the conscious experience of a particular sense. For the sake of efficiency, a lot of sensory processing in the brain is done pre-attentively (before we are aware of it), and there is a good deal of binding together of inputs from different sensory modalities, a function known as crossmodal processing. That function is highly relevant to the practice of wine tasting. What we refer to as the "taste" of a wine is actually a multimodal sensory experience with significant input from the modalities of taste, smell, touch, and vision. Indeed, the structure of a red wine is to a large degree "felt" rather than tasted. And what our vision sees strongly shapes what we "taste" (in the broader, multimodal sense explained on p.55).
All this was memorably illustrated with reference to wine in a now-famous paper by Gil Morrot, Frédéric Brochet, and Denis Dubourdieu entitled "The Color of Odors" (2001; see p.81). Of course, smells do not have colors: the title is referring to the way that even experts can be fooled by visual cues when naming odors. In one experiment, the authors invited fifty four subjects to

describe a real white wine and a real red wine. A few days later, the same group had to describe the aromas of the identical white wine and a "red" wine that was actually the same white wine but colored red with a neutral-tasting food colorant. Interestingly, subjects described the true red and the "red" wine in similar terms (this was shown statistically), even though one of the wines was actually white. Their perception of taste and smell was influenced by the color. Vision has more of an input in the wine-tasting process than most people would think.

This work has been followed up by Wendy Parr and colleagues, who studied the influence of color on wine perception. They looked specifically at the bias that color induces in wine experts and social drinkers, and sought to determine whether social drinkers' relative inexperience of wine styles would exclude them from the knowledge-driven olfactory bias demonstrated by wine

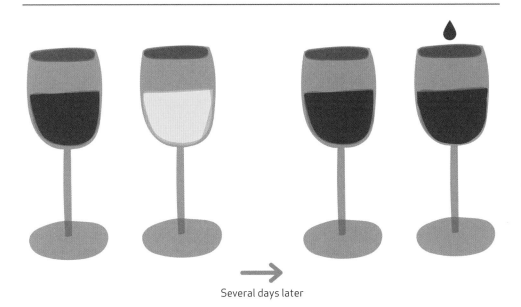

Several days later

The Brochet Experiment

Experts were asked to describe the aroma of two wines, one red and the other white. Several days later, they were asked to return for a second tasting; they were asked to describe the aroma of the same wines, but this time the white wine was colored red with a neutral food dye. That the experts used red-wine aroma descriptors to describe the white wine that had been colored red clearly demonstrated the importance of color in our perception of wine.

experts. It did, to an extent, but the novices were still influenced by the color of a white wine masked with red coloring, although not in the same way as the wine experts. The novices seemed to use wine descriptors quite randomly, and Parr thinks that they were influenced by the color through top-down processing (their thinking affected decisions made about interpretation of sensory signals). However, they did not have enough knowledge or confidence to know how to deal with the false red wine. The wine experts did better when they judged wine aroma in opaque glasses because they did not allow color to lead them astray. In contrast, novices performed worse without visual cues. In the absence of visual cues, wine experts were more data-driven than novices, and were actually describing what was there.

Perceptual bias occurs when our experience causes us to mistake what we are actually experiencing. For example, a wine judge might smell something that is not really present, because of expectations raised, for example, by the color of the wine or sight of the label. In Parr's experiments, color biases wine experts' judgments by serving as a visual misinformation cue. Social drinkers are protected from this mistake by their lack of knowledge: they do not really know what to expect. They find judging wine difficult, and instead of showing the same color-driven bias that experts do, they end up judging indiscriminately. While the wine experts showed a degree of color-induced bias, they were also fairly accurate and consistent in their aroma judgments.

Wine Color and Expectations

Charles Spence at the University of Oxford has carried out research to determine what people believe influences their perception of flavor identity and intensity. "It turns out that one of the reasons why red coloring (as in the study by Morrot et al) turns out to be such a powerful driver of what we experience (both in terms of smell and taste) is that redness typically equates with the ripening of fruits in nature." Spence thinks that semantics and experience are clearly involved. "Expectations or labels about what something might be can play a key role in how you interpret an ambiguous or ambivalent odor," he adds. "Surprisingly, expertise doesn't seem to help with the red wine color effect. I have seen experts completely fooled, perhaps even more than novices."

Spence explains that many of these multisensory interactions occur pre-attentively. "Given the overload in the amount of sensory stimulation that is constantly bombarding each of our senses, our brain tries to help out by binding what we see, hear, smell, and taste automatically, and only giving us awareness of the result of this integration. Hence, attention also fails to impact on many of these crossmodal illusions."

Also of great relevance to wine tasting, learning plays a role in crossmodal associations. "I've not seen this studied for the case of wine tasting, but for other combinations of taste and smell, your previous experience (in terms of cultural differences in exposure to certain foods, or to certain combinations of tastants and odorants) critically determines how your brain will bind the different sensory cues," says Spence.

It is not only in the world of wine that color can distort sensory judgment. A pertinent point about color and flavor is made in an amusing moment of the movie *Bridget Jones's Diary* (2001). In this scene, the inept Bridget (played by Renée Zellweger) is trying to prepare a birthday dinner party for her friends. One of the courses she chooses to make is leek soup, and in preparing this dish she ties up the leeks with string. But the string is blue, and the dye runs into the soup, turning it blue. When the guests are served the soup, they find it quite unpalatable, irrespective of its flavor. Humans really do not like blue food. Again, in their book, *The Perfect Meal: The Multisensory Science of Food and Dining* (2014), Charles Spence and Betina Piqueras-Fiszman cite an experiment in which diners were fed steak under specially filtered lighting. At a certain point in the meal, normal lighting was switched on instead and the diners saw that the steak they are eating is colored blue. The result was striking: they found the steak, which they had been enjoying, entirely unpalatable—even to the point of nausea.

A browse through the literature reveals that there are some general color associations when it comes to flavor. Red is a very important color, presumably because it is often the color of ripe fruit (a change in color from green or white to red indicates ripening, and fruit was a very important food source during humankind's evolution). Thus, making a food look more red can make us perceive it as much sweeter. Green is the color of leaves and some vegetables, and indeed some flavors in wine are described as "green." If a food is green, we are likely to think it will be sour. Blue is aversive in food, as seen above. Blue foods are rarely seen in nature, although interestingly blue is used to color medicine. It is also used to signify raspberry flavor in some drinks, perhaps because shades of red tend to suggest other fruits. Blue is also used for some alcopops and energy drinks, even though previously we have found this color aversive.

What this discussion reveals is that smell, taste, and color are much more closely linked than one might expect, but actually this is not altogether surprising. Before we smell things, we usually first recognize them by using our eyes. Once we have had a good look at something, we might then choose to explore it using our other senses. We might pick it up and feel it, and we might smell it. Because we smell things before we put them in our mouths, there is usually a co-occurrence of olfaction and vision. Indeed, the importance of vision in smell has been used as an argument to explain the "tip-of-the-nose" phenomenon. This refers to the difficulty people have in naming even familiar odors. Could this be because smells are coded in our minds in both visual and verbal ways, making it harder for us to get at the words?

Color and Smell Associations

In a famous paper (1996), Avery Gilbert and colleagues did two very interesting experiments on the connection between smell and color. First, they took twenty test odors and then asked people to describe them using color. They found significant color characterizations for all twenty odors, and when they went back two years later to test the same people, they found that these associations were stable. Second, they gave people colored chips to match with the twenty smells, and found that thirteen of the odors had characteristic hues. A decade later, Luisa Demattè and colleagues looked at the same topic, and were able to show that when participants were asked to choose the best color match to odors they were consistent in their preferred matches. They then tested the robustness of these associations, seeing how quickly the people responded to random odor and color pairings. People responded more quickly and accurately to odor–color pairings that had a strong association.

In another study (2003), Jay Gottfried and Ray Dolan showed that visual cues can help people identify smells, when the picture matches the smell. For example, if people are shown a picture of a double-decker bus at the same time as being given a sniff of diesel fumes, they can recognize the diesel fumes faster. In contrast, if there is a lack of congruence between a picture and a smell, the performance is slower: an example here would be a picture of a fish and the smell of cake. In 2013, Yéléna Maric and Muriel Jacquot asked 155 untrained subjects to match colors to sixteen natural food- and drink-related odors; the subjects chose from twenty-four colors to match the smells. They found that the results were better than simply random, but there were significant differences in the color choices reported for similar odors.

What about cultural influences? Maric and her colleagues then extended this study to compare the results of their French subjects with those of a British group. That they found a high degree of correspondence suggested that the countries are similar, at least in the way they associate colors and smells. But another study by Carmel Levitan and coworkers found some significant differences. They examined six different cultural groups with fourteen different odors and asked them to choose congruent and incongruent color matches for each. While within each group the people were consistent, there was significant variation across cultures. Does this represent differences in dietary patterns? Or might it reflect the different roles of fragrances in each culture?

It is not just the color of the food that makes a difference to our perception of flavor. The color of the plate the food is served on also has a measurable effect. White plates enhance sweet flavors in food, while black plates tend to bring out more savory flavors. Serving food on red plates reduces the amount that people eat. Lighting also affects consumption and quality; people who like strong coffee drink more of it under bright light, while those who like weak coffee drink more of it under dim light. There are also some other interesting and quite surprising observations about color, food, and drink consumption. For example, green and red light seem to add fruitiness to a wine; and men eat less under blue lighting. What is the explanation for these effects? Charles Spence suspects that it may be that we expect foods to look a certain way and we are put off by incongruence.

It is natural to find green meat aversive, because rotten meat turns a gray-green color. Blue is equally aversive, even though we do not often encounter this color in our food. One interesting

Visual stimuli may affect whether we are attracted to a dish or repulsed by it because we are trying to maintain some sort of balance across our senses. For example, it appears that we like bright light with strongly flavored food and prefer low lighting with more subtle food.

observation concerns the cultural and historical status of the color blue. It has been suggested that, until recently in human history, the color blue did not really exist in the way it does today. Ancient languages lacked a word for it, and the suggestion is that without a word to describe it, people might not have seen it. William Gladstone, who was later to become prime minister of Great Britain, researched the number of references to color in Homer's *Odyssey* (eighth century BCE) in his three-volume book, *Studies on Homer and the Homeric Age* (1858; see p.169). Nothing was described as blue. Gladstone's finding has been followed up by language researchers, and the conclusion is that virtually nothing was described as blue in the ancient world, with the exception of Egypt, where a blue dye existed. Recent research by ethnographers has shown that some tribes lack a word for blue and are particularly poor at identifying blue squares in a test where they are mixed in with green.

Some true synesthetes associate sounds, including music, with colors. While most of us cannot claim to be real synesthetes, can we use one sense to describe another with any sort of consistency? Can we carry out a sort of artificial synesthesia? And, if we can, are we doing consciously what synesthetes are doing unconsciously?

Stephen Palmer and colleagues from the University of California, Berkeley have looked at the relationship between color and music, and have asked whether this might be mediated by emotion. It has been thought for a while that different aesthetic domains might be related to each other through emotional associations shared in common. Palmer asked participants in his study to choose from an array of thirty-seven colors the five colors that went best (and later the five that went worst) with various pieces of music. Faster pieces in the major mode were associated with lighter, more saturated, yellower colors, whereas slower pieces in the minor mode were associated with darker, desaturated, bluer colors. The emotional ratings of these color choices matched the emotional ratings of the musical selections, suggesting that emotion was mediating this association.

Matching Smells and Colors

Because of the difficulties inherent in using words to communicate experiences of smells, perfume companies have found other ways to market their products aside from verbal descriptions. One option is to use the color of the liquid itself, or its bottle or package, to give consumers an idea of what it might smell like. Several studies have shown consistent relationships between smell and color. Experimenting in 2004, Rick Schifferstein and I. Tanudjaja looked at the matching of complex fragrances and colors. They found a significant association, and concluded that emotion might be the connection between the color and smell. A recent study from Nele Dael and colleagues showed that emotions and colors can also be matched in a significant way.

There is also a type of synesthesia that we all practice in relation to taste and smell. This is exemplified by the association of sweet flavors with certain smells, as occurs with vanilla ice cream. Vanilla ice cream tastes sweet—indeed, vanilla is used to flavor a range of desserts and is rarely used in savory dishes. Thus the smell

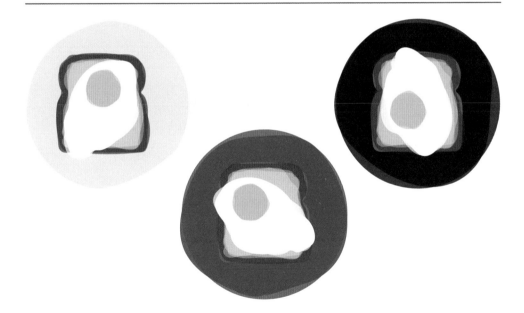

Color Affects Flavor

Plate color is highly important in flavor perception. White plates enhance sweet flavors, black plates bring out savory flavors, and red plates reduce the amount that people eat. It follows that, if you are overweight, it might be time to buy some red china to help you slim. Also, restaurants should be aware that their plates will alter customers' perceptions of their food.

of vanilla most commonly occurs alongside sweet flavors, and this sensory co-occurrence means that for most of us vanilla is a "sweet" smell, even though sweetness is something we cannot smell—it is actually one of the five basic taste sensations. Indeed, some wines—particularly some dry Gewürztraminers and Muscats in my experience—have a disconnect between the nose and the palate. The nose is "sweet," but rather surprisingly the palate is bone dry. This sweetness of smell is, strictly speaking, a form of synesthesia learned by experience.

Effects of Music on Wine Tasting

It is well known that context can affect our experience (and enjoyment) of wine. In a paper published in the scientific journal *Flavour*, Charles Spence, Ophelia Deroy, and colleagues looked at potential crossmodal correspondences between classical music and fine wine. What they wanted to know was whether listening to music affects the wine-drinking experience in measurable ways, and whether the music heard can affect taste.

To answer this question they brought together twenty-six wine drinkers; four rather good wines (Domaine Didier Dagueneau Pouilly Fumé Silex 2010, Domaine Ponsot Clos de la Roche 2009, Château Margaux 2004, and Château Climens 2001); and five pieces of music (Mozart's Flute Quartet in D major, K285—Movement 1, Allegro; Tchaikovsky's String Quartet No. 1 in D major—Movement 2, Andante cantabile; Ravel's String Quartet in F major—Movement 1, Allegro moderato, très doux; Debussy's Syrinx; and Ravel's String Quartet in F major—Movement 2, Assez vi). The participants were asked to taste the wines and rate them with and without music, and also to rate particular pairings of classical music and fine wine. In another experiment, they matched odors to different pitches of the same note.

The results revealed that there were specific music-and-wine pairings that appeared to go particularly well (or badly) together. Tchaikovsky's String Quartet No. 1 turned out to be a very good match for the Château Margaux 2004, while Mozart's Flute Quartet in D major was found to be a good match for the Pouilly Fumé. The participants perceived the wine as tasting sweeter and enjoyed the experience more while listening to the matching music than while tasting the wine in silence.

These effects were not large, but they were there. And there is so much ambient noise in experiments like this that it is remarkable that significant effects were pulled out. After all, music is very personal. Our liking of music is strongly influenced by our exposure to it, and our relationship with a particular type of music changes dramatically on repeated listening. Music also has the ability to tap into the emotions, but a particular piece of music can move one person greatly and leave another cold.

It would be fun to repeat this sort of experiment with more contemporary music, and in a situation where the music is incidental—participants should not be aware that the experiment is looking at the effect of music. You would ask them simply to rate wines while music is playing in the background. You could change the music and slip in duplicate wines later in the tasting, or in a tasting on a separate occasion. One of the more interesting findings of the Spence–Deroy study was the association of the pitch of a note with particular aromas. Some aromas are more bass; others are more treble. This finding suggests that it might be appropriate for wine writers to use musical metaphors to express their experiences in their tasting notes.

In this chapter I have explored the suggestion that our senses are not as separate as we consider them to be. Synesthesia, the jumbling of the senses, is an unusual condition where experiencing one type of sensation triggers an apparently random experience in another sense. While most of us are not true synesthetes, we mix our senses more than we realize as we experience the world around us. Color, perceived by vision, is particularly interesting in this regard: it influences what we taste and smell in significant ways. In the next chapter we will look in detail at the chemical senses, taste and smell, and then follow this up by looking at how the brain combines information from a range of senses to create our experience of flavor.

Introducing the Chemical Senses

Smell and taste are the two "chemical senses," and we have come a long way in our understanding of how they contribute to our perception of food and drink. Traditionally, the senses have been split into discrete units or "modalities," so taste and smell have been considered separately. This makes them easier to study, but has only limited usefulness because they are almost always experienced in a way that makes them dependent on each other. Further, the evidence suggests that we do not have just one sense of smell, but two. Here I will explore what we know about the chemical senses, and that information will serve as a necessary platform for the next chapter, which will consider how all the senses work together to create our experience of flavor.

Evolution of the Senses

In evolutionary terms, the chemical senses are remarkably ancient. As soon as single-celled creatures acquired the ability to move, it became essential for them to be able to "understand" their environment in order to exploit this newfound motility. The first sense to be acquired was that of detecting chemicals in the environment. Later, light sensing would become a cue for movement. As these senses became more sophisticated they were joined by the ability to detect sound and touch.

We think that the world we perceive is the entirety of the world out there, or reality. Actually, we sense just a part of what is out there. Consider how different the world must seem to a rat, living mostly in the dark, where the environment is mapped not only in terms of vision, but also in terms of smell and touch. As well as an acute sense of smell, rats, like many mammals, have a highly developed vibrissal system. This makes use of whiskers on either side of the face to detect features of the environment by the sense of touch. It is likely that a rat would have a mental map of its environment in terms of touch, just as we map our environment using vision. To give another example, the philosopher Thomas Nagel famously asked: what would it be like to be a bat? To navigate by sonar would give us a very different view of the

world. We have no mechanism for detecting some elements of the environment, such as ultraviolet light or radio frequencies, so they are not part of our view of the world, but they exist physically.

Our senses have been shaped by evolution. We detect aspects of the environment that are useful to us, and from this sensory input the brain creates a conscious representation of all that is around us: this is what we think of as reality. This modeling of reality also occurs with relation to the chemical senses. There are many chemicals in the environment that have no particular smell or flavor, and we have very different thresholds for different odors and tastes. We are capable of detecting some chemicals at minute levels, whereas for others it takes quite a lot for us even to notice them. The conscious representations of this chemical reality can differ markedly among individuals and with time. Why is this? You might argue that it is because of physical constraints on our detection systems (making them only able to pick up certain molecular structures), but a more satisfying explanation is that we have become extremely sensitive to specific compounds because it is important for us to spot them.

The Evocative Power of Smell

One night I caught a whiff of slightly off milk as I was crushing a plastic milk carton for recycling. It took me straight back to my childhood. In the U.K. in the 1970s, all children received free milk at school. It came in glass bottles, and if it was a warm day it was often slightly spoiled by the time we received it. That smell of milk on the turn is one that will stay with me forever, and it takes me immediately to the school playground, with all the memories and emotions that are associated with it. I have not drunk milk since. Another smell that has an emotion associated with it for me is that of sunscreen. Living in London, I rarely have to apply it, but when I do, the aroma takes me straight to the beach—it is the smell of vacation, and it creates a really nice, relaxing wave of emotion.

While perception of wine is fully multimodal (or crossmodal)—involving contributions from a number of senses that are then combined together—there is one that takes a lead role in this process: smell. It is possible to argue that we have two senses of smell, as Gordon Shepherd does in his book *Neurogastronomy* (2013), where he makes a distinction between the sniffing-in

The French author Marcel Proust is famous for highlighting the link between smells and memories. In *Remembrance of Things Past* (1913), the author is transported back to his childhood when he smells a tea made from lime blossom.

smell (orthonasal olfaction) and the smell that comes around the back of the mouth when we breathe out (retronasal olfaction). But I would like to propose a subtly different classification of the two different senses of smell, to categorize it by its two main functions. First, there is the sniffing-in smell that tells us useful things about the world around us. And then there is the role that smell plays in flavor: deciding whether or not food or drink is good, and rewarding us for going to the bother of finding it. It is a better distinction, because it is not just the breathing-out smell that is involved in flavor, it is a combination of both of the types of smell: ortho- and retronasal. Orthonasal olfaction (sniffing in) plays a part in both functions of smell, and so it is probably more helpful to consider smell in terms of its function (sampling the environment versus flavor) rather than using the distinction of orthonasal and retronasal olfaction.

But there is an overlap between these functions of smell. This overlap occurs in our hedonic rating of smells and flavors—how much we like or dislike them. Because smell is involved in both flavor and sampling the environment, the liking or disliking of smells will be a consequence of the functioning of the two systems together. It follows that the judgments we make about how much we like smells are bringing together two quite different biological uses of smell. Research has shown that, when it comes to liking, smell and taste are also related. A smell accompanied by a good taste leads to an increased liking for that smell. Also, repeated exposure to a smell causes us to like it more, as long as it is not a repellent smell or a really attractive one.

Retronasal smell is critical in the perception of flavor, but often we fail to recognize its contribution as coming from the sense of smell. This is because the brain localizes the signals it receives from retronasal olfaction as coming from the mouth, where the food or drink is felt as present through touch. This is logical, because it is important for us to ascribe the properties of the food in our mouth to that food, even if we are experiencing the aroma molecules in our nose; it is the sense of touch that does this for us. The brain then combines the smell signals with the sensations of taste and touch to create a seamless, single perception of flavor. Some researchers suggest that the same aroma molecules can be perceived quite differently if they are sensed orthonasally or retronasally, but not all scientists accept this proposal.

In the past, bad smells were associated with disease. During the Black Death in the fourteenth and fifteenth centuries, sweet smells were believed to keep the plague at bay. People sniffed perfumes, scented herbs, and fragrant woods to protect themselves from airborne infection. Doctors wore masks with beaklike projections filled with fresh herbs and dried petals. Even as recently as the seventeenth century, English judges wore nosegays of sweet herbs when they visited prisons, in order to ward off jail fever.

Smell is a critical sense, but it is does not get all the credit it deserves. We would likely only realize how important it is to us if we were to lose it. Anosmia—the medical name for loss of the sense of smell—may have a number of causes, including head trauma, various diseases, and congenital loss (from birth). Because smell is so vital to flavor, people with anosmia lose most of their pleasure from food and drink. And smell is also important in emotion: again, this is something we would only really think of if it were taken away. The impact of the loss of smell can be devastating, and it truly plays an underappreciated role in our everyday experience of the world.

Have Humans Lost Powers of Smell?

A common view is that while smell is a critical sense in other mammals—dog owners will be aware of how much time a dog spends sniffing around on a walk—it is less important in humans, and that we have reduced or diminished olfactory abilities. Did we trade olfaction for smell during our evolution? That is what some people think. In 2004, Yaov Gilad and colleagues published a paper in which they proposed that, during primate evolution, humans traded their sniffing skills for the acquisition of full three-color-based (trichromatic) vision. The researchers began with the observation that while humans have around 1,000 olfactory receptor genes (out of the total of 30,000 different genes in our genomes), only about 400 of them are actually functioning. The rest are what is known as pseudogenes. That is, they code for protein structures that are recognizable olfactory receptor proteins, but they do not actually make these receptors: there is something in the code that stops the genes being expressed.

We need to back up a little here, and look at the way that smell is detected in our nose. Toward the back of the nasal cavity, there are a couple of patches of yellowish tissue, covered in fine hairs called cilia, which float in a layer of mucus. These patches are around the size of a postage stamp. The cilia are attached to nerve cells called olfactory receptor neurons, which in turn are directly connected to a brain structure called the olfactory bulb. These receptor neurons—there are about twelve million of them in the average human nose—have a lifespan of only around a month and are continually being replaced, which makes them unusual

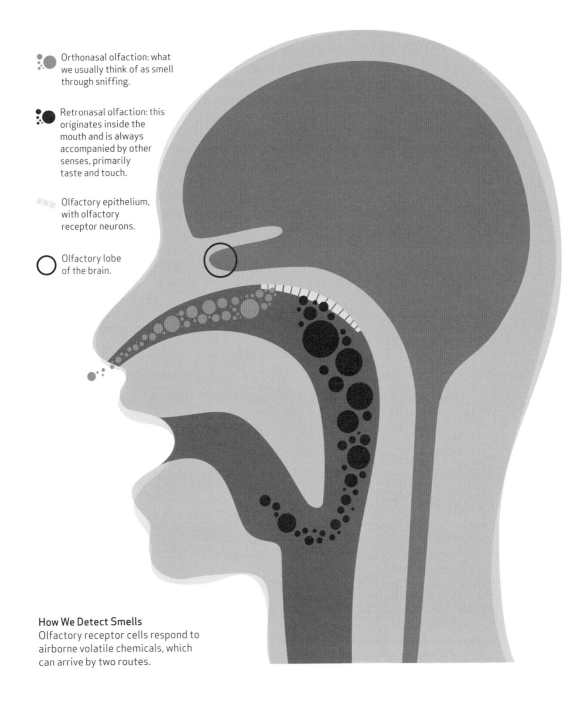

Orthonasal olfaction: what we usually think of as smell through sniffing.

Retronasal olfaction: this originates inside the mouth and is always accompanied by other senses, primarily taste and touch.

Olfactory epithelium, with olfactory receptor neurons.

Olfactory lobe of the brain.

How We Detect Smells
Olfactory receptor cells respond to airborne volatile chemicals, which can arrive by two routes.

for neurons. As air passes over the olfactory epithelium, various small airborne molecules are able to dissolve in the mucus and find their way to the cilia, where they are able to interact with special proteins called olfactory receptors. When the receptors make a connection with these molecules, which are known as odorants, they generate an electrical signal that is then sent along the nerve to a part of the brain called the olfactory bulb.

This is where the story becomes more mysterious. We are unsure how odorants interact with olfactory receptors, and how the electrical signals coming to the olfactory bulb are decoded to create a signal, which—with further processing—will create an experience of smell. But the information we do have is highly pertinent to the practice of tasting and understanding wine. In addition to olfactory neurons, we also possess trigeminal nerve endings in the nasal epithelium. These nerve endings are found throughout the mouth and their function is to sense touch, pressure, temperature, and pain. Relatively few smell molecules are "pure" in that they only stimulate the olfactory receptors.

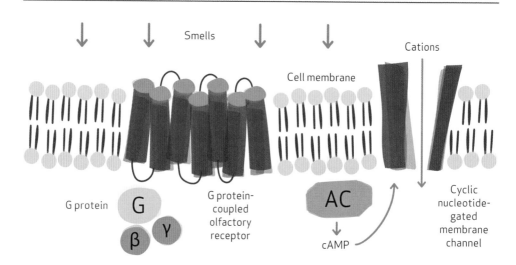

Smells

Cations

Cell membrane

G protein

G

β Y

G protein-coupled olfactory receptor

AC

cAMP

Cyclic nucleotide-gated membrane channel

Olfactory Receptors

The G protein-coupled olfactory receptor detects "specific" smells (volatile chemicals in the air), and then signals via a G protein, which activates adenylate cyclase. The resulting cAMP then causes a cyclic nucleotide-gated membrane channel to open, which causes cations to come in to depolarize the cell, resulting in a nerve signal. This biochemical process is the basis of smell.

Each of these 400 or so receptors is selective for small groups of related molecules. There is some controversy here, because we still do not know exactly how olfactory receptors detect odorants. The mainstream view is that they recognize the molecular shape of compounds, and that each receptor is matched to the shapes of bits of odorant. When the receptor binds with an odorant, it releases a chemical signal that then causes the nerve to fire. However, there is an alternative view from Luca Turin, a researcher who was profiled in the excellent popular science book *The Emperor of Scent* (2004) by Chandler Burr. Turin, a researcher who specializes in smells, and who has written widely on perfume, thinks that there are significant problems with the theory of shape recognition in receptors.

Same Molecular Shape, Different Smells

One problem is the issue of chirality. In essence, chirality is like handedness: hands are very similar, but are mirror images of each other. The same can be true of some molecules: they have the same formula and structure, but are mirror images. These are called enantiomers. You would expect enantiomers, or mirror-image molecules, to smell the same, but in fact they often smell very different, even though their structures are so similar.

The most famous example of this is a molecule called carvone. The two enantiomers of carvone, plus and minus, are structurally the same but mirror images, and one smells like spearmint and the other smells like caraway. In one experiment, Turin and colleagues took pure acetophenone, which has a distinctive smell of hawthorn and orange flower, and compared it with its fully deuterated analog. Deuterium is a heavier version of the hydrogen molecule, so both acetophenone molecules have identical structure, but one is heavier than the other.

The fact that they actually smell different despite having an identical structure is a problem for shape-based models of how smell works. If chemicals that are very different structurally can smell quite similar, and chemicals of very similar shape can smell very different, what is the explanation? Turin's exciting but controversial idea is that instead of recognizing shapes, olfactory receptors are recognizing the electrical resonance vibration of molecules. In this case, deuterated acetophenone would have a different vibrational spectrum to regular acetophenone, despite the fact that they share the same structure.

If we have 400 different functioning olfactory receptors, how do we discriminate among thousands of different smells? This is a really interesting question, and the answer seems to be that it is all about pattern recognition. As will be explained later, the brain has a way of translating patterns of olfactory receptor activation into a perceptual experience of smell.

Did Humans Trade Smell for Color Vision?

Pseudogenes tend to evolve in large gene families where there are already enough genes for the task, and having more of the same is of no extra use. In apes, around 30 percent of olfactory receptor genes are pseudogenes, while in mice that figure is 20 percent.

Let us return to the idea that, during evolution, humans traded a staggering 60 percent of our genes for olfactory receptors for pseudogenes. The idea here is that if an organism relies less on smell and focuses more on other senses, then it needs fewer olfactory receptors to do the job of smelling adequately.

Gilad and his colleagues looked at nineteen primate species, sequencing 100 olfactory receptor genes from each. Old World monkeys had a similar percentage of olfactory receptor pseudogenes as apes, but a higher percentage than most of the New World monkeys, with the exception of the howler monkey. Quite separately, the howler monkey and the Old World monkeys had developed a new feature along with this presumed loss of

The Discovery of Olfactory Receptors

In 1991, molecular biologists Linda Buck and Richard Axel made a remarkable discovery, one that was to win them the Nobel Prize in Physiology or Medicine in 2004. Until then, no one knew how smells were detected in the nose. What Buck and Axel identified was the family of membrane proteins that form the odor receptors in the olfactory epithelium.

Using the tools of molecular biology, the partners identified and studied eighteen different genes from a large family that codes for a special set of receptors called "seven transmembrane G protein-coupled receptors." The presence of these was restricted to the olfactory epithelium. At a microscopic level, the receptors are embedded into the walls of the cilia at the end of olfactory receptor neurons. These interact with smell molecules (called odorants) that enter the nose from the exterior environment and are dissolved in the thin layer of mucus that lubricates and protects the olfactory epithelium.

It is thought that each olfactory receptor neuron is home to only one type of olfactory receptor neuron. Whenever a neuron encounters a smell molecule (or molecules) of the type to which it is attuned, the neuron generates an electrical signal. Past experience of the smell and its associated molecules enables the brain to identify the smell from the specific electrical signal it receives. Strong smells trigger sustained electrical signals.

olfactory acuity: trichromatic color vision. This is where the retina has three pigments, known as opsins, that together allow for full color vision. The idea that this represents some kind of trade-off—that we have become better at seeing and worse at smelling—is attractive but has been contested.

In 2010, a group of Japanese researchers led by Yoshihito Niimura examined this issue again, but this time using high-resolution scans of primate genomes, looking at all olfactory receptor genes rather than just a small subset. From their analysis they concluded that there is no evidence of a loss of these genes occurring concomitantly with the gain of trichromatic vision—the loss appears to be gradual across lineages. Further, humans may be no worse in terms of smell performance than other primates.

In fact, the current view is that humans are actually rather good at smelling. We may have fewer working olfactory receptor genes than other mammals, but we may use our sense of smell rather differently. What we lack in actual number of receptors we make up for with how smartly we process the information. So while we may be amazed at how good dogs are at smelling, we should not automatically think that they are better than us. We are probably more reliant on retronasal olfaction and the contribution this makes to discerning flavor, and, as a result, this is something we are very good at. We cannot compete with dogs when it comes to picking up traces of scent when we walk through our local park, but once we have food in our mouths, we are rather expert, and in its contribution to flavor our sense of smell is highly sensitive. Look at the importance of gastronomy in modern societies, and how much people are prepared to pay for fine wine and top restaurants: does this suggest that our chemical senses are blunt instruments with crude detection abilities? Far from it.

In their book, *Aroma: The Cultural History of Smell* (1994), Constance Classen, David Howes, and Anthony Synnott look at how smell was once a much more recognized, important part of everyday human experience than it is in current Western culture. Among their examples, the Onge of the Andaman Islands in the Bay of Bengal define everything by smell: their calendar is based on the odor of the flowers that bloom at different times of year, and when the Onge greet each other, they typically ask, "How is your nose?" The authors suggest:

Some cultural historians suggest that the low status of the sense of smell in Western society could be the result of a demotion of smell that took place a couple of hundred years ago in intellectual circles. Somehow, in modern Western societies, we have come to regard smell as a base or primitive sense, but such an attitude is not necessarily true elsewhere in the world.

"Such a smellscape is obviously not a fixed structure, but rather a highly fluid pattern that can shift and change according to atmospheric conditions. Perhaps because of the importance their culture attaches to smell as a means of ordering the world, the Andamanese conceive of space itself not in the way most people do in the West—as a static area within which things happen, but more as a dynamic environmental flow. Consider, for example, the space of the village. This space is experienced and conceptualized as fluctuating over time: it can be more expansive or less, depending on the presence in the village of strong-smelling substances (such as pig's meat), the heat, the strength of the wind, and so on."

There are further examples. For the Bororo peoples of Brazil, body smell is associated with the life force of the individual, and breath is associated with the state of the soul. In the rain forest environment, you could imagine that olfactory cues are particularly useful, because the dense vegetation means that it is hard to see very far. It seems that native inhabitants of New Guinea, living in such a rain forest environment, are indeed alert to these cues. The Umeda people, of the Sepik River region, are known to have special skills at detecting faint traces of smoke from a campfire, or at spotting where a pungent-smelling possum might be hiding in the forest canopy.

The idea of "pleasantness" in smell may have a cultural rather than universal basis. The cattle-raising Dassanech people in Ethiopia are reported to find the smell of cows quite beautiful; apparently, they even wash their hands in cattle urine and smear their bodies in manure.

The Suya people of Brazil classify animals by odor, rather their physical characteristics or habitat. They also use similar terms to classify each other. Their human smell classification changes according to sex and age. The Suya have much higher "olfactory consciousness" than Western cultures because, for them, smells have meaning other than just provoking liking or disliking. They think in terms of smell, and smells have symbolic meanings, just as certain colors or sounds do for Westerners. Odors are not coded in our culture in the same way. We will also look in chapter 8 at how our restricted vocabulary for variations in taste and smell might be a cultural rather than biologically influenced phenomenon.

With 400 working olfactory receptor genes, how many different smells can we discriminate? Experiments have shown that in the visual system, with three different pigments (opsins), we can tell apart one to two million colors. Textbooks typically say that we can differentiate 10,000 different smells, but there is no solid evidence for this widely quoted figure. In 2014, however, a paper came out that caused great excitement. Caroline Bushdid and colleagues decided to examine just how sensitive the human olfactory sense is. They tested the ability of humans to discriminate mixtures of 10, 20, and 30 odors from a pool of 128. From the results, they used a mathematical technique to carry out an extrapolation, and concluded that, as a conservative estimate, we can detect more than a trillion different smells. This amazing result resonated with the idea that human smell is more powerful than was previously thought. But the result has been disputed. Another researcher, Markus Meister, has shown what he believes to be methodological problems in the mathematics used to calculate this number. If the same approach were applied to vision, he states, then it would predict that we can discriminate an infinite range of colors, and we cannot. That makes it unlikely that we can smell a trillion different smells and, in the absence of proper data, it is probably best to cite a few thousand instead.

The Potential of 400 Olfactory Receptors

Let us return to the issue of how a set of 400 olfactory receptors can result in perceptions of many more different smells. If each olfactory receptor were specific for one smell molecule, then we could distinguish only 400 different smells; even if we cannot distinguish a trillion smells, the actual number we can sniff is considerably more than 400. As a first step for addressing this concept, we need to separate the two dimensions of the receptor space (what is happening in the nasal cavity when smells encounter olfactory receptors) and the perceptual space (what we experience as smells). The two need not have the same dimensionality because they are doing different things. A good way to think of this relates to what happens in touch. We are not as hairy as our ancestors, but we still have hairs on our skin— around three million of them. And each hair follicle contains a mechanoreceptor that detects when the hair moves. While we can sense the bending of just one of these hairs, we do not perceive all the different patterns of hair bending. You can test this yourself if you stroke your hair twice in slightly different places. It will feel much the same, even though the patterns of hair bending, and the actual mechanoreceptors activated, will have been different.

So there is the physical activation (the receptor space), which is then experienced as a feeling of being touched (the perception space). This could be what is happening in olfaction: different patterns of activation of the various olfactory receptors might result in similar smells, with the brain interpreting these patterns in clever ways. There is unlikely to be a linear relationship between receptor activation and specific smells in most cases.

The dimensionality of the receptor space in olfaction involves the number of smell molecules of interest, the concentrations in which they are present, the design limitations of the olfactory receptor protein receptors, and the way that the smell molecules bind to these proteins. The dimensionality of the perceptual space is quite different, and is governed by what evolution has considered to be important to us in terms of our ability to smell. This would include the nature of smell cues in the environment, the sorts of decisions we have to make based on these smells, and the way in which we associate particular smells with events that are important to us. It is the processing that takes place in the brain that creates a link between the receptor space and the perceptual space. Let us think about how the brain might work here by looking at how it deals with odor mixtures.

Most of the research into smell involves working with single odorants, but in real life we are smelling a mix of chemicals, and this is especially true in the case of wine.

The challenge for our sense of smell is to extract the relevant information from a highly complex mix of odors. And we have to do this quickly: fast enough to be able to react appropriately to this information.

Each olfactory receptor neuron is thought to express one type of olfactory receptor, and each of these receptors can respond to a variety of odors. Interactions between different odors can occur at different levels of smell processing. First of all, there are interactions at the receptor sites. These interactions can be competitive and noncompetitive. A pair of odor molecules might be what is known as agonists (they both bind to and activate the receptor), or antagonists (they both bind, and one binds but does not activate the receptor). In a paper from 2012, M. A. Chaput and colleagues showed a direct link between peripheral (the receptors) and perceptual (the smell) responses to a mixture of two wine aroma compounds. The first is the woody smell of whiskey lactone, and the second is the fruity smell of isoamyl acetate.

They found that both whiskey lactone and isoamyl acetate acted simultaneously on single olfactory receptor neurons. This confirms that the responses of receptors to mixtures is not the result of the simple sum of the effects of the individual compounds. That is, there is an interaction among odorants that often occurs at the level of the receptor itself. Adding whiskey lactone to isoamyl acetate partially suppressed the olfactory receptor activation for isoamyl acetate alone, but in some mixes it can actually enhance the association.

When experiments are done in humans, a high concentration of whiskey lactone decreases the perceived intensity of isoamyl acetate. But—and here is the interesting result—at low concentrations, whiskey lactone can increase the fruity notes of isoamyl acetate. There are clear implications here for wine, because oak barrels contribute whiskey lactone to the wine, especially when they are new barrels, and even more so when they are made of American oak. Another interesting observation is that subthreshold levels of one odorant—where we cannot smell it at all—can affect the way that another odorant smells.

Desensitization and Cross-adaptation

One of the pitfalls in wine tasting is the fact that our sensory systems are quite malleable. Take vision, for example. If you are out in the sunlight and then walk into a slightly darkened room, it takes a while before you can see anything. But after a while, your visual system adapts to the ambient conditions. We take this for granted. Similarly, if you wear colored sunglasses, your visual system adapts to their tint; and when you take them off, everything you see has a strange color cast that takes a little while to disappear. A similar sort of adaptation takes place with the sense of smell, and it is called desensitization.

In a familiar example, we can enter a room or a home and find it noticeably smelly, but after a while we get used to the smell. This is an important ability: the strong smell would otherwise override more subtle smells. It is not a complete adaptation, because particularly powerful smells are merely dampened down.

Aside from desensitization, there is also a phenomenon called cross-adaptation. This occurs when the process of adaptation to smell x causes some adaptation to smell y. While desensitization is problematic for wine tasting, cross-adaptation is a greater hazard. If there is a recurring or prolonged smell in the tasting room, people become desensitized to that smell. It might be a wine

The phenomenon of adaptation can explain why some people can have a terrible body odor problem but not seem to notice it themselves—if they did, you would assume they might do something about it.

component, or it might be an environmental smell, such as coffee, paint fumes, or cooking smells. But if the smell is a wine aroma, this will change your perception of the wine without you being aware of it. Tasting a lengthy flight (or series) of the same kind of wine can be risky in this regard.

Cross-adaptation becomes even more of an issue when a smell unrelated to the wines you are tasting changes the perception of a particular wine component and thus the perception of the wine. A big problem with this is the sheer unpredictability of the process, and the fact that we are not aware that it is taking place. Have you ever sat with others and drunk a bottle over an evening, and found yourself commenting on how much the wine has changed in the glass or decanter? The common assumption is that it is the wine that has changed; but this may not be the case—it could be us.

To prevent cross-adaptation, wine judges are best advised to work in short flights. The tasting order among judges needs to be mixed up, too (ideally randomized, although having one judge work backward, and another tasting odd-numbered wines first before even, for example, is simpler to administer). Switching from a flight of wines of one type to a different type makes sense, and keeping this alternation going through the day is equally wise. Any noticeable aromas in the room should be eliminated if possible, and judges should have regular breaks.

In his book *The Scented Ape* (1990), David Michael Stoddart explores the biology and culture of human odor. His is a fascinating perspective on the importance of human smell, and how it has been treated in recent times in our culture, as though it is something we should be embarrassed about. Stoddart imagines what an observer would make of us Westernized humans. Our rigorous hygiene practices have caused us to regard body odor as unpleasant and distasteful, even though we are shaped by evolution to produce a distinctive odor (humans have more scent glands than any other higher primate), and we have a highly tuned sense of smell. Allied to this, he notes that we have relegated our sense of smell to the status of a base or vulgar sense. We go to extremes to remove our smell, yet the money we spend on perfumes and scented cosmetics suggests that the human sense of smell is far from vestigial, like the appendix or the coccyx.

Human skin is a complex organ, and most of us have around 21 square feet (2 square meters) of it. During evolution, while

Not all of the smells that we encounter in life are outside us: people also smell. But in the West, telling someone that they smell is regarded as an insult. We might amend this to saying that they smell nice, and then it is a compliment, but alone the descriptor "smell" is assumed to be negative. But it was not always this way.

we have lost most of our hair, we have not lost the glands that look after it. These are capable of secreting lots of compounds that either smell or can be metabolized by microbes to produce a broad range of aromatic molecules. The skin contains around three million sweat glands, and given certain conditions we can sweat up to 21 pints (12 liters) a day to cool ourselves through evaporation. Of the different sorts of sweat glands, the apocrine glands are most important for smell production. Many of these are found in axillary (underarm) clusters and close to the sexual organs. Interestingly, there are significant racial differences in axillary apocrine glands: Koreans and Japanese have far fewer of these. Associated with the axillary hair are large populations of microbes, capable of making quite a smell. And then there are the sebaceous glands, which create a thick oily secretion that is broken down by bacteria in the glands to create a range of smelly fatty acids. We also have saliva and urine, which are important sources of human scent. In short, we have the potential to be quite smelly—but smelly for a reason.

Influence of Smell on Choosing a Mate

There is a growing body of research suggesting that the way we smell might be important in finding sexual partners. In 1995 a famous experiment (see p.40) was carried out by Swiss researcher Claus Wedekind. In addition to considering smell as an influence in choosing a mate, he looked at the immune makeup of the participants in the study. Specifically, he examined their HLA haplotypes. "HLA" stands for human leucocyte antigen, and—to simplify—a person's HLA composition reflects their immune type. For organ transplants, surgeons seek a good HLA match between donor and recipient.

The results of Wedekind's experiments were surprising. While the women preferred the T-shirts of males with an HLA type most dissimilar to theirs, there was a twist. Those female participants who were taking oral contraceptives preferred T-shirts from men who had similar HLA patterns to theirs—the opposite result. Wedekind pointed out that, first, it seems that the smell of another person can influence how we are attracted to them. In this case, it was the females who were making the choice based on smell. Second, females choose men who are genetically dissimilar

The apocrine glands can alter their secretions in response to fear, anger, and sexual stimulation. These changes can be detected by others, and have the potential to alter their physiology. So, if you are feeling sexy, or terrified, other people can pick this up by your smell, but just how evident these states are to others is hard to say.

to themselves. As other studies have shown, the more genetically similar a couple is, the more likely they are to have trouble conceiving, aside from the well-known problems of inherited diseases associated with inbreeding. There is a phenomenon called hybrid vigor, where the more genetically different parents are, the healthier and more robust are their children. This also explains why crossbreed dogs are cheaper to insure than pedigrees.

What about the reverse result in women taking the pill? The pill mimics the hormonal state of pregnancy sufficiently that ovulation does not occur. A pregnant woman—or one taking the pill, whose body assumes she is pregnant—might want to be surrounded by kin, or people likely to be motivated by shared genetics to assist in raising the child. Wedekind also addressed the case of those couples who form while the female is taking the pill but who later

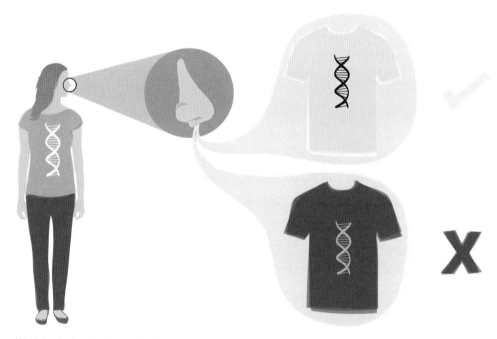

Wedekind's Smelly T-shirt Study

In 1995, Klaus Wedekind recruited forty-four males and forty-nine females. The males were asked to wear a clean T-shirt for three days without washing or using deodorant. The females were then asked to smell the used T-shirts and rate them for attractiveness. They preferred the T-shirts that had been worn by males most genetically different from themselves.

stops, or vice versa. It could be that their stability is threatened because in the new circumstances he no longer smells right.

This sort of story is very seductive, and any good scientist will be cautious about taking intriguing results and extrapolating them too far. So have there been any other studies of this topic? Unsurprisingly, given the interesting results, the answer is yes, but the results of these follow-up studies have been a little mixed. This could in part be because of the complexities of the methods involved and the different sizes of populations used.

In a study from 2006, Christine Garver-Apgar and colleagues at the University of New Mexico looked at whether sharing similar HLA profiles had any effect on existing relationships. They found that as the proportion of HLA alleles (alternative forms of a gene) that couples shared increased, the sexual responsivity of the women decreased toward their partners; they had more affairs, and their attraction toward other men increased, particularly during the fertile phase of their cycles. Interestingly, odor might also be used to signal physical symmetry. Females prefer more symmetrical males, and this can be signaled through smell. In a study from 1998 by Steven Gangestad and Randy Thornhill, twenty-nine females were asked to rate the odors of forty-one males with different degrees of symmetry. The females in the most fertile phase of their menstrual cycles gave higher ratings to the odors from the most symmetrical males—a result that has been confirmed by three subsequent studies.

Genetic Matchmaking

Commercial companies have been quick to exploit these sorts of findings. Dr. Tamara Brown, a researcher based in Zurich, Switzerland, thinks that scent cues picked up subconsciously are an important part of the "spark" that occurs when people fall for each other. Brown looked at the HLA gene patterns and came up with the formula of a matching service entitled GenePartner, which was founded in 2008. Its website states that, "The probability for successful and long-lasting romantic relationships is greatest in couples with high genetic compatibility."

How do these experiments tally with our own experience in the real world? Most of the cues we use in mate choice are quite separate from smell. We might think that a potential partner looks

Pheromone-like olfaction in humans was thought to have a role in the fascinating observation, made by Martha McClintock in 1971, that females sharing a living space will synchronize their estrus cycles. But subsequent studies have failed to find convincing evidence for this phenomenon. It seems that the idea of women living together and emitting pheromones that lead to their cycles moving into step is one that we should consign to the realms of mythology.

nice, or has an attractive personality, or a beautiful mind. Or they might just happen to be available, and we may have few other options. Indeed, it is only when we get very close that we might smell them. And this would be an almost unconscious smelling experience, rather than actively sniffing another person. Of course, things may have been different a very long time ago in Western culture, when soaps, bathing, and clothes washing were rare. And things may be very different today in other cultures where human odors are less effectively masked by hygiene practices.

Pheromones are odors that have a direct physiological response on the recipient, rather than just signaling the status of the sender. Most mammals possess a specialized structure, the vomeronasal organ, that picks up these signals, and the response to pheromones can be quite marked. Humans lack a functioning vomeronasal organ, but some people still claim that human pheromones exist. A search of the internet reveals that "pheromones" are for sale, with the promise of a new irresistibility to potential sexual partners. The fact that most of us find this sort of product implausible reflects the consensus in the scientific literature: there is no solid evidence for the existence of human pheromones.

The Anatomy of Taste

Taste is a term used to describe a specific sense, but it is also used more widely as synonym for the global experience of flavor. It is also used in the sense of aesthetic judgments: for example, "she has good taste." Here we are looking at the specific use of taste to describe what is detected in the mouth.

A taste bud consists of 50 to 150 taste receptor cells grouped together in a single structure.

The actual connection with chemicals in our food takes place at the fine hairs (microvilli) located at the tip of taste receptor cells. The cells are gathered in groups of 50 to 150 to form taste buds. In turn, the taste buds are clustered into structures called papillae. These come in three types: circumvallate, foliate, and fungiform (a fourth type does not house taste buds). Papillae are found not only on the surface of the tongue but also in the palate, larynx, and the top of the esophagus. Humans have between 3,000 and 12,000 papillae. The brain localizes flavor to where food or drink is in our mouths, so we think that taste is coming just from our tongue.

In the past, science recognized just four basic tastes: sweet, sour, salt, and bitter. To these a fifth sense was added, umami, which refers to the pleasantly savory taste of glutamate, derived from the amino acid glutamic acid. Umami was named in 1908 by Tokyo University chemist Kikunae Ikeda, who noticed this savory taste in asparagus, tomatoes, cheese, and meat, but found it strongest in *dashi*, a stock made from seaweed, common in Japanese cooking. Ikeda learned how to make glutamate industrially and became rich by patenting the process—which led to the flavor enhancer monosodium glutamate. More recently, a sixth taste has been proposed. This is the taste for fat, and it has been dubbed "oleogustus". Previously, it was thought that fat was detected by the sense of touch, as mouthfeel. But in 2015 researchers demonstrated that fats—or, more specifically, non-esterified fatty acids produced during the breakdown of fats—have a taste sensation that is distinct from other basic tastes. Previous research had shown that receptors for these fatty acids existed on the tongue. But for oleogustus to be considered a "taste," like the other five, people have to be able to distinguish it from other tastes in its own right.

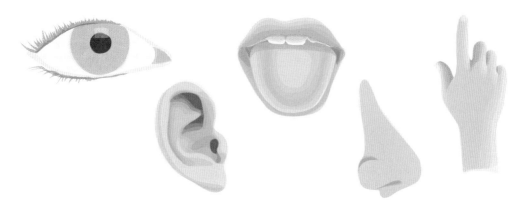

Multimodal Flavor Perception

Flavor is a multimodal perception with contributions from the five senses. Taste—from taste buds on the tongue—gives the baseline with five (or six) basic tastes. Smell, and retronasal olfaction in particular, is the most important contributor to flavor, and it is only when this sense is lost that we appreciate the importance of smell to flavor. Touch is very important: we localize flavor to the place where we can feel food or drink in our mouths, and we "taste" the heat of chili or the astringency of red wine through touch. Vision affects how we interpret flavor, and even sound, such as the crunch of potato chips, nuts, or cookies, can modify how things taste.

Taste receptors are spread more or less evenly across the tongue. This may come as a surprise to anyone familiar with the tongue map beloved of school biology texts, which shows sweet, salty, bitter, and sour flavors to be localized to different regions. This map is based on a German study from the early twentieth century that showed very small differences in sensitivity to the different tastes around the perimeter of the tongue. An influential translation of this study in the 1940s wrongly assumed that where sensitivity to the different tastes was at a minimum, it was absent altogether. The result? A diagram showing that bitter, salty, sweet, and sour are detected in distinct regions. Despite being quite wrong, it is still being widely taught to students of wine.

The tongue also has touch receptors. The feeling of the wine in the mouth, commonly referred to as mouthfeel, is detected by these touch receptors (called mechanoreceptors) in the mouth.

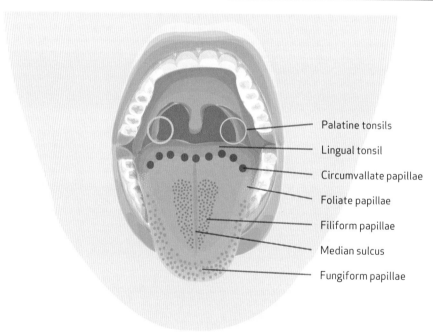

Palatine tonsils

Lingual tonsil

Circumvallate papillae

Foliate papillae

Filiform papillae

Median sulcus

Fungiform papillae

The Tongue

The muscle that houses the taste buds is called the tongue. The tongue also senses touch, and causes food to move around inside the mouth.

Taste buds are housed inside the tongue's papillae: circumvallate, fungiform, and foliate papillae contain taste buds, but filiform papillae do not.

The receptors are neurons specializing in sensing touch. With Ruffini endings, Merkel cells, Meissner cells, and free nerve endings, they are found throughout the oral cavity. Anyone who has undergone dental work that has modified the inside of their mouth in some way will know that we are very sensitive to changes in the mouth environment: we have a very well-developed sense of touch, and the tongue is especially good at exploring the inside of the mouth and helping us to map it mentally in great detail.

The subject of the inside of the mouth has been neglected in discussions about the taste of wine. But the mouth is where we interact with wine most closely, at least until it is swallowed. Most wine drinkers with more than a passing interest in what is in their glass usually smell before they taste, but then any preliminary judgment from the aroma is supplanted by a more concrete judgment made once the wine is in their mouths. For this reason, saliva is a vital component that mediates how we experience wine. It is therefore surprising that the role of saliva in the taste of wine has been so neglected.

The Role of Saliva

An increase in salivary flow usually follows some sort of stimulation. The stimulation can come from taste or smell, or from a mechanical stimulus, such as chewing. When a dentist fiddles inside your mouth, the stimulated salivary flow is sufficient that a suction tube is needed to keep your mouth from filling up. Salivary flow can even be stimulated by an association—after training, Pavlov's dogs famously began slobbering at the ringing of a bell, even in the absence of a food stimulus. The average person secretes 1–2.6 pints (0.5–1.5 liters) of saliva a day, most of which is swallowed. It is thought that around 80 to 90 percent of this is produced by stimulated flow.

Saliva contains lubricant proteins called mucins that are very slippery, capable of absorbing large amounts of water into their structure. Mucins are not unique to the mouth; they are also prevalent in the lung, where they help to form a surface layer that is constantly moved upward by the action of microscopic hairs called cilia, thus cleaning the lung surface. In the mouth, these mucins form a covering over the oral tissues that helps to lubricate the mouth (useful for talking and for masticating food) and also

Saliva is a watery secretion from three different glands: the parotid (in the cheek, under the ear), the submandibular (under the jaw), and the sublingual (under the tongue). Without any stimulation, there is a slow but steady flow of saliva. This unstimulated flow is important to keep the mouth moist, and for protecting the teeth and surfaces inside the oral cavity.

The teeth receive protection from a covering layer of salivary proteins called a pellicle. A range of different proteins are involved in the formation of this coating, which controls the colonization of the tooth surface by bacteria and helps protect against acid.

protects against irritation and unwanted microbes. The ability of mucins to absorb water into their structures helps to keep this protective lubricating layer reasonably thick, and in concert with the liquid nature of saliva, clears unwanted microorganisms and food debris from the mouth.

Saliva also contains high concentrations of calcium and phosphate ions, which help to protect dental enamel and allow remineralization of the teeth. It also protects the teeth by washing away or diluting any potentially harmful chemicals and buffering against acids in the diet.

All this protection is necessary because the inside of our mouth is a vulnerable place. It is warm and wet: ideal conditions for harmful microbes to grow. Teeth are sensitive to acidity, which can destroy them. Saliva is therefore playing an essential protective role; one that we take for granted until salivary flow is diminished or stops altogether, as occurs in some diseases, with some medications, or after radiotherapy treatments for cancer. To experience the condition xerostomia (a dry mouth due to reduced salivary secretion) is to realize just how important saliva is. If saliva flow is severely diminished, people may use artificial saliva, which is sprayed into the mouth at regular intervals. However, artificial salivas are relatively unsophisticated and do not carry out all the functions of normal human saliva.

Salivary Proteins

The saliva components of most interest to us in the context of wine tasting are two groups of proteins known as the proline-rich proteins (PRPs) and histatins, or histadine-rich proteins (HRPs). The PRPs make up about 70 percent of salivary proteins overall, and have a high proportion of the amino acids proline, glycine, and glutamine. There are three subtypes: the acidic, basic, and glycosylated PRPs. Altogether, the three groups have around twenty different members. Acidic PRPs are unique to saliva. They bind calcium strongly and are important in both forming the tooth pellicle layer and making sure that there is enough calcium present for tooth remineralization. This is because they bind calcium when it is present at high levels, and then are able to release it gradually during conditions when there is less of it available. Glycosylated PRPs are lubricants and also interact with microbes.

In contrast, basic PRPs have only one role: to bind to tannins, forming precipitates. HRPs are small proteins, rich in histidine, and only found in saliva. Twelve of them are known in humans, and they account for just 2.5 percent of saliva protein. They have antibacterial and antifungal properties, but they are also very good at binding tannins. The ability of PRPs and HRPs to bind with tannins is of real interest from the wine perspective.

The Function of Tannins

Tannins are formed by plants as defense molecules, defending against microbial attack and also acting as antifeedants. Plants are extremely vulnerable to being eaten as they are literally rooted in place, and so they have evolved to make themselves unpalatable. As well as developing physical defenses such as thorns and stings, they act as chemical factories to produce a wide range of toxic defensive secondary metabolites. Only a relatively restricted number of plant species are suitable for human consumption: in many cases, the only part of the plant we can eat is the bit we (or other animals) are intended to eat—fruits produced to aid seed dispersal. In the case of grapes, they are camouflaged green and made unpalatable by high tannins, high acidity, and no sugar until the seeds are mature enough to be dispersed, at which point the ripening process has made them attractive to eat and easy to find.

Tannins in wine are found in a variety of states: they are intrinsically "sticky" molecules and join up with other wine components such as anthocyanins (the colored pigments found in grape skin) to form pigmented polymers, or can combine with other chemicals. Seed and wood tannins are typically smaller than skin tannins, and it is thought that these smaller tannins possess a bitter taste, rather than express astringency.

One of the key roles of salivary PRPs and HRPs is to protect us from the harmful effects of tannins by binding to them and precipitating them, before they reach the gut. This makes the plants more edible than they otherwise would be, neutralizing one of their defenses. If the salivary PRPs did not cause this precipitation, the tannins would interact with digestive enzymes (which are also proteins) in our gut and render them ineffective. This would reduce the palatability of plant components by making them much less digestible. The aversive taste of unripe fruits is in part due to high tannin concentrations; the plant depends on this as a way of keeping its fruit from being consumed too early, along with color changes and high acid and low sugar. We find the bitter taste and astringent sensation of tannin aversive, and as with all such unpleasant oral sensations, the aversion can protect us from harmful consumption. Thus the PRPs and HRPs are potentially filling two roles: allowing us to detect tannins in food and to reject the food if the concentrations might be dangerous, and also helping to neutralize any tannins present in food to be ingested. In winemaking, the affinity of tannins for proteins is the basis for the use of proteins such as the albumin in egg whites as fining agents in red wines. They help to precipitate excess tannin out of the wine, to make it taste more appealing and less aggressively tannic.

The Sensation of Astringency

We sense tannins in wine largely as an astringent sensation, but there is also a contribution from taste in some circumstances. Astringency is not principally a taste, in the sense that it is not one of the primary taste modalities of sweet, sour, bitter, salty, and umami. Instead, it is chiefly detected by the sense of touch in our mouths (there is still some discussion in the scientific literature about whether or not astringency is tasted). Dietary tannins entering the mouth are bound by proteins present in saliva and form precipitates. These proteins include the PRPs and HRPs, whose role is to carry out this binding and protect us from the potentially harmful effects of tannins in inhibiting digestive enzymes. Also involved is another important protein type in saliva: the mucins. As mentioned earlier, these are involved in forming a lubricated, slippery protective layer over the internal surface of the mouth. Tannins remove this lubrication, causing a sense of dryness, puckering, and loss of lubrication in the mouth. This is what we describe as "astringent."

Related to astringency is the taste of bitterness. The majority of tannins are chiefly sensed as astringent, but they can also be tasted as "bitter" when they are small enough to interact with bitterness receptors on the tongue. Tannins seem to reach their most bitter taste at a polymerization (DP) of four (four subunits joined together, which is small), and then decrease in bitterness and increase in astringency, with this astringency peaking

The Chemical Composition of Wine

Tannins and Phenolics
Coming from the grape skins and seeds, tannins and phenolics are important wine components, especially in red wines, where they give color and structure, and help with wine ageability.

0.1%

Organic Acids
Acid is an important element of wine. Tartaric acid is the main one, but malic, lactic, and citric acids are also present. Acid decreases during grape ripening, so in warm climates it is sometimes added.

0.4%

Other Compounds
Some of the most important flavor compounds in wine are only present at very low levels. Altogether, wine contains around 800 types of aroma and taste molecules; wine flavor chemistry is thus a complicated matter.

0.5%

Glycerol
Apart from alcohol and water, glycerol is the largest single component of wine. Made by yeasts during fermentation, it can add a slight sweetness, but, contrary to popular opinion, it does not contribute to the body or viscosity.

1%

Ethanol
Alcohol adds a lot of character to wine. It makes it more full bodied and adds a sense of sweetness. It can also mask aromas and taste "hot" when the level is too high.

12%

Water
Unsurprisingly, wine is mostly water. Most of the time this is derived from the grapes, but in warmer climates, winemakers sometimes "water back" to reduce the alcohol levels, although this is illegal in many countries.

86%

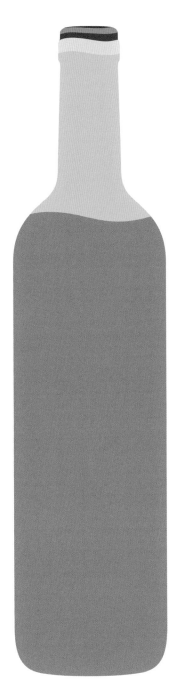

at a DP of seven (according to some studies, at least), before becoming steadily less astringent as they become larger. The astringent nature of tannins can be moderated by the presence of polysaccharides (sugars) or other wine components. It is also modified by the chemical adornments that tannins can grab, and there are many of these. In wine, tannin molecules are continually changing their length and adding things to their structure. Wine tannins can be very complicated, and researchers are still trying to correlate mouthfeel properties with their structures.

Interestingly, tannins are more astringent with lower pH—that is, wines with higher acidity taste more astringent, even with the same tannin content—and less astringent with increasing alcohol. However, the bitterness of tannins rises with alcohol level, and is unchanged by changes in pH.

As we drink wine, the wine itself will increase the flow of saliva, which in itself will change the perception of the wine. The binding of tannins may well reduce their ability to reach the bitterness receptors, and thus their bitterness may decrease and their astringency increase, both at the same time.

It is worth noting that acid is known to stimulate salivary flow. If salivary flow is increased, then there is more protein present in the saliva to form precipitates with tannins. The implication from this is that two red wines with identical tannin composition but different pH will have a different mouthfeel. This could be part of the explanation for the observation that lowering pH increases the sense of astringency. But it could be that there is some sort of additive effect between sensing acidity and astringency.

Saliva and Wine Tasting

What are the implications of this inquiry for wine tasting? Next time you taste and spit red wine, take a look at the spittoon. It is actually quite an unpleasant sight, with strings of congealed saliva, from red through purple to black in color. This is the result of interactions between wine and saliva, and chiefly the binding of salivary proteins by tannins to form precipitates. The mucins in saliva also help to create these viscoelastic strings of colored spit.

In the normal situation of drinking wine it seems likely that the production of saliva is able to keep pace with the rate the wine is consumed. With red wine, the challenge to the palate is the repeated exposure to tannins. With white wines, the tannic content is much lower, and the challenge will be the acidity, which is usually much higher than in red wines (that is, the pH of whites is lower). With Champagne and sparkling wines, the acidity is higher still. None of these should provide a major challenge to the perception of wine, unless exposure is repeated rapidly over a short space of time.

Just such an exposure takes place in many situations where wine is tasted professionally. Whether the situation is a trade tasting, or competition judging, or a critical assessment of a region's wines, it is common to find professionals tasting upward of a hundred samples a day. Repeated assessments of samples pushes up the figure considerably. I am not aware of any scientific studies that have investigated this sort of scenario, but it is possible to predict what might be happening in terms of salivary flow.

In the first instance, with red wines, tannins will be interacting with salivary proteins, precipitating out and causing a sensation of astringency and mouth drying. The initial layer of mucins lubricating the mouth will be stripped. Then, with repeated exposure the deeper layer of mucins will be stripped; this is something that would normally not happen with a typical wine-drinking as opposed to tasting scenario.

Normally, repeated exposure to the same taste or smell will result in a degree of adaptation. However, with astringency, repeated exposure results in the sensation of astringency increasing. Wine ingestion stimulates saliva production, but this is not sufficient to deal with repeated samples of red wine in close succession, in that it fails to replenish the lubricating layer of salivary mucins on the mouth surfaces. The result is that the sense of astringency increases with each fresh sample, to the point where it can become uncomfortable. Usually, the last thing I feel like after a day of thorough tasting is another glass of wine: my mouth is feeling utterly fatigued.

With acidity, frequent exposure to a high-acid stimulus is likely to overwhelm the buffering and dilution capacity of the saliva. This can leave the mouth feeling sensitive to subsequent samples, and might lead to acidity being misjudged. However, my experience as a taster is that it is less fatiguing to taste many white wines in a single session than it is to taste many red wines.

This is not meant to read as a counsel of despair for professional wine tasting. But it is an observation that should encourage us to approach tasting with a degree of humility. Tasting lots of wines in succession carries with it risks, not just of palate fatigue, but also of the effects of presentation order. The perception of any one wine can be influenced by the nature of the preceding wine. For

this reason, it is good practice to have tasters on a panel do their work in different orders, even if it is as simple as some tasting in reverse order. It is significant that, in sensory analysis at an academic level, presentation order is randomized.

Given that saliva is unable to cope well with the sort of frequency of wine tasting typically carried out by professionals, what can we do to help? At the most basic level, we need to hydrate properly. Dehydration reduces saliva flow. If we spit, we not only eject the wine, but also the saliva our mouths have produced. If we are producing around 1.75 pints (1 liter) of saliva a day, and spitting rather than swallowing it, this fluid shortfall needs to be made up. Often tasters clear their palates with water plus solids such as crackers, bread, or black olives. This may help by absorbing some of the tannins that have built up and not been cleared by the overworked salivary flow, but it is not a sophisticated solution.

Restoring Palate Sensitivity

Researchers have examined the effectiveness of palate cleansers in restoring the palate to baseline conditions in sensory analysis. One study compared astringency buildup using a number of different cleansers: deionized water, a pectin solution of 1 gram per liter; a CBMC (carboxymethlycellulose) solution of 1 gram per liter, and unsalted crackers. Subjects tried the same wine six times, using a cleansing process after the third wine. The unsalted cracker was found to be the most effective measure at reducing astringency buildup, while water alone was the least effective; astringency built up whatever cleanser was used. Another study showed that a pectin rinse was the most effective cleanser, followed by unsalted crackers. CBMC has been shown to be effective in some instances.

In sensory analysis work, the hundred or more samples that professional tasters regularly undertake daily would not be tolerated. The "noise" produced from this sort of palate fatigue would likely render any statistical analysis insignificant. Under these circumstances, experienced, competent judges remain able to make good decisions in discriminating wine quality. However, with fatigued palates they would find it more difficult to make the fine discriminations that are important in judging top-quality wines.

Certainly, results would be cleaner and better if fewer wines were tasted, and gaps between flights were sufficient to allow palate recovery. For fine wines, small differences in quality are significant. And for top red wines, mouthfeel is one of the key components of the wine. Elegance and harmony, much prized in older wines in particular, depend in large part on mouthfeel. For assessing these sorts of wines, the number of samples that can be reliably assessed is reduced.

There is one further point that must be made in relation to saliva and wine tasting, and this concerns inter- and intra-individual differences in saliva production. People differ in the composition and production of saliva, and each person's salivary flow rate will change with a number of factors including hydration state, time of day, emotional state, and the influence of medication. In addition, 10 to 15 percent of the population breathe largely through their mouths, resulting in significant evaporation of saliva; they are estimated to lose 0.6 pint (350 ml) per day.

In conclusion, we encounter wine most profoundly when it is in our mouths, and the internal environment of the mouth clearly has a significant impact on wine perception. Saliva is vital in mediating our experience of wine, and so any attempt to understand the practice of wine appreciation must take into account saliva and the mouth environment as an intrinsic component of flavor perception.

In this chapter I have explored the chemical senses of taste and smell. I have looked at the way that the human sense of smell has been underestimated, and considered its importance in our daily lives. I have also explored taste itself, and pointed out that it forms only a basic contribution to the sense of flavor, although we think of flavor as originating in our mouths because that is where the sensations are localized, through touch. Touch is very important for wine, because mouthfeel is an undervalued component of our appreciation of wine, and saliva plays a vital role here. In the next chapter we will look at the brain, and how it constructs a multimodal perception of flavor.

Both intra- and inter-individual differences in saliva are likely to affect the mouthfeel of red wines. This adds another level of inter-individual variation to wine tasting, in addition to factors such as taste bud density, olfactory receptor repertoire, and knowledge and experience. The extra level of intra-individual variation is something we must be aware of as tasters.

Wine and the Brain

The emerging view among scientists is that sensation is multimodal. That is, the different sensory modalities, including taste, smell, touch, hearing, and vision, overlap to an extent, with our perception being a unity, containing input from different senses. This understanding has important consequences for the way that we think about wine tasting.

The Role of the Brain

In this chapter, I explore the way that the brain processes the sensory input gained during wine tasting, and its implications for our understanding of this practice.

In the previous chapters, I have touched on how our chemical senses do not act as measuring devices. When we encounter wine, our tongue and nose do not just detect tastes and smell molecules present in the wine, as a laboratory instrument does. Instead, there is a distinct sense called flavor, which is the result of the brain combining information from taste, smell, touch, vision, and even hearing to enable us to choose what to eat and drink, and also which allows us to experience pleasure during the process. Increasingly, scientists are recognizing that sensation is multimodal, combining lots of different kinds of information at a preconscious level, before constructing the experience that we become aware of consciously.

Inside each of our heads, we have a mushy, jellylike organ weighing around 3 pounds (1.4 kg), and containing around 100 billion specialized information-processing cells called neurons. It is by far the most complicated organ in our body. These neurons are each capable of making an astonishing number of connections with other neurons, and it is this interconnectivity that codes the very heart of what makes us "us": our memories, personalities, emotions, hopes, fears, and dreams are all dependent on the proper functioning of the brain.

The neurons in the brain signal to each other electrically, and also through neurotransmitter and neuromodulator chemicals. Brain structure itself is complicated, and there are various

If we are going to understand wine tasting in an intelligent way, our starting point must be that we are not measuring devices. However much we train ourselves, we can never get away from the fact that our consciousness does not present us with an exact, true version of reality. What we are aware of has already been edited by our brains.

schemes for classifying the different bits and what they do. Until recently, the most popular concept of how the brain works was the triune brain model (see right) devised by Paul MacLean in the 1960s. Taking as his guide the way that the brain has developed through evolution, he divided it up into three competing systems that have been bolted onto each other. First, there is the ancient reptilian brain, which keeps our basic functions ticking over and is involved in sex, aggression, and appetite. Then there is the limbic system, which is known as the paleomammalian brain. This is the seat of emotions. Finally, we have the neomammalian brain: the cortex, which is responsible for cognition, and which in MacLean's model dominates the more primitive regions. In some ways this hierarchical model is an allegory, and it has proven quite popular. Even today, people are drawn to the idea of the reptile brain leading us astray with its base instincts, as if this somehow absolved us from blame when we behaved in inappropriate ways.

But modern brain science contradicts the triune model, with its strictly linear, hierarchical manner of information transfer. While it might be convenient to divide up the brain and attribute certain functions to specific areas, there is a lot of interconnectivity in the brain, with signals being sent one way and then back again, and multiple areas participating in the same tasks. Also, MacLean's model places reason over emotion, and there is every reason to believe that emotion is involved in decision making and should not be relegated like this.

The brain uses about 20 percent of our calorie intake. People looking for ways to lose weight will perhaps be disappointed to learn that thinking harder or being smarter does not cause us to use up more calories: most of the energy is used in general maintenance of the brain so that it can work properly, rather than in performing specific tasks.

Modeling the World Around Us

Rather than deliver sensory input from our tongue, nose, eyes, and ears to our conscious awareness in a linear fashion, the brain models the world around us. Our sensory systems are bombarded constantly by a mass of information, which, if attended to uniformly, would swamp our perceptive and decision-making processes. Instead, the brain is able to extract from this sea of data just those features that are most relevant. This is done by a procedure known as higher-order processing.

Let us look at this another way. We often think that our sensory systems are revealing to us the world around us in an accurate and complete way. But in reality, what we experience is an edited version of reality that is based on the information that is most

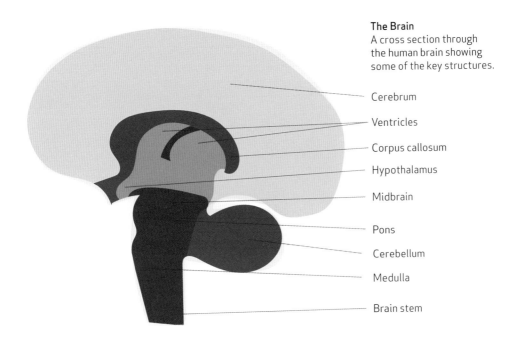

The Brain
A cross section through the human brain showing some of the key structures.

Cerebrum

Ventricles

Corpus callosum

Hypothalamus

Midbrain

Pons

Cerebellum

Medulla

Brain stem

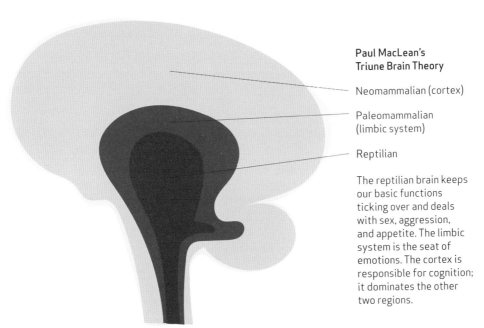

Paul MacLean's Triune Brain Theory

Neomammalian (cortex)

Paleomammalian (limbic system)

Reptilian

The reptilian brain keeps our basic functions ticking over and deals with sex, aggression, and appetite. The limbic system is the seat of emotions. The cortex is responsible for cognition; it dominates the other two regions.

relevant to our survival and functioning. For almost all purposes it does no harm for us to think of the world around as revealed to us to be "reality"—indeed, life would become quite complicated if we operated any other way—but for the purposes of this discussion it is useful to realize that the version of reality we experience is an edited and partial one. And quite a personal one, too.

Reality and its Representations

This can be illustrated in a number of ways. Think about your household pets, if you have any. Dogs live in a world of smell that is almost completely closed to us, and which is just as vivid to them as the visual world is to us. Rats and mice, like many small mammals, get almost all the information they need about their environment from a combination of sniffing and using their whiskers: they are nocturnal, and vision is not so useful at night. Now switch on your radio or television, or take a call on your cell phone: it is clear that the air is full of information that we cannot

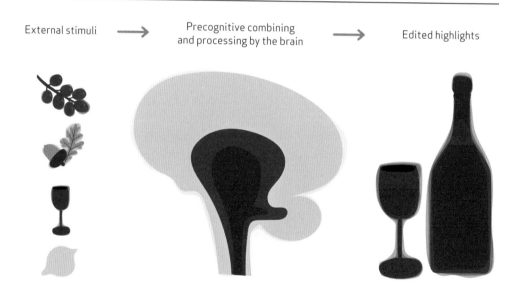

External stimuli → Precognitive combining and processing by the brain → Edited highlights

Creating a Model of Reality
The brain models the world around us, and our conscious perception is a highly edited version of reality. By the time we are aware of perception, a lot of editing has already taken place.

access unless we have a device to decode it. Third, take a look at a visual or optical illusion, such as Gaetano Kanizsa's triangle, the café wall illusion (see p. 60), or Louis Necker's cube. They show that in some cases what we perceive is not present. These are just some of the many tricks that "fool" the visual system. They give us clues about the sort of higher-order processing that is taking place, and demonstrate that what we "see" is not always what is there. Synesthesia, discussed in chapter 1, also does this nicely.

Let us also consider the metaphor of a map. A "perfect" map in terms of accuracy would be an exact correspondence to the physical reality. So, for London, where I live, the ultimate map would be exactly the same size as London and have every detail marked on it. But this map would be entirely useless. What a good map does is provide you with just the information that you need. Consider one of the classic maps of all time: Harry Beck's map of the London Underground routes (1931). Beck's genius was to separate the subway lines from the constraints of the actual overground geography, which suddenly resulted in a highly functional, uncluttered, and rather beautiful map that contained all the important detail, but presented it in a clear way. Thus we have the geographical reality, which the map then represents in a different, but more useful way. It is what the brain is doing as we perceive. This map has since been the model for subway maps for cities around the world. The version of reality that our brains presents us with is in many ways similar to what a good map does: it is what we need to function, without too many of the unnecessary details. It is a representation at a different level, based on reality, but different from it.

Higher-order Brain Processing

Scientists understand the higher-order processing in the human visual system better than that of any other of the senses. For instance, they have worked out how visual processing extracts features of the environment that are most likely to be relevant. Our peripheral vision is sensitive to motion: moving objects immediately stand out, because neurons are tuned to respond to them. This ability to detect motion is much stronger in the periphery than it is in the central visual field. Faces are also likely to be significant cues, so our visual systems have special brain mechanisms for face processing. This is the reason why so many advertisements and magazine covers rely on human faces, even where the face is not particularly relevant to the publication.

Although it is less well studied, this sort of higher-order processing is also important in flavor detection. We are bombarded with chemical stimuli all the time and the brain has to filter this information so that only the important bits get through. It seems that much of the brain is dedicated to producing a suitably edited view of reality, just as the staff in a newsroom work hard all day sifting through the output of journalists to produce a fifteen-minute news bulletin for broadcast that evening.

A further illustration that our brain is working without our awareness of it comes from blindsight. This occurs in people who have specific damage to areas of their brains involved in visual perception. Although they are effectively blind in certain areas of their visual field (they cannot "see"), they can do things with their visual system in that field that shows that their vision is working at a preconscious level—for example, to guide their hand

The Café Wall Illusion

What we see here is not what is present. The lines are actually parallel, but we see them as strikingly curved. This shows that our visual perception is not an exact representation of reality.

movements in grasping an object. This was first described in 1974 in a paper published by Elizabeth Warrington and Lawrence Weiskrantz on a patient who had completely lost sight on one side of their visual field. In a series of experiments they found that even though he could not see anything in this region, he had an 80 percent success rate at pointing at a circle when it appeared, or deciding whether a line was horizontal or vertical after he was asked just to guess. Interestingly, these subjects can even sense emotion with their blindsight, but they have absolutely no access to this information consciously. It is intriguing and slightly scary to think that the functioning of our brain in sensing the world, and thus some of our decisions, might be out of our conscious control.

We have already looked at how our perception of flavor, and of course our perception of wine, is multimodal, drawing on input from all the senses and recombining it in interesting ways before we are already conscious of it. The brain is doing interesting things to create the perception of flavor. We know this is true theoretically, but what about in practice? Perhaps the leading figure in actually studying the impact of multisensory (or crossmodal) perception is Charles Spence at the University of Oxford. His book with Betina Piqueras-Fiszman, *The Perfect Meal* (2014), looks at all the elements that go together to create the ultimate dining experience. He poses the question: can science and neuroscience get us closer to the perfect meal? The answers to this question that have come from his research are highly relevant to wine tasting.

Spence regrets that this topic has been little studied. "My colleagues aren't interested in food: it is dirty and messy, people get full up and they spill it, and they'd much rather test people on computers with flashing images." He cites William James, writing in 1892: "Of the food lover's prized possession—taste, smell, thirst, hunger—little of psychological interest is known."

When the world's top chefs are writing about the perfect meal, they think of their creative process in terms of senses. Ferran Adrià (formerly of the Spanish restaurant El Bulli) claims that cooking is the most multisensory art: "I try to stimulate all the senses." In the United Kingdom, Heston Blumenthal (who achieved fame with his restaurant, The Fat Duck) has claimed that eating is the only thing that we do that involves all the senses: taste, smell, touch, vision, and hearing. They are all involved in

"Once at least in the lifetime of every human, whether he be brute or trembling daffodil, comes a moment of complete gastronomic satisfaction. It is, I am sure, as much a matter of spirit as of body. Everything is right, nothing jars. There is a kind of harmony, with every sensation and emotion melted into one chord of well-being."
M. F. K. Fisher, 'The Pale Yellow Glove' from *The Art of Eating* (1937)

"[Heston Blumenthal] has been a key figure in going to science labs every few months to find out what scientists have discovered about the mind on flavor, and then try to interpret this to create something wonderful on a plate that is memorable and stimulating, because it is built on the brain science and can more effectively stimulate the senses."

Charles Spence

experiencing and enjoying the flavor of the food on the plate. "None of us realize how much influence the senses have on the way we process the information from the plate into our brain, and construct the flavors that we like or dislike, enjoy, crave, or remember," says Spence, who has collaborated with Blumenthal.

But the perfect meal is not just about the senses. "It is also about memories and emotions," says Spence. "Increasingly the perfect meal is about the theatricalization: the imagination and storytelling are all brought to bear to turn the food into something memorable." Spence claims to be a poor cook, but his contribution here is the science. "Every day in the lab at Oxford we are thinking about how what we see might change what we taste, how what we feel might change what we smell, and how changing smell might change what we taste. All the senses are connected in ways that we do not understand. They interact more than we realize in ways that the science is only just beginning to elucidate."

Spence sees value in gaining insights from the chefs who have picked up intuitively on the various elements of what makes a great meal experience, and then trying to study these aspects. He gives the example of a restaurant where you have to book two months in advance. This is raising expectations. Then a month before the meal you get a note in the mail, scented with a fragrance that you then experience as you enter the restaurant. As you leave, you are given a bag of candies, which you take home, extending the experience.

What about cutlery? The Fat Duck, for example, is known for its heavy cutlery—is this part of the perfect meal? Does the weight in your hand make things taste better? Spence mentions an experiment that looked at this, involving 160 diners in the Sheraton Grand in Edinburgh. Half used the regular heavy cutlery, the other half used lighter cutlery; those using the heavier were willing to pay an extra premium for the same food.

He gives the example of Denis Martin, whose restaurant in the Valais, Switzerland, has two Michelin stars. It is located in the middle of a knitting museum, and Martin saw that when people walked through the door, they were not going to enjoy his modern Swiss cuisine fully; they are uptight, suited Swiss businessmen dining on expense accounts. The solution? People are told to arrive at 7:00 p.m. and there is nothing on the tablecloth except for a toy Swiss cow. Nothing happens until someone picks up the cow and it moos; before long, the restaurant is filled with the sounds of laughter and mooing cows. Changing the mood, this is a psychological palate cleanser, preparing people for the meal to come. Then there is "digital seasoning." This began with Blumenthal's "Sound of the Sea" dish, where diners were given a conch with an iPod shuffle in it, and listened on headphones to a marine sound track that works to enhance the flavor of the dish. A residence at the House of Wolf in Islington, London, took this idea more midmarket, with theme music accompanying each dish across the whole restaurant.

Spence notes that some high-profile new restaurants have been multisensory. The Ultraviolet in Shanghai is a ten-seater restaurant in a secret location (customers are taken there). In the high-tech experiential dining room, each course is enhanced by a taste-tailored atmosphere. For example, fish and chips are served with sounds of the sea, projections of the Union Flag of the United Kingdom on the table, and a device squirting out marine smells: it is a true multisensory experience. Another example is Sublimotion in Ibiza, Spain, which at $1,600 (£1,200) a head is thought to be the world's most expensive restaurant. "At this sort of price it cannot just be about the food and taste and flavors," says Spence. "It has to be about the whole experience."

The Visual Component of Flavor

One of the strongest influences on flavor is visual. "We are led by our eyes," says Spence. He refers to a dish—again, from Blumenthal—a scoop of pink–red food that looks like strawberry ice cream. It is actually a crab bisque; Blumenthal thought it tasted wonderful but people found it overseasoned and too salty. The eyes suggest "sweet" and the palate says "savory," and, given this expectation, the dish ends up tasting too salty. "The first experience of this dish has to be right and involve the right name," says Spence. "If you call this dish 'Fugue 386,' it is enough to suspend expectations and you come at it with a fresh palate and it will taste seasoned just right—the chef has to get into the mind of the diner and to lead their expectations."

How food looks matters now more than ever, in the age of smartphones and sharing pictures of our dishes on social media. Back in the 1960s, French chefs did not care how things looked: food was about the taste, and it was served on the plate as it might be at home. Then came nouvelle cuisine and things began to change. "In the twenty-first century the perfect meal should look just so," says Spence. The way a plate looks is a key element in our enjoyment, but does it make a difference with taste? The answer is yes. Many of today's chefs use asymmetric plating, but studies have shown that people prefer it symmetrical; if the plating is asymmetrical, they enjoy the food less and want to pay less for it.

The color of the plate matters, too. In an experiment, Adrià took one of his desserts and served it to half of his diners on a white plate and to the other half on a black one. It tasted 10 percent sweeter and 15 percent more flavorful on the white plate. Again, in a hospital setting, patients ready for procedures are sometimes given food on a red tray. But red says "do not eat me": put anything on a red plate or tray and people will eat less.

Perhaps more importantly, Spence states that insects may be the food of the future because current dining practices are unsustainable. Most people find the idea of eating insects unappealing, so the challenge for Spence and his colleagues is to apply their knowledge of the psychology of food to persuade us that the foods of our future are delicious rather than unpalatable.

Spence and colleagues have taken this approach to food further, to study how changing the environment might change the perception of wine. Over four days in May 2014 they ran what is probably the world's largest multisensory taste experiment, on Southbank in London. During the four days, almost 3,000 people sampled a glass of red wine in a room in which the color of the lighting and/or the music were changed repeatedly. The wine—a Campo Viejo Rioja—was presented in a black tasting glass, and the tasters had to rate it over a number of taste, intensity, and liking scales. For the first two days they tasted the wine while exposed to white, red, and green lighting with music designed to enhance sourness, and then under red lighting paired with music associated with sweetness. For the final two days, tasters rated the same wine under white, green, and red lighting with "sweet music," and then green lighting with "sour music" (this shift was to rule out any order effects). The results? For all four days, the wine was perceived as fresher and less intense under green lighting and sour music, and people liked the wine most under red lighting while listening to sweet music. How significant were these influences? The authors noticed a swing in ratings of 9 to 14 percent, which seems quite large. Considering the large number of people involved in the study, the results were robust and impressive.

Spence and colleagues have also looked at how hearing might be involved in flavor perception. They have studied whether people can tell apart the sounds of pouring sparkling water, Prosecco, and Champagne. Interestingly, people perform better than chance in this test, suggesting that hearing may well have a role in altering the perception of sparkling wine. And what of the pop of the cork (or the crack of the screwcap)? Could this lead to expectations when wine is about to be consumed?

Gathering Data from the Brain

Flavor seems to be complicated and multimodal, but how can we link up the production of electrical currents at the receptor level when food and drink are encountered, with the unified conscious experience of flavor in the brain?

A relatively new technology, functional magnetic resonance imaging (fMRI), has transformed brain research in recent years by allowing researchers to visualize the brain in action. During a regular MRI scan, a subject is placed inside a large cylindrical magnet and exposed to a massive magnetic field. A sophisticated detection device then creates three-dimensional images of tissues and organs from the signals produced. fMRI is a twist on this theme, where the technique is used specifically to measure changes of blood flow in the brain. When brain cells become more active, they need more blood, and this demand generates a signal in the scan. Although there was initially some controversy about whether a direct correlation exists between the bloodflow detected in an fMRI scan and actual brain activity, the consensus in the field is that this is so. The power of fMRI is that it can show which parts of the brain are used when, for example, we think of chocolate or move our middle finger.

Spence worries that some of this research is too reliant on results from fMRI studies. "If you were to volunteer to take part in an experiment, you would be put on a tray, your head would be clamped still, you would be given headphones to black out the 120 db of background noise, a tube would be inserted into your mouth, and you would be slowly inserted into the coffin. Periodically you would be given a four-milliliter squirt of liquid."

For the reliable detection of brain signals in an fMRI scan, subjects are required to lie inside a large metal cylinder with their heads completely still. Because of the practical and experimental difficulties of these sorts of studies, this remains an area where there is still a lot of uncertainty.

Color Influences the Taste of Wine

A Spanish wine (Campo Viejo Rioja) was served to each person in a black glass under a range of sound and lighting conditions, which were changed repeatedly. The test was conducted under red, white, and green lights, and with both "sweet" and "sour" music. People were asked to rate the wine on a scale of taste, intensity, and liking. They found the wine fresher and less intense under green light with sour music, and they liked the wine most of all under red light with sweet music.

Yes, various brain areas light up in these experiments, but their context is hardly a real-world, natural setting. "I think this is taking things too far: no one has had their perfect meal lying in one of those machines with a periodic puree being pumped into their mouth," says Spence. "It tells you something and it is important, but I do not think it tells you about the perfect meal and how to get closer to it." However, even the limited data obtained so far are highly relevant for wine tasting and are important if we want to provide a robust theoretical basis for the human interaction with wine.

Taste Perception and Memory

Let us return to the theme of flavor processing in the brain. The senses of taste and smell work together to perform two important tasks: identifying nutritious foods and drinks, and protecting us from eating things that are bad for us. The brain achieves this by linking food that we need with a reward stimulus—it smells or tastes "good"—and making bad or unneeded foods aversive. To do this, flavor perception needs to be connected with the processing of memory (we remember which foods are good and those which have made us ill) and emotions (we have a strong desire for food when we are hungry, and this motivates us to seek out a proper meal). Because seeking food is a potentially costly and bothersome process, we need a strong incentive to do it. Hunger and appetite are thus powerful physical drives.

As we discussed in chapter 2, taste begins on the tongue, where sensory cells convert chemical information into electrical signals, which then pass through to the primary taste cortex in the brain. This is located in a region called the insula. Taste provides us with relatively little information compared with the sense of smell. Whereas there are just five or six basic tastes, we can discriminate among the many thousands of volatile compounds known as odorants. Our olfactory epithelium contains olfactory receptor cells that, on detecting odor molecules, create electrical signals that pass to the olfactory cortex via the olfactory bulb.

At this stage, with the information that exists at the level of the primary taste and smell areas of the brain, it is likely that nothing is coded except the identity and intensity of the stimulus. Alone, this information is of relatively little value. But what the

brain does next is the complex higher-order processing mentioned above; it extracts the useful information from the mass of data, and begins to make sense of it. This is where we turn to Edmund Rolls, a professor of experimental psychology at the University of Warwick (and previously Oxford University, where most of his work was done), who has studied a region of the brain called the orbitofrontal cortex; fMRI is one of the tools that he used.

Rolls and others have shown that it is in the orbitofrontal cortex that taste and smell are brought together to form the sensation of flavor. Information from other senses, such as touch and vision, is also combined at this level, to create a complex, unified sensation that is then localized to the mouth by the sense of touch—after all, this is where any response to the food or drink, such as swallowing it or spitting it out, must take place. Rolls has also demonstrated that the orbitofrontal cortex is where the reward value (the pleasantness or "hedonic valence") of taste and smell is represented. It is here that the brain decides whether what we have in our mouths is delicious, bland, or disgusting. Another fMRI study has shown that the brain uses two dimensions to analyze smells: intensity and hedonic valence. In the brain, the amygdala structure responds to intensity while the orbitofrontal cortex region decides whether the smell is good or bad.

Crossmodal Processing

Some nerve cells in the orbitofrontal cortex respond to combinations of senses, such as taste and sight, or taste and touch, or smell and sight. This convergence of inputs, known as crossmodal processing, is acquired by learning, but it is a process that occurs slowly, typically requiring many pairings of the different sensations before it is fixed. This suggests an explanation of why we often need several experiences of a new food or wine to be able to appreciate it fully. It is also at this level that stimulus–reinforcement association learning takes place. For example, if you are faced with a new food (the stimulus) that tastes good but which makes you vomit (the association), the next time you pop some of it into your mouth you will immediately spit it out in disgust. This saves you from having to vomit again, and therefore is a protective mechanism. This aversive mechanism is weak, however, and may be wilfully ignored.

One aspect of Rolls's research on the orbitofrontal cortex that has direct relevance to wine tasting is his work on sensory-specific satiety. This is the observation that when enough of a particular food is eaten, its reward value decreases. However, this decrease in pleasantness is greater for that food than for others. For example, if you like both banana and chocolate, and eat a lot of banana, you may not want another banana but you will still fancy a chocolate. This trick of the brain makes us desire the particular sorts of foods that we need at a given time, and helps us to balance our nutritional intake. Using fMRI, Rolls has shown that in humans the response in the orbitofrontal cortex to the odor of a food eaten to satiety decreases, but the response to the odor of another food that has not been eaten does not change. Perception of the intensity of the smell of the consumed food does not change, but perception of its pleasantness (hedonic valence) does.

In another study he showed that swallowing is not necessary for sensory-specific satiety to occur. Quizzed about this in relation to wine, Rolls was rightly cautious about speculating, but agreed that sensory-specific satiety might have some effect during a wine tasting where a taster is repeatedly encountering the same sort of taste or smell. At a large trade tasting it is quite common to taste as many as a hundred wines in a session. If sensory-specific satiety does occur in this sort of setting, it is likely that the brain will be processing the taste of your last wine differently to that of the first—assuming that the tastes or smells have some components in common, such as tannins, fruit, or oak.

This all makes perfect sense at a practical level. I love raspberries, but they would lose their appeal if I had already eaten five punnets of them. While I would still recognize them as raspberries, my brain is changing how attractive I find different flavors according to other information it is receiving.

When you have not eaten for a long time, even simple foods can taste great; their hedonic valence has been altered by your state of hunger.

How the Brain Turns Molecules into Smell

Smell research has typically focused on receptors and molecules. Ever since the molecular nature of olfactory receptors was pinpointed in 1991, scientists have tried to match the 400 or so functioning olfactory receptors that humans possess to chemical structures on smell molecules. The goal of this research? To identify specific molecular features recognized by olfactory receptors, and from there to be able to design specific artificial smell compounds. This would greatly benefit the multibillion-dollar perfume and cosmetic industry, for example.

Theoretically, the simplest way our olfactory system could function would be for each olfactory receptor neuron to carry one type of receptor (this is thought to be the case), and for each of these receptors to recognize a single aromatic molecule. If you were to design a robot that could smell, this would likely be your approach. This is the concept behind an electronic nose: it is tuned to recognize the chemical structures of specific molecules.

To develop this line of thinking, when the receptor detects the molecule, the result is an electric signal; this is processed by the brain, which in turn presents our conscious perception with the experience of that molecule. Again, if you were designing a robot's sense of smell, you would need to take that electric signal from your tuned receptor and find some way of representing it so the robot can act on this information. How may the concept of "representing" be explained? Probably, the simplest way is to use the analogy of a laptop. When I strike the key "A," it creates a signal that the computer then represents as the letter "a" on the screen, or the capital letter "A" if I hold the shift key down. In a simple smell system, a smell—such as strawberry or vanilla—would be detected by a receptor; this would fire an electric signal that the brain would represent to my consciousness as the smell of strawberry or vanilla. I would experience the initial receptor–molecule interaction as a smell, based on electrical activity and processing in my brain that is just as mysterious to me as the link between pressing a computer key and seeing a letter on a screen.

But we know that this simple, robotic view of smell is far too simplistic, because we have 400 or so olfactory receptor types, and yet we can recognize perhaps 10,000 different smell molecules. This means that many, if not all, olfactory receptors are recognizing more than one smell molecule. In turn, there must be some combinatorial signal that leads to the perception of each individual smell.

There is a further problem. Consider the smell of wine or coffee. These are smells that are blends of many hundreds if not thousands of aromatic compounds. And yet we regard them as a single smell. The simple robotic smell system where one receptor recognizes one smell molecule, which is then represented in some

readout, simply is not adequate to deal with the real-life situation where we encounter mixtures of many smell molecules. If you want an olfactory system that functions in a biologically useful way, you will need a rather different way of organizing it.

So there is a problem with the traditional approach to understanding smell—that of trying to identify how the molecular features of a smell are represented. This receptor–molecule focus has not really explained much about how we actually experience olfaction. A new theory of smell, though, looks like it may have a lot more explanatory power. It is called the perceptual learning approach, and it draws heavily on the way that we carry out vision, by dealing with the world in terms of objects.

Smell objects are created through learning by what is called synthetic processing. This is where we learn to recognize combinations of smells that occur together. These objects might also include information from other senses, such as taste and color, and also "affective" input (how much we like or dislike them). Researchers Donald Wilson and Richard Stevenson have proposed this new object-based theory of smell. They state: "We propose that experience and cortical plasticity play a critical, defining role in odor perception, and that current views of a highly analytical, 'receptor-centric' process are insufficient to account for current data." According to this view, we learn to recognize odor objects. This is very similar to what occurs in vision. Wilson and Stevenson say: "Odorants and odorant features that co-occur are synthesized through plasticity within central circuits to form single perceptual outcomes that are resistant to background interference, intensity fluctuations, or partial degradation."

"Learned odor objects may include multimodal components, and recognition of familiar odor objects can be shaped by context, attention, and expectation."
Wilson and Stevenson

Simplicity Derived from Memory

One observation that has led to this shift in thinking is the way that we treat multicomponent mixtures as single odors. As I mentioned earlier, complex mixtures are dealt with as one odor object, such as the smell of wine or coffee. This is because we are recognizing objects when we smell. Knowledge of the molecular features that are being detected by the olfactory receptors is not sufficient to predict the nature of the smell that is perceived. How the receptor activity is "read" by the brain depends on past experiences and current expectations.

In order to dig a little deeper in explaining this concept, let us consider vision. On the retina, the image seen by the eyes is inverted and back to front, and it consists of pixels: single dots of information about the light reaching that bit of the retina. It is the higher-processing systems in the brain that begin to extract information from this collection of pixels. It looks for features that are meaningful, such as edges, contrast differences, things that are moving, and so on. Our visual system is looking for objects. We understand the world around us in terms of objects; indeed, as infants develop into young children, a lot of their interest is taken up in recognizing and naming these objects.

Recognition of Objects

In our memory, we have developed lots of templates for various objects through our experience. So, when we look at a visual scene, the first thing we do (quickly and unconsciously) is to look for objects. We see something, and we check against our templates whether it fits the criteria for a particular type of object. If the answer is yes, we conclude that is an object of that type. Further, based on our experience of how this sort of object behaves and how we should interact with it, we can decide whether it is significant or not in this current context.

As an example, there are certain features that we associate with a car. Once we have this car object in our memory, whenever we see a scene with a car in it, we immediately identify it as "car." We can recognize cars of all shapes and sizes immediately as cars, independently of the specific details of each particular car object. These objects stay the same regardless of major changes in lighting and intensity. For example, colors change from morning to evening, and yet we still recognize objects and their colors. Dealing with the world by identifying and manipulating objects makes the computational problems of vision a lot easier.

A face is a particularly important and relevant object in any visual scene, and so we are very good at picking out faces in scenes, even if they are crowded. Our brains have dedicated face-detection modes, and we are so good at this that we only need a very few features to do it.

Cartoons provide a great example of how we only need a restricted set of features to recognize important objects in our

Humans have exceptional abilities in recognizing faces, to the extent that we can recognize "faces" where there are none, like a bearded face of Jesus on a piece of toast, or a large-nosed face in a cloud. This phenomenon is known as face pareidolia, the illusory perception of nonexistent faces.

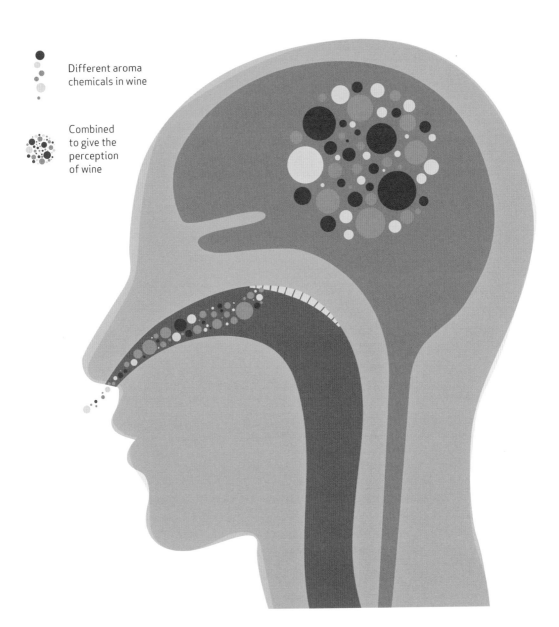

Different aroma chemicals in wine

Combined to give the perception of wine

How We Deal with Complex Odor Mixtures

Wine contains a complex mixture of odor molecules, yet we are able to recognize it as the single odor object we call "wine." Even wines that are quite different in composition are recognized very quickly to be wine. We can then examine these further to separate them into types of wine.

environment. With a few small strokes of a pen, a good cartoonist can create objects that we recognize very clearly as people, and from these very limited features we can make inferences about the intent or emotional state of the characters. Animations do this beautifully. Uta Frith and colleagues devised a set of simple animations with just two triangles. The two triangles move around and interact. One is larger than the other, and just from this simple animation most people with normal abilities to "mentalize" (work out the intentions and emotional state of others) can report on the nature of the interaction of these two shapes. From virtually no information at all we can attribute mental states to triangles, and empathize with them as if they were human.

A related phenomenon in animation is known as the "uncanny valley." When we see animated movies featuring human characters, we like those characters more when they are realistically human, but only up to a point. Once the characters become too realistic, they enter the "uncanny valley," where we find them a bit disturbing, and like them less. The animation of one popular film, *The Polar Express* (2004), is often cited as being realistic enough to enter this uncanny valley, and thus be slightly uncomfortable to watch. This probably explains why some of the more successful super-realistic animated films have featured toys or animals as their leading characters.

The Brain's Recognition of Smells

Ernest Polak came up with a new model of olfaction in 1973. He envisaged a large set of diversely tuned olfactory receptors that signal the pattern of odor features in a stimulus. He postulated that "the brain attempts to recognize this odor image by scanning it and resolving it into previously stored patterns." This would be similar to object perception in vision. This idea is supported by the fact that we can complete degraded inputs and recognize familiar patterns despite changes in odor intensity or the presence of background odors. Just as we pick out familiar visual objects from a crowded scene, we are able to pick out odor objects against what would seem to be a confusing mix of smells. Also, our familiarity with a smell (an odor object) enhances our ability to discriminate it.

Think of an orange. An orange has shape properties (it is spherical), texture properties (it has dimpled skin with two poles), color properties (it is called an orange for a reason), and also properties of smell and taste. It also has touch properties; we know what an orange feels like in our hands. Yet we think of an orange as a single object, and this object is fully multimodal.

For people with normal senses, wine tastes and smells of wine. It is a liquid that usually comes from a bottle, which is opened (with a corkscrew, or by twisting off a screwcap) and then poured into a glass. It is then drunk. Our experience of the wine is one in which the wine is a whole. Most people do not sniff the wine first: they will take a sip. And then they respond to the wine in its entirety. Usually, their response is a hedonic one: I like it or I do not like it. It is relatively rare for people outside of the wine trade to separate out liking from quality. Wine, a complex mixture of smells and tastes, has become an object. Within the set of wine there are subsets: white, red, pink, sweet, dry, and so on. But these subsets are still dealt with as objects.

What we do when we try to examine a wine as professionals is to fight against our understanding of wine as an object. We are trying to distinguish individual components in a complex mix, and that is quite difficult, because it is not how our sense of smell normally works. Our sense of smell, as we have discussed, is tuned to recognize patterns that we can then treat as smell objects.

Extending the Idea of Smell Objects to Flavor

I have discussed how flavor is multimodal, drawing on a number of sensory systems. The latest thinking about how this single perception of flavor comes about is that it might also be an object-based system, similar to olfaction. Here it is the oral referral of olfaction when food or drink is in our mouths that binds together all the different senses in a flavor "object." We imagine that the retronasal smell that contributes to flavor is coming from where the food or drink is activating the sense of touch. But although our brains may have encoded flavor objects that we can access consciously, we have only a limited ability to identify the separate smells that contribute to a flavor object. It is likely that any object recognition in smell and flavor resembles face processing in vision. It is configurational, based on perceptual fusion. We see the whole thing, but we are also able, in a very limited way, to access the components that make up the object.

In some ways, all of our object-based perception of the world around us is truly multimodal. While not all objects have input from all the senses, considering each of the senses in isolation does not necessarily give us full insight into how we experience the world.

These are quite complicated ideas, but they are important concepts to grapple with if we are to understand what is happening in flavor perception. But a word of caution: "Flavor objects, assuming there are any multisensory objects, gets very philosophical pretty quickly," says Spence. "I'm not saying it is wrong, but my gut feel is that there is more work to be done defining what exactly flavor objects are."

Trained Tasters Experience Wine Differently

In 2002, researchers of the Functional Neuroimaging Laboratory of the Santa Lucia Foundation in Rome, headed by Dr. Alessandro Castriota-Scanderbeg, put together a simple yet elegant study addressing a key question: do trained tasters experience wine differently from novices? The researchers asked seven professional sommeliers and seven other people, matched for age and sex but without specific wine-tasting abilities, to taste wine while they monitored their brain responses.

But getting someone to taste wine while they are having their brain scanned is no trivial feat. "The experience was pretty uncomfortable," recalls one of the sommeliers involved, Andrea Sturniolo. "I was under a tunnel with four plastic tubes in my mouth, totally immobile." Through these tubes the researchers fed the subjects with a series of four liquids: three different wines, and a glucose solution as a control. Subjects were told to try to identify the wines and form some sort of critical judgment about them. They were also asked to judge when the perception of the wine was strongest: while it was in the mouth ("taste"), or immediately after swallowing ("aftertaste"). "The experiment lasted a good fifty minutes," says Sturniolo, "which seemed endless." He added: "certainly they were not the ideal conditions to carry out such a delicate experiment, but as these conditions were identical for all participants, I think the results are reliable."

So what did the scans show? Some brain regions—notably the primary and secondary taste areas, in the insula and orbitofrontal cortex—were activated in both sets of subjects during the "taste" phase. But during this initial period, another area was activated, but only in the sommeliers. This was the front of a region known as the amygdala–hippocampal area. However, in the "aftertaste" phase the untrained subjects also showed activation of this amygdala–hippocampal area, but only on the right side, whereas in the sommeliers this zone was activated on both sides. In addition, during the aftertaste the sommeliers exclusively showed further activation in the left dorsolateral prefrontal cortex.

Given its importance in the processing of flavor, it is not surprising that the orbitofrontal cortex was one of the regions activated in the brains of both trained and nontrained wine tasters in this study. But what about the other areas—the ones that were highlighted specifically in the sommeliers?

First, we have the amygdala–hippocampal area. This is a zone that plays a key role in processing motivation (the amygdala) and memory (the hippocampus). According to Castriota-Scanderbeg, "the finding of an early and consistent activation of the amygdala–hippocampus complex in the sommelier group suggests a greater motivation for the recognition process." This may indicate that the sommeliers were expecting a reward and thus pleasure from the wine-tasting process. The other key area is the left dorsolateral prefrontal cortex, which is a zone involved in the planning and use of cognitive (thinking) strategies. The sommeliers' unique

Object Recognition in Smell

According to the theory of object recognition, we learn to recognize broadly similar olfactory receptor activation patterns as particular smell "objects." Here, the concept is illustrated in a simple way. The colored dots indicate receptors that are activated. In each case, the wine is recognized as an object, even though there is some variation in the receptor patterns.

activation here is consistent with the idea that only experienced tasters follow specific analytical strategies when wine is in their mouths. The researchers speculate that these strategies might be of a linguistic kind, associating words with specific flavors. We will return to this important concept later.

It seems that the sommeliers were experiencing something different to the average person when they tasted wine, just as fMRI studies on musicians have shown that music activates different areas of trained musicians' brains to those of casual listeners. "There is clear evidence that the neural connections of the brain change with training and experience," says Castriota-Scanderbeg. He explains that "there are two apparently contradictory ways that the brain adjusts its structural network in parallel with the increasing expertise of the subject." The first, and most common, is to assign a specific function to a smaller cluster of cells higher up in the brain's hierarchy. The second strategy is to recruit more brain areas to help with a complex task. Experienced wine tasters seem to follow this second strategy, drawing on new brain areas to help with the analysis of sensory stimuli.

During rehabilitation of stroke patients it is common to see a particular task activate a much smaller but higher region in the brain at the end of the process than it did at the beginning.

More recently, Lionel Pazart and colleagues did a similar study, attempting to address this issue but ironing out some of the methodological problems they thought that the Castriota-Scanderbeg study contained. In this study, published in 2014, they looked at ten famous sommeliers and ten gender- and age-matched controls. Two wines were included in the experiments: an Arbois Chardonnay and a Jura Pinot Noir. They put their twenty subjects in an fMRI machine and sent wine into their mouths by tubes while their brains were being scanned. The goal was to identify differences in brain activation, comparing wine and water tasting in both groups, to see what effect expertise was having. They found that in both experts and novices there was both overlapping and integration of gustatory (taste), tactile (touch), and olfactory (smell) inputs in the insular cortex. This flavor percept was then conveyed to upstream regions in the brainstem and thalamus, and downstream regions in the amygdala, orbitofrontal cortex, and anterior cingulate cortex.

That it is difficult to categorize and recognize odors is widely recognized. However, trained wine experts such as sommeliers develop the ability to describe the sensations they experience when they taste wine, while novices find it very hard to use words to describe what they experience. As I will discuss in chapter 5, wine expertise is thought to be based more on cognitive power than on enhanced perceptual ability. In Pazart's study, the sommeliers' numerous activations were seen in brain areas involved in memory processes, predominantly in the left hemisphere. These experts seemed to process the sensory information more economically than the control group, who showed activation in different associative cortices, predominantly in the right hemisphere. The experts are using their brains more efficiently. The results also showed that wine experts work simultaneously on sensory quality assessment and on recognizing wines that they are trying.

Brain Changes Wrought by Experience

The implications of these experiments for wine tasting are clear. Assuming that you have drunk a resonable amount of wine over a number of years, do you remember one of the wines that first really appealed to you? If you were to go back in time now and taste that wine again, while possessing your current wine-drinking history, you would actually perceive something quite different as you sipped that wine the second time around. Your brain has been changed by drinking all that wine (and not in the sense of alcohol-induced neural degeneration). By paying attention as you have been drinking—just as the sommeliers in this study had done—your response to wine has come to differ from that of untrained subjects. This underlines the importance of the learning component in wine appreciation.

Another study, carried out by a group of researchers from California working in the new field of neuroeconomics, reinforces the idea that knowledge changes perception. The researchers used fMRI to show that the information people are given about the wine can change their actual perception of the wine, and how pleasant they find it. The authors discuss a term in economics called Experienced Utility (EU), and describe how marketing frequently aims to change the EU of a particular good without changing the nature of the good.

The researchers chose to use wine as a test case of how price can modify EU. They gave a group of twenty subjects five different Cabernet Sauvignon wines while they lay in an fMRI machine. The subjects were told the retail prices of the wines they were tasting,

People versed in one culture of wine may need to relearn about wine when exploring another. Even if you have years of expertise in Australian reds, for example, you may have to start from scratch when trying to appreciate German Riesling.

and were told to focus on the flavor of the wines and say how much they liked them. However, there was a clever twist to this experiment. In reality, only three wines were being presented to the subjects; two of the wines were presented as different wines at different price points. What the subjects actually tasted were a $5 wine (wine one, at its real price); a $10 wine (wine two, which was actually a $90 wine); a $35 wine (wine three); a $45 wine (wine one, at a false price) and a $90 wine (wine two, at its real price).

Unsurprisingly, there was a correlation between price and liking. Significantly, subjects preferred wines one and two when they were told they were drinking the higher-priced wines. The brain scans, comparing the response of subjects when tasting the same wines but believing them to be different and at different prices, showed that the parts of the brain that experience pleasure are more active when subjects think the wine is higher priced. The price is not just affecting perceived quality—it seems to be affecting the actual quality of the wine by changing the nature of the perceptive experience. The importance of these results are that they demonstrate that our expectation as we approach wine—perhaps caused by sight of the label—will actually change the nature of our wine-drinking experience.

Verbal Representations of the Tasting Experience

Cognitive psychologist Frédéric Brochet has created a body of important work that is highly relevant here. Following studies of the practice of wine tasting as it is usually carried out by professionals, he claims that the practice and teaching of tasting rests on a fragile theoretical basis. "Tasting is representing," says Brochet, "and when the brain carries out a 'knowledge' or 'understanding' task, it manipulates representations." A "representation" is a conscious experience constructed by the mind on the basis of a physical experience, which in the case of wine tasting is the taste, smell, sight, and mouthfeel of a wine. Brochet uses three methodologies in his work: textual analysis (looking at the sorts of words that tasters use to verbalize their representations); behavior analysis (inferring cognitive mechanisms from looking at how subjects act); and cerebral function analysis (looking at how the brain responds to wine directly through the use of fMRI).

While we will be discussing words for wine in depth in chapter 8, Brochet's work on textual analysis, which involves the statistical study of the words used in a text, is worth mentioning here. Brochet used five data sets, consisting of tasting notes from *Guide Hachette*, Robert Parker, Jacques Dupont, Brochet himself, and notes on eight wines collected at Vinexpo from forty-four professionals. Employing textual analysis software called Alceste, Brochet studied the way that the different tasters used words to describe their tasting experiences.

Brochet summarizes his six key results as follows. First, the authors' descriptive representations are based on the types of wines and not on the different parts of the tasting. Second, the representations are "prototypical," that is, specific vocabularies are used to describe types of wines, and each vocabulary represents a type of wine. Putting this another way, when a taster experiences a particular wine, the words they use to describe it are those that they link to this sort (or type) of wine. Third, the range of words used (or lexical fields) are different for each author. Fourth, tasters possess a specific vocabulary for preferred and nonpreferred wines. No taster seems able to put aside their preferences when their representations are described. Brochet adds that this result, the dependence of representations on preferences, is well known from the fragrance world. Fifth, color is a major factor in organizing the classes of descriptive terms used by the tasters, and has a major influence on the sorts of descriptors used. Sixth, cultural information is present in the sensorial descriptions.

Brochet then invited fifty-four subjects to take part in a series of experiments in which they had to describe the smell of a real red wine and a real white wine (see p.15). A few days later the same group returned to describe the smell of the same white wine, and also that of the same white wine that had been colored red with a neutral-tasting food colorant. Interestingly, on both days they described the "red" wine using identical terms, even though one of them was actually a white wine. Brochet concluded that the perception of smell conformed to color: vision is having a significant input in the wine-tasting process. Brochet points out that this is known in the food and fragrance industries; it is the reason that no one sells colorless syrups or perfumes anymore.

In a second and equally mischievous experiment, Brochet served the same average-quality wine twice to people with an interval of a

Brochet states that "certain descriptive terms referring to cognitive representation probably come from memory or information heard or read by the subject, but neither the tongue or the nose could be the object of the coding." In other words, judgments about wine call upon elements outside direct sensory experience of the wine.

week. The twist was that on the first occasion it was packaged and served to people as a Vin de Table, and on the second as a Grand Cru wine. The subjects believed they were tasting a simple wine and then a very special wine, even though it was one and the same. What Brochet found in the subjects' tasting notes made telling reading. For the "Grand Cru" wine versus the Vin de Table, "a lot" replaces "a little"; "complex" replaces "simple"; and "balanced" replaces "unbalanced"—all because of the sight of the label.

Brochet explains the results in terms of a phenomenon called "perceptive expectation": subjects perceive what they have pre-perceived, and then they find it difficult to back away from that. For us humans, visual information is much more important than chemosensory information, so we tend to trust vision more. This explains enologist Émile Peynaud's observation that "blind tasting of great wines is often disappointing."

A further study in Brochet's series examined how the qualitative ratings of a series of wines differed among a group of wine tasters. This group of eight tasters were asked to rank eighteen wines, which they tasted blind in order of preference. The results differed widely. With a similar methodology to that employed by the researchers of the Santa Lucia Foundation (see p.76), Brochet used MRI to assess the brain response of four subjects to a series of wines. One of the most interesting results obtained was that the same stimulus produced different brain responses in different people. In terms of brain area activated, one person was more verbal, another more visual.

When a person tastes the same wine several times, the images of each tasting are somewhat different. Brochet concluded that this demonstrates the "expression of the variable character of the representation." The representation is a "global form, integrating, on equal terms, chemo-sensorial, visual, imaginary, and verbal imagination."

Undoing the Brain's Work

In this chapter, we have been looking at the way that the brain combines information from different senses to create the perception of flavor. Much of this combination is taking place before we are consciously aware of it, just as a newsroom edits material to present a daily fifteen-minute news bulletin. What we perceive is not an exact correspondence with reality; the brain presents us with only the information we need, just as a good map helps us to navigate a city or find a destination on a journey, without overwhelming us with unnecessary information. Yet when it comes to analytic wine tasting of the sort practiced by the wine trade, we are trying to do something that is at odds with the way our perception works. Barry Smith, codirector of the Centre for the Study of the Senses at University of London's Institute of Philosophy, comments:

> "Serious wine tasters are trying to undo the brain's work, which is a crazy thing to be doing. The brain has beautifully put all this information together for you below the level of consciousness, so it appears in your experience as an integrated unified whole. Then what tasters do is pull those bits apart again and make themselves notice them. What is the texture like? How fine are the tannins? What is the astringency? Which acids or sugars am I getting? How do the aromas persist? It is trying to look behind the curtain, by reflection from the top level. If they weren't integrated, you'd have all that information lying around in bits: they would be there for you to notice separately. But the brain's job was to find the thing that has got all of that together, and tell me how collectively it tastes. So wine tasting is odd."

Smith goes on to say:

> "[Master of Wine] Jasper Morris said [that] when you are teaching people to taste, and you are getting them to taste the relative acidity in ten wines, and you ask them to rank the wines, if you ask them whether they like the wines they say, I do not know. Then you say forget all this, just drink as you would at home. And they say, oh, I quite like that. It is as if, when you are concentrating on the parts, you are not getting the synthetic experience of the whole, which is where I think the hedonics resides. The unification the brain does is the vehicle for the pleasure and hedonics."

This is an interesting perspective. Smith is suggesting that analytic wine tasting is an activity quite different from normal wine drinking. It is almost as if critics should take a step back after their analytical work and just drink the wine as a normal person might, in order to understand it properly. In the next chapter we will look at the chemical composition of wine, and relate this to the perception of wine. We will be returning to the brain in chapter 7, where we will explore the nature of conscious experience, and look a little more deeply at how we interact with the world.

Wine Flavor Chemistry

Wine is a chemical "soup," and many of these chemicals have tastes and smells. The traditional understanding of wine flavor chemistry has been that flavor is additive. Sensory scientists have explored the individual flavor and aroma impact of these chemicals and then tried to relate this to the overall properties of the wine. But now this view is being questioned. Some chemicals may have relatively low impact on their own—they may even be below the threshold of perception—but reconstitution experiments in which single or related groups of compounds are selectively removed have revealed that these seemingly unimportant chemicals can have a large impact on overall wine flavor. In this chapter, our new understanding of wine chemistry is explored in depth.

The Complexity of Wine Flavor

We will start with the assumption that the flavor of wine is based on chemicals present in the wine. But, as we have already discussed in the previous chapters, things are not quite this straightforward. As you and I taste the same glass together, while our sensory systems are encountering the same molecules, we are probably having rather different experiences, although our experiences are sufficiently similar to allow us to discuss the wine. For the purposes of this chapter, though, we will ignore this extra level of complication, and talk about the chemicals in wine as they might be experienced by an average person with a normally functioning sensory system and an average amount of wine-tasting experience.

Wine is a complicated mix of many hundreds of flavor-active compounds. The exact number of volatile molecules found in wine is unknown, but estimates generally fall in the range of 800 to 1,000. There are clearly many of them, although in each wine only a limited number of these are found above the level at which most humans would detect them, known as the perception threshold. A recent development has been the application to wine of a chemical analytical approach called metabolomics. This uses powerful analytical techniques to analyze everything that is present in the wine at the same time, generating a huge amount of data. Then, equally powerful statistical tools are used to analyze these data and assess the chemical composition of the wine as a whole. This unbiased approach has the benefit that it is neutral: the study does not start with any assumptions about what is there in the first place. There is a lot of interest in this approach because it could, for example, create a fingerprint of what might be specific to wines of a certain place. For example, it might be possible to look at a range of wines from Gevrey-Chambertin in Burgundy, France, and then prove which ones came from specific terroirs, even though this is very hard to do from tasting alone. Also, it could be a valuable tool in authenticating valuable or old wines.

Ultimately, though, a reductionist/additive approach—in which we break down wine into its many components, examine what each of those components smells and tastes like, and then work back to the flavor of the wine—is not going to work.

Wine aroma and flavor are not additive (simply the sum of the different smells and tastes of the various chemicals it contains). Instead, there are many interactions between the different components, including masking interactions (where one compound interferes with the perception of another) and synergistic interactions (where a perception is created by a combination of two or more different compounds).

The volatility of various flavor compounds can be altered by other components of the wine. Added to this, human perception of various flavor chemicals is altered by their context—the suite of other chemicals present in the wine. Thus chemical "A" might be below detection level in one wine, and above it in another, even though its concentration is the same in both. The smell of the wine can also influence the way we interpret what is in our mouths. One study showed that smelling something sweet makes us rate the sweetness of a sugar solution in our mouths more highly. And, in a remarkable twist, even imagining smelling something sweet can change our rating of the sweetness of the sugar solution.

One further complicating factor is that many of the most important chemicals that shape a wine's specific character are present at very low concentrations. Look at winemakers' old adversary 2,4,6-trichloroanisole (TCA), the chief culprit in cork taint, as an example. This musty-smelling taint is detectable at extremely low concentrations of less than five parts per trillion—a concentration that is often compared to drops in an Olympic-size swimming pool, or seconds in many centuries; it is not many of either. Conversely, the most prevalent constituents of wine are often relatively unimportant in terms of the sensory qualities of the wine. Also to be remembered is that those compounds that we currently know most about are not necessarily the most important in determining wine flavor; they are simply those that we can sample using the techniques available to us.

Vicente Ferreira of the University of Zaragoza in Spain is one of the leading experts in wine composition and aroma. His research has been really interesting because he has taken a global look at wine flavor. Ferreira separates the various flavor compounds of wines into three different groups, a structured way of thinking that helps us to grapple with this difficult subject. In addition, there is his important concept of the wine matrix. While some wines contain what he terms "impact" compounds, many lack these, instead containing a large number of active odorants, each of which adds nuances to the wine.

We saw in chapter 3 how the sense of smell works by object recognition. We process the world around us in terms of objects, and smell looks at patterns of multiple odorants that make up objects that we can identify. So, for the wine expert, there is the object that represents the smell of Sauvignon Blanc, or Pinot Noir, or mature Bordeaux. We recognize the objects but find it hard to identify the components. It follows that if we are to understand wine flavor chemistry, we must deal with mixtures of smells simultaneously, rather than in isolation: the wine is a whole.

Wine Odor

Ferreira describes the basal composition of what he refers to as "wine aroma," which is the result of twenty different aromatic chemicals that are present in all wines to make a global wine odor. Of these twenty aromas, just one is present in grapes (β-damascenone); the rest are produced by the metabolism of yeasts, in many cases working on precursors present in the grape juice. These include higher alcohols (for example, butyric, isoamylic, hexylic, phenylethylic); acids (acetic, butyric, hexanoic, octanoic, isovaleric); ethyl esters from fatty acids; acetates and compounds such as diacetyl; and ethanol.

In addition, there are sixteen "contributory compounds" that are present in most wines but at relatively low levels. Their odor activity value (OAV; the ratio of the concentration of the compound to its perception threshold) is usually below one, but they have odor activity that is synergistic, contributing to characteristic scents despite being at lower concentrations than would normally lead to them being smelled. The perception threshold is the concentration at which a normal person can smell

One of the challenges for sensory scientists is that in many cases it is not possible to establish a clear link between a sensory descriptor and a single-aroma molecule. Instead, what tasters refer to by specific descriptors is often the result of the interaction of two or more odor-active chemicals. In the past, wine aroma research was all about finding a molecule to explain everything, but Ferreira's work has caused people to think about combinations of aromas.

the compound, and it differs according to whether it is in water or wine. The type of wine will also affect its detection. Included in contributory compounds are volatile phenols (guaiacol, eugenol, isoeugenol, 2,6-dimethoxyphenol, 4-allyl-2,6-dimethoxyphenol); ethyl esters; fatty acids; acetates of higher alcohols; ethyl esters of branched fatty acids; aliphatic aldehydes with eight, nine, or ten carbon atoms; branched aldehydes (such as 2-methylpropanol, 2-methylbutanol, 3-methylbutanol, ketones, aliphatic γ-lactones); and vanillin and its derivatives.

Impact Compounds

Impact compounds are a group of chemicals that are responsible for giving characteristic aromas to certain wines, even when they are present at extremely low concentrations. These are of great interest because they often contribute to distinctive varietal aromas. However, many wines lack distinct impact compounds. For example, Sauvignon Blanc is very interesting as a grape variety because much of its characteristic aroma is believed to come from a small number of impact compounds, chiefly methoxypyrazines (of which the most significant is 2-methoxy-3-isobutylpyrazine) and three thiols (4-mercapto-4-methylpentan-2-one [4MMP], 3-mercaptohexan-1-ol [3MH], and 3-mercaptohexyl acetate [3MHA]). Impact compounds, some of which are detailed below, have become the focus of intensive research.

- Methoxypyrazine: the most important one is 2-methoxy-3-isobutylpyrazine (MIBP; known widely as isobutyl methoxypyrazine), which has a detection threshold of 2 ng/liter in water and white wine (slightly higher in reds), and is responsible for green, grassy, green pepper aromas. 2-isopropyl-3-methoxypyrazine (isopropyl methoxypyrazine) is also important, but likely secondary to MIBP.
- Monoterpenes, such as linalool, which is important in many white wines, such as Muscat, and has floral, citric aromas.
- Rose-cis oxide: characteristic of Gewürztraminer, this has a sweet, flowery, rose petal aroma.
- Rotundone: a sesquiterpene that gives pepperiness to Syrah at incredibly tiny concentrations. Remarkably, one-fifth of people cannot smell it.

The methoxypyrazines are one of the few classes of impact compounds formed in the grapes, and are highly stable throughout wine fermentation and aging.

- Polyfunctional thiols (mercaptans). These include 4MMP, which has a box tree aroma (4.2 ng/liter detection threshold); 3MHA, which has a tropical fruit/passion fruit scent (60 ng/liter); and 3MH, which smells of grapefruit. These three are important in the aroma of Sauvignon Blanc. A number of other thiols are also important in wine aroma, usually as fault compounds.

In addition to the actual aroma molecules, some of Ferreira's most interesting recent work has been on what is called the nonvolatile matrix of wine. The idea here is that wine constituents that do not have any aromatic characteristic of their own may still strongly influence the way that the various aromatic molecules present in wine are perceived. In effect, the nonvolatile matrix influences how we interpret the smell of wine. Ferreira and his colleagues carried out an interesting experiment in which they showed that the nonvolatile matrix is critical in determining the aromatic character of wine, even to the point that when the aromatics from a white wine are put into a red wine matrix, the wine smells like a red wine. "Knowledge of volatile and nonvolatile composition alone is not enough to completely understand the overall wine aroma and in general its flavor," state the authors in the introduction to the paper. "Interactions among odorants, perceptual interactions between sense modalities, and interactions between the odorant and different elements of the wine nonvolatile matrix can all affect the odorant volatility, flavor release, and overall perceived flavor or aroma intensity and quality."

For this study, they selected six different Spanish wines, three white and three red. The aromatics from samples of each of these wines were removed by the use of a process called lyophilization (freeze drying) and any remaining aromatics were removed by using a chemical called dichloromethane. The dichloromethane was itself removed by passing nitrogen through the sample. The extract was then dissolved in mineral water to produce the wine matrix.

In a separate series of manipulations, aromatic extracts were collected from each of the wines, producing six aroma extracts. Then a series of reconstituted wines were made by combining different wine matrices with different aroma extracts. In total, eighteen reconstituted wines were made and analyzed by a trained sensory panel. The results showed that the nonvolatile extract

(the matrix) had a surprisingly large impact on aroma perception of the wine. As an example, when the aroma extract from a fruity white wine was reconstituted with the nonvolatile extract from another white, there was relatively little effect. But when it was combined with the red wine nonvolatile matrix, there was a large difference. The sensory panel went on to use terms relating to red fruits, rather than terms typically used to describe white wines. Other red wine terms that started to appear were "spicy" and "woody." A similar effect occurred when red wine volatiles were added to a white wine matrix: "white," "yellow," and "tropical fruits" all start to appear in judges' tasting notes.

These results surprised the authors. Previous studies showed that nonvolatile components of wine can affect wine aroma, but this is largely through binding to them and making them less releasable. The remarkable thing about this study is that it

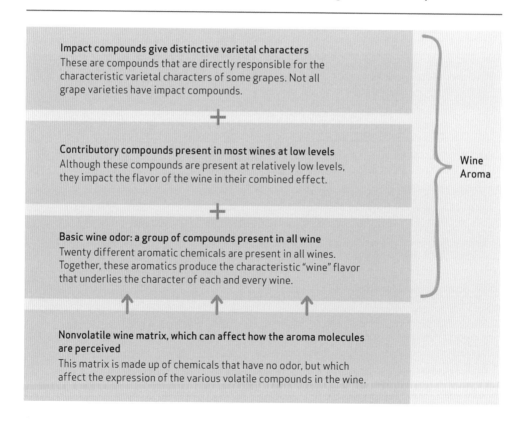

Impact compounds give distinctive varietal characters
These are compounds that are directly responsible for the characteristic varietal characters of some grapes. Not all grape varieties have impact compounds.

+

Contributory compounds present in most wines at low levels
Although these compounds are present at relatively low levels, they impact the flavor of the wine in their combined effect.

+

Basic wine odor: a group of compounds present in all wine
Twenty different aromatic chemicals are present in all wines. Together, these aromatics produce the characteristic "wine" flavor that underlies the character of each and every wine.

Wine Aroma

Nonvolatile wine matrix, which can affect how the aroma molecules are perceived
This matrix is made up of chemicals that have no odor, but which affect the expression of the various volatile compounds in the wine.

demonstrates that the nonvolatile matrix is having an important effect in modifying the perception of the volatile components of wine. It is well known that crossmodal sensory effects can modify perception, especially when vision is involved (as we saw in chapters 1 and 3, experts tasting a white wine colored red will describe its aroma in red wine terms). This factor was avoided in the study by serving the wine in black glasses and asking participants to describe the aromas before they tasted the wine.

What is emerging from these sorts of studies is a more holistic view of wine. While the reductionist approach attempts to study wine flavor by breaking it down into its constituent chemical compounds and then studying these in isolation, the field of wine flavor chemistry is maturing with the realization of the limits of reductionism. With this in mind, let us take a look at some of the key components of wine.

A view of the flavor of wine that treats the wine as a whole, and takes the human side of perception into account, is likely to lead to a more complete understanding of wine flavor.

Organic Acids

Acid helps wine to taste fresh, and also helps to preserve it. White wines with higher acidity usually age better than those with low acidity. Red wines can get by with a little less acidity because they contain phenolic compounds that help to preserve them. The main organic acids found in grapes are tartaric, malic, and citric. Tartaric acid is the key grape acid, and can reach levels of 15 grams per liter in unripe grapes. It is quite a strong acid and is specific to grapes. In musts it is found in the range of 3 to 6 grams per liter. Malic acid is abundant in green apples and, unlike tartaric acid, is widely found in nature. Before veraison (where grapes change color and their skins begin to soften) it can hit levels of 20 grams per liter in grapes. In warm climates, it is found in musts in the range of 1 to 2 grams per liter, and in cooler climates it occurs at 2 to 6 grams per liter. Citric acid is also widespread in nature, and is found in grapes at 0.5 to 1 gram per liter. Other organic acids present in grapes include D-gluconic acid, mucic acid, coumaric acid, and coumaroyl tartaric acid. Succinic, lactic, and acetic acids are among those produced during fermentation. Ascorbic acid may be added during winemaking as an antioxidant. If malolactic fermentation takes place, the malic acid is largely converted to lactic acid by the action of lactic acid bacteria. Lactic acid tastes less acid than malic.

Musts and wines are known as acidobasic buffer solutions. This means you have to work quite hard to change their pH levels (pH is a measure of the number of hydrogen ions in solution; the more acidic wines have lower pH). In contrast, if you add acid to water, you can shift its pH quite quickly because water has none of the buffering effect. It is the presence of compounds in musts and wines that makes it less easy to shift the pH (although it is a bit easier to shift pH in wine than must). It is difficult to predict the pH of a final wine by looking at the pH of its must because several things occur during the winemaking process that can change pH. Where acidification is needed, it is usually done with tartaric acid. Legally, pH may be changed with malic or citric acid, but because these are weaker acids, quite a bit more is required. Adding citric acid is not a good idea where malolactic fermentation is going to take place, because the bacteria turn citric acid into diacetyl, which has a buttery taste and can be quite off-putting.

High pH is not necessarily a bad thing: it can confer on a wine a deliciously smooth mouthfeel (as in some Provençal rosés or northern Rhône whites). Generally, though, winemaking at lower pH levels is safer because of the reduced risk of oxidation and microbial spoilage. The pH affects the amount of sulfur dioxide (SO_2) that is present in the active molecular form. At pH 3.0, 6 percent of SO_2 is in the molecular form, whereas at pH 3.5 only 2 percent is. In a wine that is less acidic, up to pH 4, 0.6 percent of SO_2 is in the molecular form, and so lots of acid would have to be added for it to have any significant effect in protecting the wine.

Confusingly, "TA" stands for both total and titratable acidity, and is used in analyses of wine. Total acidity is the total amount of organic acids in the wine. Titratable acidity is the ability of the acid in the wine to neutralize a base (an alkaline substance), which is usually sodium hydroxide. Total acidity is hard to measure in practice, so titratable acidity is used as an approximation; by definition it always going to be a lower figure than the total acidity. When the "TA" of a wine is given, it is usually the titratable acidity; it is expressed in grams per liter, but here is another potential source of confusion. Most countries use "tartaric acid equivalent," but some European countries use "sulfuric acid equivalent," which is two-thirds of the value of tartaric acid equivalent.

When it comes to the taste of acidity, what is more important, pH or TA? Most of the literature on this suggests that it is the TA

Winemakers can use malic acid to make small changes in pH because it does not fall out of solution in the same way that tartaric acid tends to, especially when there is potassium in the must or wine. Some winemakers in warmer climates use sulfuric acid illegally to change pH, because it is very effective at doing this.

that gives the taste of acidity, and so the figure that is important to look out for is not pH but TA. The confounding factor here is that pH and TA are usually correlated so they are hard to separate, in that low pH wines usually have high TA. But you can get higher pH wines with high TA, and here the acid would taste quite sour. The different organic acids do seem to have different flavors: tartaric is hard, malic is green, and lactic is softer with some sourness. Often, where tartaric acid is used to adjust the pH of wines from warm climates, the levels of acid needed result in the acid sticking out as very hard and angular, even where the pH is not especially low. Another issue is that added tartaric acid reduces potassium concentrations in the wine (they bind to form potassium bitartrate), and potassium is thought to play an important part in contributing to the weight or body of the wine.

Sugars and Sweetness

Sweetness in wine is a combination of three factors. First of all, there is sugar itself. This is sensed by sweetness taste receptors on the tongue. Second, there is a sweetness that comes from fruitiness. While sweetness is tasted, some wines can also smell sweet, even though sweetness is a taste modality. Most commercial red wines are dry in terms of sugar content, but many have sweet aromas from their fruitiness. Very ripe fruity flavors taste and smell sweet, even in the absence of sugar. The third source of sweetness is alcohol itself, which tastes sweet. It is really instructive to try the same red wine at different alcohol levels, where the alcohol has been removed by reverse osmosis or the spinning cone. As the alcohol level drops, with all other components remaining the same, the wine tastes progressively drier and less rounded and full. Where alcohol has been reduced substantially, such as in the new breed of lighter, 5.5 percent alcohol wines, it is necessary to add back some sweetness, usually in the form of residual sugar. It helps if the original wine has a very sweet fruit profile to begin with, too. Makers of lower alcohol whites sometimes blend in some Muscat or Gewürztraminer, which have sweet aromas, to increase the impression of sweetness.

In sweeter white wines and also Champagnes, sugar and acid balance are vital. The two play against each other. Sweetness is countered by acidity, such that a sweet wine with low acid seems

much sweeter (and often flabbier) than the same wine with high acidity. In Champagne, a typical dosage for a Brut (dry) Champagne is 8 to 10 grams per liter, which helps to offset the acidity but does not make the Champagne taste sweet. Botrytized sweet wines are prized because, as well as concentrating sweetness and flavor, the shriveling process of noble rot on the grapes concentrates the acid levels. The great sweet wines of the world have very high sugar levels as well as high acidity.

Polyphenols

These are probably the most important flavor chemicals in red wines, but are of much less importance in whites. Polyphenols are a large group of compounds that use phenol as their basic building block. An important property of phenolic compounds is that they associate spontaneously with a wide range of compounds, such as proteins and other phenolics, by means of a range of noncovalent

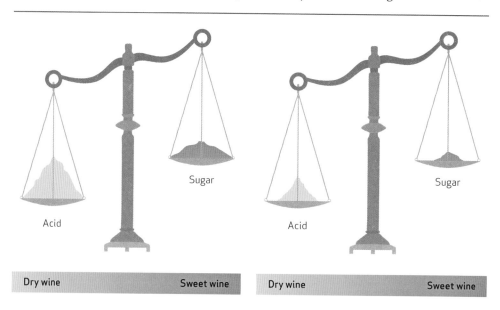

Acidity and Sweetness

Sweetness and acidity balance each other out: a wine with quite a lot of sugar can taste as dry as one with very little sugar if the acidity is high.

The flavor comes from the ratio between the sugar and the acid, rather than the quantity of either.

forces (for example, hydrogen bonding and hydrophobic effects). Phenolic compounds are widely thought to have health-enhancing effects, but their propensity to bind with proteins such as salivary proline-rich proteins (PRPs) will conspire against them reaching active sites in the body where they might be active. Among the polyphenols are the following important groups:

Non-flavonoid polyphenols There are two types of these smaller non-flavonoid polyphenolic compounds, the benzoic acids (such as gallic acid) and cinnamic acids. They are often present in grapes in a conjugated form (for example, as esters or glycosides).

Flavan-3-ols These are important in wine, and include catechin and epi-catechin. They are particularly important in their polymeric forms, where they are called procyanidins (often referred to as condensed tannins).

Flavonoids Comprising the flavonols and flavanonols, these are yellow-colored pigments found in red and white grapes.

Anthocyanins These are the red, blue, and black pigments in grapes, almost always found in the skins. Five different anthocyanin compounds are found in red wines, the dominant one being malvidin. They are not stable in young wines, but react with tannins to form complex pigments that gradually become larger as wine ages, to the point where they become insoluble and precipitate out. Oxygen has an important role in facilitating the process of phenolic polymerization. The color of pigments depends on the acidity of the grape must and the concentration of sulfur dioxide: they tend to be redder at lower pH (more acid) and more purple at higher pH.

Tannins The term "tannin" is chemically imprecise but is used by almost all wine tasters. It describes a group of complex plant chemicals found principally in bark, leaves, and immature fruit that form complexes with proteins and other plant polymers, such as polysaccharides. It is thought that the role of tannins is one of plant defense: they have an astringent, aversive taste that is off-putting to herbivores. In wine, tannins come from grape skins, stems, and seeds, and their extraction is heavily dependent on the particular winemaking process involved. Other tannins come from new barrels used to age wine. Tannin management is a crucial step in making red wines. Tannins are thought to taste astringent because they bind with salivary proline-rich proteins and precipitate them out. They may also react directly with tissues in the mouth, a topic discussed in chapter 3.

Alcohol

In considering chemicals that contribute to the flavor of wine, let us not forget alcohol. Produced by yeasts during fermentation, it is typically present in concentrations of 10 to 15 percent in most wines, although it can be lower or higher. As well as contributing its potent effects on our central nervous system, it affects the flavor of wine quite significantly.

Ethyl alcohol is the most important component of wine, and is produced by fermentation of sugars by yeasts. On its own, it does not taste of much, but the concentration of alcohol in the final wine has a marked effect on its sensory qualities. This is evidenced by the "sweetspot" tastings carried out during alcohol reduction trials. If a wine with a high natural alcohol level is subjected to alcohol reduction via reverse osmosis, a series of samples of the same wine can be prepared differing only in alcohol levels, say at half-degree intervals from 12 to 18 percent alcohol. Panels of tasters show marked preferences for some of these wines over others, and different descriptors are commonly used to describe the sensory properties of the samples. Excessive alcohol can lead to bitterness and astringency in a wine. It may also taste "hot." Hildegarde Heymann and colleagues studied the influence of alcohol on red wine perception in a study from 2013. They pointed out that alcohol levels had risen in many wines over the last twenty years, as a result of both climate change and market demand for more fruit-forward wines. The rise has come with flavor implications that may, in some cases, be unintended. Overall, alcohol influences taste and mouthfeel descriptors more than aroma descriptors. It enhances bitterness and astringency, but it suppresses sourness. It also alters the perception of sweetness (making the wine taste sweeter).

Alcohol has been shown to modify the solubility of many of the aroma compounds, making them less likely to leave the solution,

Although many would agree that alcohol levels have risen lately, there are few firm data points to back up this claim. The levels indicated on the label are not always totally accurate. Winemakers in the United States have 1.5 percent leeway below 14 percent and 1 percent thereafter. The European Union allows a 0.5 percent leeway. In New World countries under-reporting averages 0.45 percent, and in Europe it is 0.39 percent. So, a wine that is labeled as 14.5 percent may well be closer to 15 percent.

and thus making the wine less aromatic. An analytical chemistry experiment by R. S. Whiton and Bruce Zoecklein in 2000 showed that as alcohol rose from 11 to 14 percent, there was reduced recovery of typical wine volatile compounds. In 2007, Ferreira's group identified a range of esters responsible for the berry flavors in a series of red wines. But adding more of these to the wine did not increase the fruity impact because of the suppressing effect of other wine components, including alcohol. In another experiment they added increasing levels of ethanol to a solution of nine esters at the same concentration that they found in wine; they discovered that the fruity scent quickly fell as alcohol rose, to the point that, when alcohol reached 14.5 percent, the fruity aroma was totally masked by the alcohol. Alcohol also contributes a burning sensation and increases the perception of viscosity.

Heymann and colleagues showed that fresh fruit aromas decreased with increasing alcohol, along with floral aromas. Meanwhile, rising alcohol levels increased "wood," "pepper," and "chemical" flavors.

An interesting study was conducted in 2010 by French researcher Sophie Meillon and her colleagues, who took an Australian Syrah and reduced it in alcohol from its original strength (13.4 percent) down to 8 percent, also producing three wines at intermediate levels between these extremes. The researchers introduced the wines to seventy-one French consumers who drank red wines at least once a month, and measured how much they liked them and how complex they thought them to be. The Syrah at 8 percent was liked significantly less, but for the other wines there was no significant difference. Adding sugar to the 8 percent Syrah increased its liking considerably. They found they could segment this population by their reaction to the wines. Group One (eighteen individuals) liked the 11.5 percent wine the best, and liked the two lowest-alcohol wines much less than the other groups. Group Two significantly disliked the Syrah at 8 and 11.5 percent, but they liked the 13.5 and 8 percent wines. Group Three preferred the two lowest-alcohol wines. The more consumers disliked the alcohol-reduced wine, the more bottles they had in their cellar—an interesting finding.

Glycerol

After alcohol and water, glycerol is the most abundant component of wine. It is produced by yeasts during fermentation, and the final level will vary depending on the strain of the yeast, ripeness of the grapes, the fermentation dynamics, and the source of nitrogen in

Some people wrongly think that there is a relationship between the "tears" or "legs" that form on the side of a wineglass and the wine's glycerol content. These tears are formed by the difference in surface tension between water and alcohol, and their extent relates largely to the alcohol content of the wine, not wine quality. Known as the Marangoni effect, it is seen quite beautifully in young, deeply colored port.

the must. It is usually found at 4 to 9 grams per liter in dry wines, and is sometimes much higher in sweet wines made from nobly rotted (botrytized) grapes. It is widely thought that glycerol is desirable in wine because it adds body or viscosity. Certainly, on its own it has a slightly sweet taste, but you would need to have a lot of it in a wine for it to have a real effect on viscosity or mouthfeel. Glycerol's main contribution to quality is to add a slight sense of sweetness, which can be attractive. In sweet wines, it can pass the threshold—around 25 grams per liter—that has been shown necessary for it to change viscosity in a detectable way.

Acetaldehyde

Acetaldehyde, also known as ethanal, is produced by the oxidation of alcohol (ethanol). It has a distinctive appley, nutty taste, and it is an important part of the flavor of Fino Sherry, Manzanilla, and Vin Jaune from the Jura in France. In red wines it is typically found at levels of around 30 milligrams per liter, in white wines at 80 milligrams, and flor-aged Sherries at 300 milligrams. Its sensory threshold in wine is around 100 milligrams per liter.

Wine Faults

This book may not be the right place for a lengthy exploration of the fascinating world of wine faults, but it is worth mentioning the key classes of fault. But first, some clarification. When is a fault a fault? With the exception of the musty taint caused by bad corks, the other fault compounds are not always faults, even when they are present at above-threshold levels. For example, oxidation is often a fault, but oxidative characters in wine can be attractive. Reduction can be used as a stylistic tool when it is nice reduction, and in the right context. And the spicy, slightly animal flavors associated with the yeast *Brettanomyces* are appreciated by some—again, when they are in the right context.

Cork taint This musty taint is caused by fungal metabolites present in some corks, chiefly 2,4,6-trichloroanisole (TCA). It is almost always caused by bad corks, but there are some instances where related haloanisoles (the class of compound to which TCA belongs) are present in winery timber or barrels and can taint the wine. TCA is thought to affect around 3 percent of all natural cork. There is some suggestion that historical rates were higher: in Australia in the mid-1990s there was quite a crisis of cork taint. Cork taint probably will always be with us, as long as natural cork is used to seal wine bottles.

Brettanomyces Usually shortened to just brett, *Brettanomyces* is a yeast that is present in the vineyard and winery environment and, given the right conditions, can grow in wine, particularly once alcoholic fermentation is complete. It can utilize the last bit of sugar that is present in the wine that other yeasts cannot, and can also grow using other wine components as food. It creates a range of by-products with a sensory impact, predominantly ethyl phenols and isovaleric acid, giving wines a meaty, spicy, animal, horse-sweat character. Many famous wines have reasonably high levels of brett. The key ethyl phenol in its flavor impact is 4-ethyl phenol, and this is used for diagnosis because it is a unique product of brett in wine.

Reduction This refers to problematic volatile sulfur compounds, which often develop when wines are kept protected from oxygen. They are produced by yeasts during fermentation. The key volatile sulfur compound is hydrogen sulfide, which smells of drains and rotten eggs. If it is detectable, it is always a problem. More complex compounds, such as disulfides, mercaptans (also known as thiols), thioesters, and dimethylsulfide can be problematic, or they can be complexing, depending on their concentration and their context. They contribute characters such as onion, cooked cork, matchsticks, smoke, or minerals. The struck-match, mineral character from some mercaptans is actually quite sought after in Chardonnay and white Burgundy. But toying with reduction as a complexing factor is a slightly dangerous winemaking game.

At low levels the savory characteristics caused by brett can add complexity—at least in some wine styles; at higher levels they can be overpowering. As well as having this aroma impact, brett can also make the wine finish in a short, metallic sort of way. Some people cannot stand brett, while others quite like it.

Oxidation and volatile acidity These are two faults that often occur together. Oxygen can be very damaging to wine, although some is needed during fermentation and the aging process. So it is really a question of appropriate oxygen management. One concept that has been popular in recent years is that of macro, micro, and nano oxygenation. During primary ferments, quite large doses of oxygen are welcomed to keep the yeasts doing their job. This is

If oxygen is not managed properly at the various stages the wine can develop oxidative characters that could lead to the fault of oxidation. White wines begin to taste nutty and appley and darken in color, taking on "sherried" aromas. Red wines lose their bright red or purple-red color and become more orange and brown in hue, losing their fruity aromas and beginning to taste baked and stewed. They can also take on rather open, fruity, appley aromas during the early stages of oxidation.

macro-oxygenation. Then, once alcoholic fermentation is complete, the wine needs to be protected from oxygen, but not entirely. Barrels allow the wine just a little oxygen: enough for the positive changes of aging to take place. Some wines, however, need very little and develop best in inert containers, such as stainless steel tanks that exclude all air. Sometimes, small amounts of oxygen are introduced deliberately, in a process called micro-oxygenation, especially with tanked red wines. Finally, once the wine is bottled, a tiny amount of oxygen transmission via the closure can help it develop and age in attractive ways: this is nano-oxygenation. Coupled with these changes, however, there is often the development of volatile acidity, which is basically the wine turning into vinegar, caused by the action of acetic acid bacteria. At very low levels, a little bit of volatile acidity can be complexing, adding lift to the nose of the wine. But as it increases, it becomes unpleasantly sweet and vinegary, and is often associated with the gluelike, nail varnish smell of ethyl acetate (this is formed by the esterification of acetic acid). Some people are more susceptible to volatile acidity than others. Having said that, some wines are deliberately made in an oxidative style, most famously Oloroso and Amontillado Sherries, Madeiras, and Tawny Ports.

Mousiness This fault is on the rise, largely because of the reduced use of sulfur dioxide by winemakers wishing to work more naturally. It is caused by microbial action, and the compounds responsible are 2-acetyl-3,4,5,6-tetrahydropyridine; 2-acetyl-1,4,5,6-tetrahydropyridine; 2-ethyltetrahydropyridine; and 2-acetyl-1-pyrroline. You cannot smell these in the glass because they are not volatile at wine pH, but when the wine is in your mouth the pH changes, and you smell them retronasally. The smell is of mouse cages or mouse urine—not very nice.

Geosmin With its earthy, musty, beetroot aroma, geosmin is a metabolite made by soil bacteria, hence its smell of freshly turned earth. It is produced by fungi on grapes during damp harvests. Many whites from the Loire Valley in France showed this character in 2011.

Smoke taint Because of the increased incidence of bushfires in many wine regions, smoke taint is increasingly a problem. If grapes are ripening on the vine, they pick up this ash-like taint, coupled with a dry finish. One of the compounds responsible is guaiacol. It is detectable at 6 μg per liter in white wines and 15 to 25 μg per liter in reds. Another smoke taint compound is 4-methylguaiacol, which has a charred, spicy aroma.

Eucalyptus taint Grapes grown near eucalyptus trees can pick up a distinctive minty, medicinal character. This is because of the distinctive-smelling oil from their leaves, which contains eucalyptol (1,8-cineole). The oil vaporizes and finds its way onto the grapes. The character is stronger in red wines because of the skin maceration during fermentation. In vines growing near eucalyptus the level of cineole in the wines can be as high as 20 μg per liter; the detection threshold is 1.1 to 1.3 g per liter in red wines.

Holistic Approach to Studying Flavor Chemistry

The New Zealand Sauvignon Blanc research program provides a great example of how a holistic approach can be used to study wine aroma. One of its objectives was to characterize the aroma and flavor compounds present in Sauvignon, with a view to identifying why New Zealand (and specifically Marlborough) Sauvignon Blanc is so distinctive. How is it different? Is it because it possesses smells and tastes that other Sauvignons lack? Or is it because it has particularly high levels of compounds that it shares in common with Sauvignons from other regions? Laura Nicolau and PhD student Frank Benkwitz set about answering these questions using analytic chemistry and reconstitution experiments. As Benkwitz put it, "the perception of mixtures of flavor-active compounds is a complicated human response that currently cannot be predicted from knowledge of the separate components."

Nicolau and Benkwitz adopted a clever two-pronged strategy. In the first part of his work, Benkwitz aimed to provide a list of Sauvignon compounds in order of estimated importance for overall aroma. To do this, he used a range of analytical techniques, including GC-O (gas chromatography–olfactometry), AEDA (aroma extract dilution analysis, a quantitative GC-O technique), and GC-MS (gas chromatography–mass spectrometry). Those compounds present at concentrations above their threshold

"I teach wine aroma to students, and we used to say that compounds which have lower odor activity values, where the concentration is under the perception threshold in the wine, are not so important. But the more research we do, the more we see that they are important, able to influence the perception of other components in the mixture."
Laura Nicolau

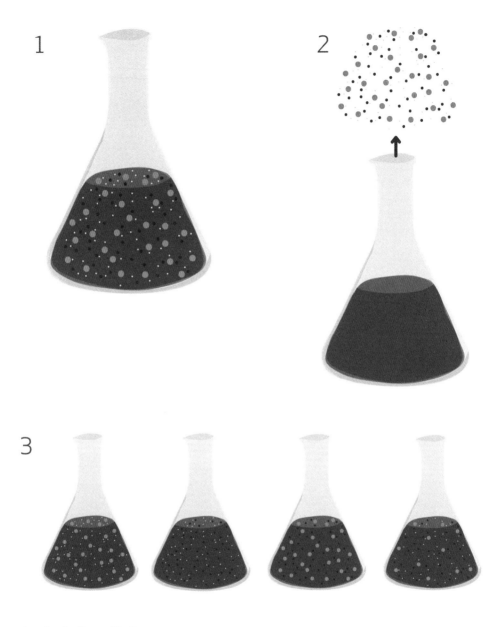

Imaginative Reconstitution

1. Take a wine with its mix of flavor molecules.
2. Strip the wine of all its aroma molecules.
3. Add back the main aroma molecules at their original concentrations, then omit specific molecules singly or in groups to assess their impact on the overall wine aroma.

detection level were highlighted as significant. Next, he conducted a reconstitution experiment in which he created a "model" Sauvignon Blanc by deodorizing an actual Sauvignon Blanc wine, then adding back the key aroma-active molecules at the same concentrations as were found in the original wine. He used this model wine to do omission tests, looking at the effects of omitting either related groups of compounds, or single compounds on their own, and seeing their effect on the perception of the wine by trained panels of tasters. This is a particularly elegant experiment that treats the wine as a whole, getting away from the limits of more reductionist approaches.

Characteristics of Marlborough Sauvignon Blanc

Yet Marlborough Sauvignon is clearly different from most other Sauvignons in a number of respects. First, it shows high levels of methoxypyrazines. These are a group of compounds including 2-methoxy-3-isobutylpyrazine (MIBP; known widely as isobutyl methoxypyrazine); 2-isopropyl-3-methoxypyrazine (MIPP; known as isopropyl methoxypyrazine); and 2-methoxy-3-secbutylpyrazine (MSBP; known as sec-butyl methoxypyrazine). Of these, MIBP is the key methoxypyrazine in Marlborough Sauvignon. While other Sauvignon Blancs also share high levels of methoxypyrazine, the Marlborough examples were consistently quite high in this respect. Second, a group of compounds known as polyfunctional thiols are present at unusually high levels in Marlborough Sauvignon. Three are considered to be particularly important in Sauvignon: 3MH; 3MHA; and 4MMP. Of these, 3MH and 3MHA are found at extremely high levels in Marlborough Sauvignon. There is a striking variation within the region and from year to year, but on average, Marlborough Sauvignon has much higher average levels than wines from other regions.

The purpose of this stage of the research was to produce a list of compounds with an odor activity value (OAV) of greater than one. Initially, a quantitative form of GC-O, AEDA, was used to identify target compounds. AEDA relies on calculating the maximum dilution at which a compound can be detected, by recording the flavor dilution (FD) factor. The FD value produces a hierarchical list of odorants ranked in terms of importance. This can be used as a screening method before the OAVs are defined, a step that takes

Benkwitz looked at eighty-three different examples of Sauvignon Blanc and identified some forty-nine different aroma compounds, many of them present in only trace amounts. This initial study showed all the Sauvignons to be qualitatively similar: that is, they all contained the same compounds but at different levels. There are no compounds that are unique to the distinctive Marlborough style.

more time to carry out. OAVs are calculated by working out the concentration of an odorant in the wine under scrutiny, and then dividing this by the perception threshold. A compound with an OAV of one is present at its perception threshold, and one with an OAV of two is present at twice its perception threshold.

Then, once the deodorized wine was created, they added back the aroma–flavor compounds at their original levels. Initially, they used a "complete" model with nineteen compounds added back, but later a model, using just the eleven compounds having an OAV of more than two, was sufficient. The model wine created was significantly different to the original wine, but Benkwitz speculates that it might be a closer match if the differences in pH, alcohol, and polyphenols (created by the deodorization process) were corrected.

Experimenting with a Model Wine

The two terpenes linalool and α-terpineol had a huge impact when they were omitted from the model wine. Reduced "apple lolly," "stone fruit," and "tropical" characters were all detected. Monoterpenes have ten carbon atoms in their backbone, and include linalool, nerol, geraniol, citronellol, and α-terpineol. They interact synergistically and have pleasant floral aromas, but individually they are usually below threshold level in Sauvignon Blanc. Thus it is of great interest that they are so influential.

Nicolau explains the idea behind creating the model wine. "You deodorize the Sauvignon Blanc, and put back the compounds at the level that you know they were present in the wine. Then you omit some of them in different combinations. We might look at a group of compounds, such as taking out all the esters, or all the thiols, or taking one ester or thiol at a time." The analysis of the reconstituted wines was carried out by the sensory science group at Plant and Food Research, Auckland. "The surprise in Sauvignon came from the terpenes," she reveals. "If you take them out, it makes a huge difference to the overall perception of the wine."

"The esters also have a huge influence," says Nicolau. More than 160 of them are found in wine, and they are produced during fermentation. They are described as being fruity and floral, and are rapidly hydrolyzed in wine over the first year after bottling, with lower pH accelerating this hydrolysis. "They have a broad impact, so they can influence the fruity aromas generally, including the tropical fruit," says Nicolau. Removing the esters showed a small drop in intensity for most of the descriptors, as well as a large decrease in "passion fruit skin–stalk" and "sweet, sweaty passion fruit." "Previously we thought this was from the thiols, but the esters have that note as well," says Nicolau. She adds that, "when you take out the thiols, there is a more subtle difference than when you take out the terpenes, for example." Indeed, when the three thiols 3MH, 3MHA, and 4MMP are taken out, the effect on overall aroma is not as significant as would have been expected. The descriptors "flinty" and "passion fruit skin–stalk" are significantly less intense, while "capsicum" is more intense.

The C_6 compounds seem to be quite important. These include 1-hexanol, cis- and trans-3-hexenol, and cis and trans-2-hexenol, and they are described as having "herbaceous, green, grassy" aromas. Eliminating these reduces tropical characters as well as "passion fruit skin–stalk." The key methoxypyrazine MIBP is described as having aromas of "capsicum, vegetative, and green," but its omission does not change the intensity of the capsicum character in the wine. The only significant change is the decrease in intensity for "flinty." This is surprising, because methoxypyrazines are considered impact compounds in Sauvignon Blanc, but the results from this experiment do not support that hypothesis.

In the initial study, β-damascenone, a norisoprenoid that smells of fruit and roses, was omitted. In a later study it was included, and Benkwitz found that it enhanced the perception of the thiols, but it only had a minor impact when it was omitted alone. He thinks that β-damascenone may turn out to be a very important compound in Sauvignon Blanc. Norisoprenoids are 13-carbon compounds produced by the degradation of chemicals called carotenoids during the ripening process in fruit. As well as β-damascenone, α- and β-ionone are also important, and have a violet aroma.

Another single compound with a relatively large effect if left out is β-phenylacetate. While its OAV in the model wine was just over one, it has a significant impact if omitted, reducing the overall intensity of the aroma profile, while slightly increasing the scores for "banana lolly" and "apple lolly." When ethyl hexanoate is removed, it also has a significant effect, increasing "banana lolly" and "apple lolly," as well as "tropical" and "sweet, sweaty passion fruit." "Passion fruit skin–stalk" and "flinty" are decreased.

The reductionist model of wine flavor chemistry, in which one compound is studied at a time, is clearly out of date. A new, more holistic approach to understanding the flavor and aroma of wine is now emerging, and it promises to give greater insight into why different wines taste different. It might one day be possible to say, chemically, why certain famous wines taste the way they do. Might this increased understanding enable winegrowers one day to produce exact replicas of, say Chave Hermitage or de Vogüé Musigny from lesser sites? And is that even desirable?

Surprisingly, in reconstitution experiments, taking out a single compound can have more of an effect than taking out whole groups of related compounds, including that single compound. This is hard to explain. For example, if the three polyfunctional thiols (3MH, 3MHA, or 4MMP) are removed together, there is a relatively small change in the aroma profile. If 4MMP or 3MH alone are removed, there is a more significant difference.

Individual Differences in Flavor Perception

Individuals differ, in many ways. We are quite used to the idea that if you take a hundred people at random, they will show a spread of physical characteristics such as height or eye color. We are less comfortable with the notion that our senses of taste and smell may show a similar range of variation. To what extent do we differ in our perception of flavors and aromas, and is this variation in taste along a continuum, or—more intriguing—are there more-or-less discrete groups of individuals living in different, shared taste worlds? And do different cultures experience wine differently? In this chapter we will explore the world of individual differences, and how they might be important for wine tasting.

Polar Opposites in Wine Appreciation

Consider this scenario: two wine critics walk into a bar offering "natural" wines, made using natural fermentation, with little intervention in the winemaking process. The first, a pugnacious middle-aged guy, snatches the list from the bartender, scans it briefly, and passes it to the second, a placid but determined-looking younger woman. "I cannot believe you can drink any of this poison," he says. "It is just filthy. A complete joke. The emperor has no clothes." Her eyes rise to heaven for a moment, but he fails to spot the gesture because he is busy rooting around in his bag for a bottle that he has brought along. "Let me pick something that might surprise you," she responds. The wine arrives: a natural Grenache from South Africa with no added sulfites. The wine is poured, pale red in the glass, and with a faint haziness. She takes a sip; it is fresh, sapid, slightly leafy, with lovely vibrant red cherry fruit, kept fresh with keen acidity. Her colleague wrinkles his brow, and shakes his head. "Thin, weedy, light, and without any concentration," is his verdict. He calls for some fresh glasses and pours the wine he has brought. It is purple-black and dense, with immense concentration. They both take a sip. He smiles, convinced of victory. She spits out the wine ostentatiously and plonks her

glass back firmly on the table. "Undrinkable," is her verdict. "But this is an immense wine," he replies. "No. Oak, over-ripeness, soupy texture," she says. "It is just big: huge, in fact. A complete caricature of a wine. I cannot drink that." Neither of them will budge. There is no way they can agree. They part, each convinced that the other is utterly crazy in their tastes.

Disagreement among Supercritics

That was just an illustration, but critics can come to equally opposite conclusions in real life. In 2003 the Saint-Emilion property Château Pavie in the French wine region of Bordeaux produced a wine that polarized critics. In particular, there was a well-publicized spat between two of the world's most famous wine writers, Jancis Robinson and Robert Parker.

Robinson's tasting note reads: "Completely unappetising overripe aromas. Why? Porty sweet. Oh really!! Port is best from the Douro not Saint Emilion. Ridiculous wine. More reminiscent of a late-harvest Zinfandel than a red Bordeaux with its unappetising green notes." She scored it 12/20.

At this stage, Parker had not released his scores for the wine, but immediately hit back on his bulletin board. A war of words broke out between the two. When Parker did write about the wine, he scored it initially 96/100 (on subsequent tastings he has scored it as highly as 99/100), and said the following about it:

It seems that for Jancis Robinson an important element of wine quality is its typicity. So a wine may taste attractive but could be marked down because it does not taste according to accepted notions of how a wine from Saint-Emilion should taste. But is her extremely low score of 12 out of 20 explicable solely as a protest vote over lack of typicity?

"Another off the chart effort . . . A blend of 70 percent Merlot, 20 percent Cabernet Franc, and 10 percent Cabernet Sauvignon, it is a wine of sublime richness, minerality, delineation, and nobleness. Representing the essence of one of St.-Emilion's greatest terroirs, the limestone and clay soils were perfect for handling the torrid heat of 2003. Inky/purple to the rim, it offers up provocative aromas of minerals, black and red fruits, balsamic vinegar, licorice, and smoke. It traverses the palate with extraordinary richness as well as remarkable freshness and definition. The finish is tannic, but the wine's low acidity and higher than normal alcohol (13.5 percent) suggests it will be approachable in 4–5 years. Anticipated maturity. 2011–2040. A brilliant effort, it, along with Ausone and Petrus, is one of the three greatest offerings of the right bank in 2003."

Were they tasting the same wine? Both Parker and Robinson are world-famous wine critics. Had they been incompetent tasters, they would never have achieved the success they have, so this is an unlikely explanation for the different verdicts. What other explanations are there? One, suggested by Parker in a comment on the internet, is that Robinson has a personal dislike of the style of wine produced by Pavie owner Gerard Perse. But Robinson tasted this wine blind, so that could not be the explanation. Another is that both Parker and Robinson were experiencing the same flavors when they tasted, but were interpreting these differently. There is a further explanation of the divergence of opinion between these two accepted critics, and this is the concept of individual differences in taste perception—the subject of this chapter.

As an aside, I was served the same 2003 Pavie blind at a dinner in 2006, and scored it 91/100, noting that it had a nose with rich, chocolately, roast-coffee notes and some very sweet dark fruits, and a palate that was bold, full, and concentrated, with lots of oak influence, along with the sweet fruit. My conclusion was that, apart from slightly excessive oak, it was very good, and in its style. But it certainly did not taste of Bordeaux to me.

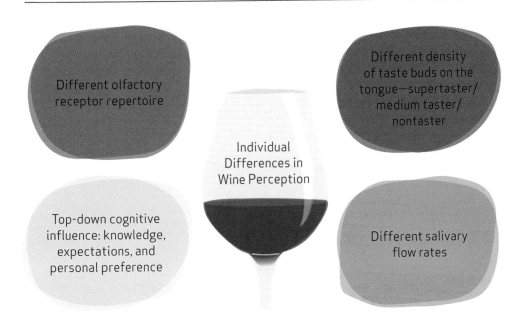

Different olfactory receptor repertoire

Different density of taste buds on the tongue—supertaster/ medium taster/ nontaster

Individual Differences in Wine Perception

Top-down cognitive influence: knowledge, expectations, and personal preference

Different salivary flow rates

We are all different. Save for genetically identical twins, everyone on this planet has a unique genetic code. No one is exactly alike. But many of these individual differences occur on a continuum. Line up a hundred people in height order, and the differences among them will appear gradual, from shortest to tallest in relatively small increments. Height, along with many other biological traits, varies in the population on a normal distribution, appearing on a graph as a bell-shaped curve, with a lot of people somewhere in the middle, and progressively fewer very tall people and very short people. If you are marketing a product to a normal distribution, you would usually aim somewhere in the middle, where most people are.

When it comes to flavor perception, such a continuum of differences would not be all that interesting. You would want to make a wine or any other food or drink that appealed to most people, right in the middle of that distribution. But what would be far more interesting would be if there were discrete differences in taste and smell, so that you could separate the population into a number of groups, each of which was living in a unique flavor world. Then, rather than target the average person with a product, you could target these groups separately, and have a number of products that much more closely matched the preferences of people in the real world.

Some researchers have claimed that people live in different sorts of taste worlds. If this were true, it would have profound implications for wine tasting, judging, and education.

Individual differences in wine perception comprise three elements. The first is the physical apparatus that each of us has for tasting with. We have a different distribution of taste buds, with some genetic differences in the ability to taste certain flavors, coupled with a different suite of olfactory receptors, which suggests that we might each smell things differently. In addition, our salivary flow rates can affect the mouthfeel of wines, and we differ in salivary output. Then we have different experiences with flavor. As we have already discussed in previous chapters, we learn to recognize smells as objects, and there is learning involved in associating tastes with smells, and in associating these senses with other senses such as vision. Finally, there is a top-down cognitive input to our wine-tasting experience: our knowledge, expectations, and personal preferences can influence our perceptions, and will certainly play a role in forming our verdicts on a wine. In this chapter we will tease these issues apart and decide exactly how significant these individual differences are.

New Zealand-based cognitive psychologist Wendy Parr warns researchers not to see consensus where it does not exist:

> "Research demonstrates that perception involving taste and smell, important to wine tasting, is much more diverse amongst people than is perception involving vision, hearing, and trigeminal stimulation. Hence, contrived methodologies that attempt to align tasters both conceptually and linguistically, often in an effort to align sensory data with wine chemical composition or to limit variability for other reasons, are unlikely to produce valid data in the sense of real-world, wine-tasting phenomena. If a certain degree of consensus is desired, it can be achieved by selection of a tasting task and wine evaluation context to maximize such. None the less, research based in methods and theories of cognitive psychology makes clear that aiming for within-taster and between-taster consensus is an ideal, rather than a reality."

Supertasters, Nontasters, and Thermal Tasters

In 1994, while I was working as a scientific editor, I attended a conference that our organization had convened on the molecular

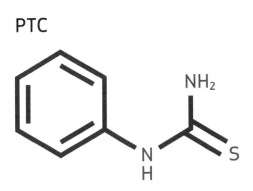

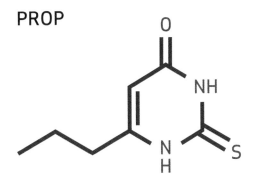

The Structures of PTC and PROP
People differ widely in their ability to perceive PTC and PROP molecules. Future work on PTC and PROP taster status is likely to have significant implications in the wine-tasting world.

In 1931 a chemist named Arthur Fox was busy at work in his lab when one of the chemicals he was synthesizing blew into the air. It was phenylthiocarbamide (PTC). While he could not taste it, the colleague working with him found it extremely bitter. The variation in bitter taste perception that he had discovered turned out to be genetic in origin. Closely related to PTC, but safer to use, is the propylthiouracil (PROP) employed by researchers today.

basis of taste and smell transduction. One of the speakers was psychophysicist Linda Bartoshuk, who at that time was Professor of Surgery at Yale University. During her talk, Bartoshuk handed out small pieces of blotting paper that had been soaked in a chemical called propylthiouracil (PROP), and we were instructed to place these on our tongues. One-quarter of the room tasted nothing; half found the taste quite bitter; the remainder of the group found it to be extremely unpleasant, intense, and bitter. We had discovered what is known as our PROP taster status.

Bartoshuk explains that the PROP compound and its chemical relatives contain molecules that stimulate a specific bitter receptor in the taste membrane. Nontasters of PROP carry two recessive alleles of a gene that has recently been localized to chromosome 7; tasters carry either one or both alleles. "My lab discovered a large variation among tasters; those with the most taste buds are called supertasters and those with fewer are called medium tasters," says Bartoshuk. "Supertasters live in a neon taste world; taste sensations are roughly three times as intense to them as nontasters." But it is not just taste that is affected by these genetic differences. "Since taste buds are surrounded by nerve fibers carrying oral burn/pain, supertasters perceive more oral burn from stimuli such as alcohol, and supertasters also perceive more intense oral touch sensations," she adds. Tannic structure in wine is perceived by the sense of touch, so this is highly relevant here.

Bartoshuk continues: "Perhaps the most important attribute of the sensory experience produced by wine tasting is retronasal olfaction. When we sniff odors from the outside world, this is called orthonasal olfaction. When we put things in our mouth, chewing and swallowing pumps volatiles up behind the palate into the nasal cavity. This is retronasal olfaction." Supertasters, it seems, perceive more intense retronasal olfaction, presumably because they perceive more intense oral sensations.

PROP taster status has been a subject of great interest in the wine world because it is a genetic variation that will have an effect on the way we taste wine. But there is more. The types of PROP sensitivity are attributable to genetic mutation in a gene encoding a taste receptor called TAS2R38. This comes in two forms: PAV (proline-alanine-valine) and AVI (alanine-valine isoleucine). If you have two PAVs, you are a supertaster; if you have two AVIs you are a nontaster; and if you have one of each, you are a medium taster. It has also been shown that supertasters have a higher concentration of fungiform papillae—that house taste buds—on their tongues.

Is PROP taster status due solely to the mutations in TAS2R38, or is the number of taste buds on the tongue also significant? It is hard to see how the two could be connected. Recent research indicates that there is not a correlation between taste bud density and the TAS2R38 genotype, which muddies the PROP story somewhat. And how generalizable is PROP taster status to other flavor sensations? Bartoshuk refers to supertasters as living in a "neon" taste world, but is the failure to taste PROP and PTC more a specific ageusia (loss of taste function of the tongue) or simply a loss of the ability to taste one group of compounds?

Uses of PROP Taster Status

Gary Pickering of Brock University in Ontario, Canada, has studied wine tasting and PROP taster status. "Not all of the variation in PROP tasting is attributable to TAS2R38," he explains,

Without the aid of PROP testing strips, one way to work out whether or not you are a supertaster is to put blue food coloring on your tongue and count the number of papillae, which are visible to the naked eye. Those with more papillae will also have more chorda tympani and trigeminal nerve fibers. This might explain the overall enhanced taste sensitivity of PROP supertasters.

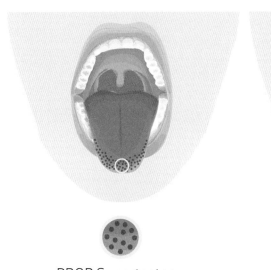

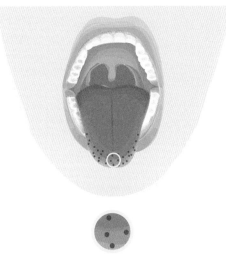

PROP Supertaster

PROP Nontaster

The PROP Supertaster Test

Blue food coloring on the tongue reveals the high density of papillae of the PROP supertaster.

PROP nontasters will note that their papillae concentrations are relatively sparse.

while also emphasizing that much of it is so. Pickering says that gustin, a growth factor for taste buds, has been shown in some studies to associate with PROP taster status. This could explain why supertasters also have more papillae on their tongue. "The interesting thing about PROP tasting status is that it has some predictive value with respect to general taste sensitivity, including wine perception," says Pickering. Is it useful for wine tasters to know their PROP taster status? "I think so," he replied. "But . . . the peer-reviewed scientific literature is where the truth lurks."

In one study, Pickering and colleagues looked at 331 wine drinkers, and classified them as experts (111) and consumers (220). The PROP taster status of all of them was ascertained, and PROP bitterness sensitivity turned out to be higher among the wine experts than the consumers. The team concluded that people might self-select themselves for the wine profession on the basis of their sensory ability: if you are more sensitive to flavor, you may be more likely to become a wine professional. In another study, they looked at 1,010 U.S. wine consumers, examining the influence of selected factors on self-reported liking and consumption of fourteen different wine styles. The factors were experiential (their wine expertise), psychological (their adventurousness with alcoholic beverages), and biological (their age, sex, and PROP responsiveness). On the basis of statistical tests, they came up with three distinct groups with regard to wine liking, and postulated that these clusters of consumers could represent plausible market segments. The groups were "red wine lovers," "dry table wine likers and sweet dislikers," and "sweet wine likers." The clusters differ in key demographic measures, including sex, age, household income, and education, as well as wine expertise and PROP responsiveness. They then extended the study with wines placed into five categories—dry table, sparkling, fortified, sweet, and wine-based beverages—to identify the factors affecting wine liking and consumption. Wine expertise was the most important factor, but PROP responsiveness and alcoholic beverage adventurousness were also important; age and sex were not.

In 2000 a new sort of taste sensitivity was discovered by Alberto Cruz and Barry Green: thermal taste. These are taste "phantoms" caused when the tongue is heated or cooled; up to 40 percent of the population experience this, and are therefore thermal tasters (TTs). In TTs, temperature changes commonly create a metallic

taste, and a consistent finding is a sweet sensation at the tip of the tongue when it is warmed after having been cooled, and a sour or salty taste when the tip of the tongue is cooled. TTs are reported as having a heightened response to taste and also some trigeminal stimuli (touch sensed in the mouth). TT status and PROP taster status have been shown to be independent of each other.

Specific Anosmias: "Smell Blindness"

Most of our 400 or so olfactory receptor genes respond to more than one smell molecule. But there are examples of specific anosmias (losses or impairments of the sense of smell) that result from mutations in single genes. The most famous is that of OR7D4. This gene codes for an olfactory receptor protein that enables us to detect androstenone, a smelly steroidal compound produced by pigs. Depending on the version of the OR7D4 gene people have, they find androstenone unpleasant, or sweet, or they cannot smell it. Overall, some 40 to 50 percent of the population cannot smell it at all.

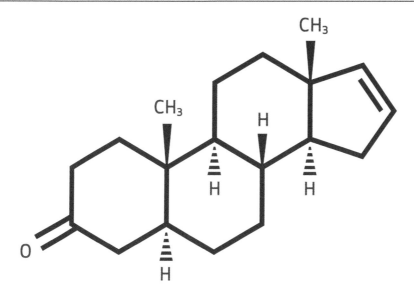

The Structure of Androstenone
Androstenone is a smelly steroidal compound produced by pigs that is described as sweaty, urinous, and musky by those who can smell it.

Depending on the version of the OR7D4 gene people have, they find androstenone unpleasant, or sweet, or they cannot smell it at all.

People from Africa tend to find the smell of androstenone distasteful. Pork from uncastrated male pigs is strong in androstenone, and they find it unpalatable. There may have been evolutionary pressure to lose the sense of smell for androstenone because doing so would make eating pork more palatable, and make pig herding a more acceptable activity.

In 2015 a research group in Alaska led by Kara Hoover looked at the sequences for OR7D4 in 2,200 people from different populations around the world, and found evidence that this gene had been subject to evolutionary selection. But there is an interesting twist. First, insensitivity to androstenone changes though adolescence, especially in males. Secondly, the ability to smell it can be induced by exposure, which is very surprising for a trait that has a strong genetic component. How might that work? It suggests that those who cannot smell it might still be able to detect it unconsciously, and that somehow this induces sensitivity, perhaps by affecting the number of olfactory receptors that can detect it, so that more are made.

One example of a specific anosmia highly relevant to wine is that of rotundone. Discovered by scientists at the Australian Wine Research Institute in 2007, it is the molecule responsible for the "black pepper" aroma in some wines made with the Shiraz (Syrah) grape variety. Technically speaking, rotundone is a bicyclic sesquiterpene. In addition to making wine taste peppery, it is responsible for similar aromas and flavors in herbs and spices, including peppercorns. It is detectable at tiny concentrations. Remarkably, one-fifth of people cannot smell it at all. Thus, in the Australian survey, while most of the panelists they used for sensory analysis could detect rotundone at the miniscule concentration of 8 nanograms per liter in water, 20 percent of them failed to detect it at 4,000 nanograms per liter.

Cilantro, also known as coriander, is a green herb that is widely used in Eastern cooking. Some people love it and some hate it; people who dislike it say they find it pungent and soapy. It is now believed that this preference is due to a difference in olfactory perception, even though we talk of the "taste" of cilantro.

Given the fact that we all have different subsets of olfactory receptors, it is strange that there are not more examples of specific anosmia. One explanation might lie in the way that we detect smells: it is by pattern recognition, with most single odorants being recognized by more than one receptor type, and each receptor type usually recognizing more than one odorant. In chapter 7, we discuss how we learn through experience to recognize smell "objects" where combinations of several or even hundreds of different smell molecules are recognized together as a single smell. The existence of specific anosmias, especially when these involve wine flavor compounds such as rotundone, are of great relevance to the practice of wine tasting and criticism. Specifically, in rotundone we have a compound that is responsible for the pepperiness that is such a valued character in many Shiraz/Syrah-based wines, yet 20 percent of tasters cannot sense it. Imagine there are two judges in a wine show, one of whom is able to sense rotundone and one who cannot. What to the first judge may be a beautifully peppery Shiraz might be quite a different wine to the second one.

Cultural and Age Differences in Wine Tasting

In chapter 6 we discuss the importance of learning in the experience of flavor. If theories that smell and flavor are represented as objects in the brain are correct, then learning plays a critical role in developing the set of flavor and aroma objects that each of us recognizes. People from different cultures therefore will approach wine from different perspectives, because they may well have different sets of aroma and flavor objects encoded in their brains.

However, most of us come to wine for the first time as adults. Before that occurs, we lack a flavor object called "wine," or a set of flavor objects for different kinds of wine. So all of us, whatever our cultural backgrounds, have to build these objects through learning. We are probably making new objects and refining existing ones as we carry on experiencing new wines. This late start in adulthood will offset some of the impact of cultural differences, which otherwise might be expected to be quite pronounced.

Another source of individual differences is in age. The sense of smell typically declines as we age, in a nonspecific way. That is, we gradually lose sensitivity to all smells, not just certain smells. This sort of decline is gradual and often goes unnoticed. The good news, particularly for professional tasters, is that age-related decline is not universal—some eighty-year-olds can smell as well as young adults. But in others, the sense of smell pretty much disappears.

So what is the nature of olfactory expertise? And, by extension, do naturally gifted wine tasters exist? We are familiar with skilled performers in other areas, such as sport or music—people who just seem to have exceptional talent that, when combined with appropriate training, manifests itself as an ability for highly skilled performance. Could smell be similar? Is it possible to train someone to become an expert smeller or wine taster?

Generally speaking, people are fascinated by high-level skill acquisition. Many of us watch top sports stars perform with awe. But are these stars born or made? Professor Anders Ericsson and colleagues studied virtuoso violinists and produced a well-known paper, "The Role of Deliberate Practice in the Acquisition of Expert

Those of us who plan to be tasting wine for a living into our old age are presumably hoping to retain our sense of smell, although there are famous examples of tasters who have continued to be influential after claiming that most of their sense of smell was gone.

Performance" (1993). Ericsson's conclusion was that rather than innate ability, it was practice that made perfect.

"Our civilization has always recognized exceptional individuals, whose performance in sports, the arts, and science is vastly superior to that of the rest of the population. Speculations on the causes of these individuals' extraordinary abilities and performance are as old as the first records of their achievements. Early accounts commonly attribute these individuals' outstanding performance to divine intervention, such as the influence of the stars or organs in their bodies, or to special gifts. As science progressed, these explanations became less acceptable. Contemporary accounts assert that the characteristics responsible for exceptional performance are innate and are genetically transmitted."

All the violinists in this study started playing at around age five. By age eight, practice times had started to diverge, and this difference persisted until age twenty when the elite performers had put in 10,000 hours compared with the 4,000 hours of the nonelite group. No super-gifted performers emerged at, say, 5,000 hours' practice, suggesting that there were none with so much innate talent that they did not need as much practice as their peers to reach genius level. Ericsson and colleagues also extended this discussion to look at people gifted in other realms, such as playing chess, long-distance running and even science, finding similar broad conclusions. These gifted individuals got there not because of some luck of genetics, but because they put in an extreme amount of directed practice.

Canadian journalist Malcolm Gladwell popularized the idea that practice makes perfect, and that 10,000 hours of practice are required for success, in a chapter in his book, *Outliers* (2008). The 10,000-hour "rule" is now firmly established in popular culture.

But could it be that only the very most gifted will be rewarded enough by their practice to be committed to work so hard? Ericsson commented: "Contrary to the popular 'talent' view that asserts that differences in practice and experience cannot account for differences in expert performance, we have shown that the amount of a specific type of activity (deliberate practice) is consistently correlated with a wide range of performance including expert level performance, when appropriate developmental differences (age) are controlled."

This conclusion clashes somewhat with the prevalent view in society. Most people would think that, in order to produce a genius, it is important to spot early innate differences and then to take the seemingly gifted children and coach them intensively. According to this view, early talent is what results in the commitment to increased practice needed for expert levels of achievement. But Ericsson stresses the importance of effort:

> "We agree that expert performance is qualitatively different from normal performance and even that expert performers have characteristics and abilities that are qualitatively different from or at least outside the range of those of normal adults. However, we deny that these differences are immutable, that is, due to innate talent. Only a few exceptions, most notably height, are genetically prescribed. Instead, we argue that the differences between expert performers and normal adults reflect a life-long period of deliberate effort to improve performance in a specific domain."

With the exception of factors such as height, which is not modifiable, many of the physiological attributes of elite athletes are inducible by training. Ericsson and colleagues suggest that if you take a child and subject them to the appropriate training regime you can produce exceptional talent. Of course, one factor here has to be the willingness of the child to stick to this regime.

Criticism of the 10,000-hour Rule

The idea of the 10,000-hour rule does seem wonderfully egalitarian. Just think: with sufficient deliberate practice we can all achieve our goals, and our kids can all be geniuses. But, as attractive as it sounds, Ericsson's paper has come under fire. In a meta-analysis (a study that combines all the published evidence on a topic) of 2014, Brooke Macnamara and colleagues found a much weaker contribution of deliberate practice to outstanding success across a range of fields.

> "In terms of percentage of variance in performance explained, the effect of deliberate practice was strong for games (26 percent), music (21 percent), and sports (18 percent), and much weaker for education (4 percent) and professions (less than 1 percent and not statistically significant). Why were the effect sizes for education and professions so much smaller? One possibility is that deliberate practice is less well defined in these domains. It could also be that in some of the studies, participants differed in amount of prestudy expertise (for example, amount of domain knowledge before taking an academic course or accepting a job) and thus in the amount of

deliberate practice they needed to achieve a given level of performance."

There is a lot of money in soccer, and top stars are highly sought after. Developing young talent is therefore a priority, because if you scout a young genius and then take them through to first-team level, you will have a valuable asset on your hands. So all clubs have a rigorous scouting system, based on spotting talented young soccer players. Yet the attrition rate is extremely high. Young players are recruited to soccer academies, but very few make it as professionals.

In many ways, this chimes with reality more than the 10,000-hour rule does. Take professional sport, and specifically soccer, as an example. Within the ranks of professional soccer players, the number of world-class performers at "genius" level is tiny. If giving young soccer players 10,000 hours of directed practice were sufficient to produce a genius, this would not be the case.

Is It Possible to Have a Superior Sense of Smell?

Let us return to our topic of interest: smell, and by extension the ability to become a gifted wine taster (given that smell represents the largest proportion of the sensory space of wine). Patrick Süskind, in his novel *Perfume* (1985), explores the idea that some people might have a spectacularly enhanced sense of smell. His tale is set in eighteenth-century France, when perfumes were widely used to offset the stench of urban living. The lead character, Jean-Baptiste Grenouille, is born into poverty, but possesses a remarkable talent: he can smell much better than anyone else. After a chance encounter with a failing master perfumier, Grenouille finds his vocation, creating wonderful scents. But he knows he is missing a magic ingredient, and to find this he embarks on a grisly, murderous quest. The novel explores some interesting issues. Chiefly, the idea that for most of us the sense of smell is imprecise and somehow incomplete. It is a sense that has the ability to communicate in a very direct and raw way with our emotions, but much of the time it is strangely muted. There is a whole world of olfactory sensations out there, which, to us humans, is out of our reach. The idea that someone could inhabit that world is a really interesting one.

In *The Man Who Mistook His Wife for a Hat* (1998), neurologist and author Oliver Sacks recounts the true story of a (temporarily) real-life Grenouille. This was Stephen D., a twenty-two-year-old medical student who had experimented with psychoactive drugs. In a vivid dream, Stephen saw himself as a dog and entered a world unimaginably rich and significant in smells. When he awoke he had an incredible transformation. Not only could he see enhanced colors ("I could distinguish dozens of browns, where I had just seen brown before"), but also he had a dramatic enhancement in smell. He experienced the exaltation of what is often called a base sense to the plane of a higher sense: "I went into a scent shop. I had never had much of a nose for smell before, but now I distinguished each one instantly—and I found each one unique, evocative, a whole new world." Stephen found he could tell his friends apart just by their smell, and his patients, too. "I went into the clinic, I sniffed like a dog, and in that sniff recognized, before seeing them, the twenty patients who were there—each had his own olfactory physiognomy, a smell face, far more vivid and evocative, more redolent than any sight face." This ability lasted only for some three weeks. Sacks reported that sixteen years later it had not returned, and that Stephen was occasionally nostalgic for the loss of this enhanced smell world.

This remarkable account raises some interesting questions. Do our brains deliberately limit the extent of our olfactory perceptions? The case of Stephen suggests that our sense of smell is potentially much more powerful than the version we experience. As I argued in chapter 2, we tend to underestimate our olfactory abilities because we make the wrong comparisons. We often compare ourselves with dogs, who clearly are able to inhabit a world that is quite different to ours in terms of using smell to sniff the environment. For a while, Stephen experienced this doglike sense of smell—a world that is closed to us. His case suggests that the brain might in some way be limiting our smell worlds, somewhere between the olfactory epithelium and where the conscious experience of smell is perceived. Lurking within us is a potentially much more powerful sense that has been downgraded through evolution. In chapter 2 we saw how sexual attractiveness is mediated by smell, and the idea that we make mate choices partially based on their smell, which we barely consciously perceive—if at all—is tantalizing.

Sacks also tells the story of a man who lost his sense of smell through a head injury. The shearing of the olfactory nerve projections as they pass through a part of the skull called the cribriform plate is not unusual. While we think we could cope well with losing smell, compared with other senses, it is by all accounts quite a loss. This man was startled by the dramatic impact the loss of smell had on him. "The sense of smell? I never gave it a thought. But when I lost it, it was like being struck blind. Life lost a good

Our sense of smell is very powerful, but it is different to that of dogs. It has been shaped by evolution to be relevant to our needs. As well as being a means of detecting and avoiding danger, it serves as an exquisitely sensitive tool for the selection, enjoyment, and appreciation of food and drink. Further, with scents and perfumes, we can create an ambience of emotional significance.

deal of its savor—one does not realize how much 'savor' is in smell . . . my whole world was radically poorer."

A few months later, he began to smell his coffee. He tried his pipe, catching some of the aromas he loved. Excited by the prospect of regaining his sense of smell, he went to see his doctor, only to be told that his smell was still lost. It was instead the development of olfactory imagery that was causing these sensations of smell, and this was enough to fool him that he was really experiencing odors. We will return to this topic of olfactory imaging a little later.

How Do Novice and Expert Wine Tasters Differ?

Jordi Ballester is a researcher at the Institut Universitaire de la Vigne et du Vin, which is part of the University of Bourgogne in Dijon, France. He has studied how experts differ from novices when it comes to assessing wine. "Novices use basically bottom-up processes," he says, "which means that they take most of the information from the sample itself since they have very little information to bring to the tasting besides affective hedonic judgments." An "affective hedonic judgment" is basically deciding how much you like something, and this is the information that novice, untrained wine drinkers focus on in wine tasting.

So is the improved performance of experts largely because of improved cognitive ability, or is their perception better—either naturally, or because they have worked to improve it? "In terms of detection (sensitivity), experts are not more sensitive than novices for alcohol or tannin perception," says Ballester. "They do not have better olfactory equipment than novices. However, [Sophie] Tempere and colleagues recently showed that training could slightly lower detection thresholds, therefore this is most likely to benefit experts." He adds, "Experts' ability in discrimination tasks is slightly better than novices', but nothing very impressive."

Ballester confirms that, "Experts' superiority is due basically to their improved cognitive ability, for instance, the ability of focusing on attributes that according to their knowledge would be relevant in a given tasting."

"There is a small literature on changes in sensitivity with experience/expertise, especially in terms of olfaction," agrees New Zealand-based psychologist Wendy Parr. "But I think that it is generally considered, on the basis of research to date, that

Jordi Ballester suggests that the theoretical knowledge that experts possess helps in wine tasting, but that it can be a trap if this knowledge triggers the wrong expectations: "Experts usually follow a tasting method," he says. "They know how to improve the signal from the glass, they know the effect of temperature, of exchange surface between liquid and air, they may even have a sensitivity map of their tongue, know their PROP status, and so on."

it is experientially based cognitive change in processes such as perception, memory, and decision making/judgment that contributes by far the most to 'expert' performance in many domains [wine included], and that any changes to sensitivity [that is, sensory phenomena measured by detection levels or discrimination ability] are small." Parr reckons that it is the higher-order cognitive processes of classification and storage of domain-specific knowledge that are particularly important here.

Parr, working on the perception of Sauvignon Blanc, claims that professionals and novices approach wine in quite different ways:

"We have recently done a study that is quite cognitive. We gave people a large A1 sheet of paper, and had around seventy descriptors of Sauvignon that had come out of our previous studies. Each one was written on a separate sheet of paper with a sticky back. We asked people to draw a picture of a high-typicality Sauvignon in a hierarchical structure, like a tree shape. We had a group of wine consumers and a group of wine professionals. People had to sit and think. They did this experiment twice: they came and did it totally from memory [for example, they were asked to think about a good example of a Marlborough Sauvignon] and they drew these pictures. They came back two weeks later and we gave them three Sauvignons that had been rated in a previous experiment as highly typical. They tasted these wines, and did the picture again. So this is a perceptive condition, versus a conceptual condition [doing it from memory]. The findings showed some interesting results and differences. Some people had broad pictures of Sauvignon; others had more linear ones."

The idea behind these two separate experiments is that the first condition, what is known as a "semantic" condition, relies on top-down cognitive processes of memory and linguistic skill. The second is a "perceptive" condition, in which tasting the wine takes place at the same time as a classification task: this is a bottom-up experiential process. The three questions being posed were: first, would experts and novices employ the same descriptors in the same way?; second, would expertise influence reproducibility across both semantic and perceptive conditions?; and third, do both groups exhibit a shared concept of Sauvignon Blanc?

"An efficient storage in long-term memory of sensory and theoretical wine knowledge (organized into interrelated categories) is clearly an asset in wine tasting. This allows experts to actively search specific attributes, which are likely to co-occur. This strategy is more effective than simply screening all the characteristics of a given wine, which can lead to missing something. Even if the incoming signal is almost the same, perception is somehow shaped by knowledge and expectations."
Jordi Ballester

Experts need to make sure that their knowledge does not stop them tasting what is actually in the glass. Jordi Ballester says that, "Language is very important. Efficient communication is more important than how nice the wine note sounds. I make [students] play communication games to make them understand how difficult wine tasting is."

The results showed that experts classified the properties of Sauvignon Blanc according to their own internal descriptions of typical New Zealand Sauvignon Blancs, while the novices were much less consistent in their descriptions. The experts had a stronger underlying cognitive concept of New Zealand Sauvignon Blanc, producing stronger hierarchical trees. They were also more consistent among themselves: this higher within-group consistency indicates a shared conceptualization of Sauvignon Blanc knowledge. The experts and novices used different levels in their hierarchical descriptions, with stronger superordinate nodes. That is, the top descriptors for Sauvignon are seen as more important. From this, Parr concludes that the experts use top-down processes in their wine judgments, involving prototypes shared by all experts. For the novices, it seems that their descriptions are driven by bottom-up processes, and are based on the taste of the wine. Ballester emphasizes that theoretical knowledge should not overshadow bottom-up processes during tasting.

The Role of Mental Imagery

Earlier in this chapter, we looked at the case of the anosmic man who experienced phantom smells by imagining them. Sophie Tempere and colleagues studied this type of mental imagery with relation to wine tasting. Novices, undergraduate enology students (intermediates), and wine experts were asked to imagine smells repeatedly, while they were presented in picture form. Their smell abilities, sensitivities, and identification performance were compared before and after this mental training. Just as with repeated smell exposure, the repeated imagination of odors was able to enhance olfactory performance, improving the identification and detection of smells. But this ability was only improved in the experts and it was specific rather than general for the actual odors imagined. The researchers suggest that olfactory mental imagery could be used as a training strategy.

We have looked at the theoretical basis for inter-individual differences in wine perception. What about in the real world? In agreement with these observations on individual differences are the experiences of companies who use large panels of consumers for sensory research. Jane Robichaud has considerable experience in assessing people's sensory perceptions of wine. A trained

The Expert Versus the Novice

Uses cognitive approaches: memory plus smell, mental representation

Has increased ability to detect and name smells

Takes longer and is better at recognizing wine aromas

The Expert

Has ability to detect and name smells

Takes less time but is less able to recognize wine aromas

The Novice

winemaker as well as a sensory scientist, she was one of the authors of the celebrated Wine Aroma Wheel, and worked for California wine producer Beringer before moving to the U.S. company Tragon. Robichaud's work at Tragon was part of a process known as "product optimization," in which quantitative consumer sensory research provides winemakers with practical information that can help them make "consumer-defined" wines.

Learning What Wine Consumers Prefer

For the "optimization phase" of Tragon's work, typically 150 to 200 or more of the "target" consumers are recruited. "We find that people are wired quite differently such that they like different things," says Robichaud. "Taking coffee as an example, some people like it strong, dark and rich, some like it medium and coffee-ish, and some like brown water." Robichaud explains that it is possible to find discrete "preference segments," meaning groups of consumers exhibiting similar and distinct likes for specific combinations of attributes.

"About 30 percent of the population are not good measuring devices," concludes Robichaud. This seems to tally well with the work on PROP sensitivities (see page 114), but Robichaud does not think that PROP status is all that useful a measure. "We did a bit of PROP testing at Beringer and it did not work very well: it bore no relation to who was a good bitterness taster." The problem here seems to be that there are many chemical compounds that elicit bitter tastes, with quite different structures, and PROP is just one of them. Robichaud thinks that about one-third of people do not seem to get bitterness in wines at all.

Wes Pearson is a senior sensory scientist at the Australian Wine Research Institute (AWRI), and he agrees that inter-individual differences are quite significant. "In some of our work we attempt to minimize that effect, in others we will use it to our advantage," he says. The AWRI has an external descriptive analysis panel that does a lot of the sensory work at the institute, and for this panel he wants to minimize inter-individual differences. "We do this by using a large panel of as many as fifteen, so that individual sensitivities come out in the wash," he says. "We run panel performance after we have completed the data collection phase that measures each panelist's ability to, first, discriminate between

Tragon recruits members of the public and puts them through a two-day course in sensory analysis. The tasters do not need to be connoisseurs, but they need to be regular consumers who are good at group dynamics. Typically, 70 percent of them pass the course and 30 percent drop out. The job of this trained panel is to come up with the descriptive language that will be used to describe the wines being examined.

the samples; second, their deviation from the group mean; and third, their repeatability, as they would normally see all samples in triplicate. Looking at this we can get an idea of what panelists can see and what they cannot, and who is sensitive to what." In addition to this panel, the AWRI also have a different internal panel made up of staff who are winemakers or wine show judges, and this smaller panel is used for troubleshooting commercial wines with potential issues. This is a less expensive and more rapid way of assessing the problems without using costly analytical techniques or using a full panel. "After running this panel for years I know who is sensitive to what," says Pearson. "Consequently, when certain judges say they see a certain taint or fault, I know I can trust their assessment, as I know individually they see that attribute or character at levels below most other judges."

The AWRI also uses PROP testing to screen panelists for its descriptive analysis panel, but Pearson knows its limitations: "I like PROP because it is easy to use and it is a pretty cut and dried result. But it is not something I am going to set my watch to. The more we learn about bitter receptors the more we see how big a role genetics plays, and the less you can rely on [PROP] as an effective screening tool. "

For the student of fine wines, these observations mean that there is no "single truth" about a wine. While much of the quality of fine wine can only be appreciated by experience and learning—a realm that is accessible to almost all—the existence of specific anosmias and aguesias means that, at the most basic level, the same wine is not the same to all people. We do indeed live in different taste worlds. We can learn to love flavors that initially we find quite difficult but there is also a level at which aesthetic decisions on style and balance will be affected by our biological differences. While we may be in broad general agreement, it is in these fine distinctions—so important in wine appreciation—that we will find ourselves disagreeing.

"Once they have done the initial PROP test, we do not continue to test them with that compound. We do not only look for 'supertasters' of PROP, we are usually satisfied if they can just taste something bitter, but if they cannot taste it at all that would be a red flag for their inclusion in our descriptive analysis panel."

Wes Pearson

Why We Like the Wines We Do

Of all sensory experiences, it is with food and drink that we see most clearly others' preferences. Some restaurants offer scores of dishes and hundreds of wines. In part this caters to the mood of the diners (no one wants to eat or drink the same thing all the time), but it also reflects individual likes and dislikes. What is particularly interesting is that these preferences are not static, but change with time. Our tastes mature, and we have the ability to develop new preferences—even for things that initially tasted unpleasant to us. This is highly relevant to wine tasting, and this chapter will explore how our preferences are shaped, and why there is no universal consensus on what is nice and what is nasty.

Where Do Our Flavor Preferences Come From?

The topic of flavor preferences is complicated because, as we all know from personal experience, they change over time. Not long ago I was on a wine press trip in northern Portugal when I was offered some Queijo Serra da Estrela, a mountain ewe's-milk cheese that is highly prized. It has a hard skin, under which there is a soft, gooey, stinky mass of cheese. I have never liked cheese, but at that moment I made the choice to try it, hoping that by gritting my teeth I might develop a taste for it. And now I love cheese. I continue to be averse to some of the stinkiest, most pungent, runny cheeses (although I will try them), but I have developed a liking for interesting cheese, simply on the basis of making the decision that I will like it and then trying different types with an open mind and a responsive palate. This tale illustrates that it is quite possible to acquire tastes that are initially aversive. Conversely, I have a persistent phobia for butter; I can use it in cooking, but if I see it spread on bread or toast, I cannot eat it, even though I think I might like the taste. This shows that a food can be disliked for reasons other than the flavor. Everyone's flavor preferences are a blend of the innate and the acquired, and can change with time.

We are all born with a liking for sweet tastes. Sweetness is a good guide to foods with plenty of energy in them, and during human evolution sweet-tasting fruits would have been an important calorie source. Human breast milk is quite sweet, too, so it is natural that we should enjoy this taste right from the beginning of our lives. Another taste that is with us from the start is that of umami, the savory taste of glutamic acid, which signals the presence of protein. Umami is found at high levels in foods such as Parmesan cheese and tomatoes. Newborns have been shown to prefer the flavor of vegetable soup with a dollop of added monosodium glutamate (an artificial source of umami flavor). Interestingly, the diet of a mother can influence the later food preferences of her child, because of the exposure of the fetus to low levels of certain compounds from the mother's diet. The liking of salt develops later, after the age of six months, and increases into adulthood. Once we have left childhood, we strongly prefer salt, and we like it even more when our body needs it.

Sourness in foods and drinks, together with carbonation in drinks, are acquired tastes. In evolution, we would have come across these flavors only when some microbial activity had taken

Tastes Change with Development

Infants usually dislike salt, bitter, and sour tastes, but as adults, we can grow to like them.

Our tastes seem to be quite malleable and some of the most enduring tastes are acquired.

place, and often the foods displaying them would have been beneficial, so we do not have an innate liking for them. Bitterness is an aversive taste because many potential foodstuffs that are bitter are also toxic. It makes sense that children should find potentially harmful tastes aversive, but later in adulthood we are able to acquire the taste for such foods when we learn from the experience of others (or even from our own experience) that bitter, sour, or fizzy foodstuffs can be okay. Our ability to acquire tastes opens up potential new food sources, but clearly there are risks involved in exploring unknown potential dietary items.

Some people are much more likely to try new foods than others. I remember an uncle who came to stay with us when we were children. His dietary choices were so restricted that most of the time a separate meal was prepared for him—a piece of meat, some potatoes, some boiled vegetables; the rest of us ate as usual, because there was no way we could all survive on such a dull diet, even for a short time. The term for those who are afraid of novel foods is neophobia, and this can be inherited. Around one-quarter of adults are moderately to severely neophobic.

Choice in food is highly personal. It is rare to find a restaurant that does not offer a broad range of menu options. We like to eat different things, and choose food that matches our mood. And wine lists? They are long and varied for a reason. Clearly, choice is something we appreciate when it comes to flavor.

Learning to Love Wine

I remember first becoming interested in wine. I was in my early twenties, living in Wallington, London. Nearby, there was an independent wine merchant called The Wine House; this was the source of most of my good early experiences of wine. When you are an inexperienced wine drinker, you fall in love with some wines, but then find it hard to explain why, or to replicate what it was that made it stand out. There were a few wines that grabbed me to the point where I was desperate to replicate the experience. One was a 1985 Forest Hill Shiraz from Western Australia. There was something about the flavor that I found irresistible. In particular, it had a smooth, rounded mouthfeel: it was like drinking silk. But I knew the wine had sold out, so I went back to The Wine House to find something similar. "I would like a red wine, with sweet fruit, and no tannin," I said. The honest response came: "Are you sure you would not rather have a fruit juice?" It seems odd now, but that was what appealed to my palate at the time.

On another occasion, a friend was bringing to dinner a Crozes-Hermitage, from the northern Rhône in France. It was a stinky, old-fashioned wine that had lots of the animally, meaty flavors that I would now be able to identify as caused by *Brettanomyces*, a controversial rogue yeast that can be a fault, but which also, in some cases, can add complexity. I did not like the wine at all.

Now, faced with the same wine, I might have a different view. Even though I do not necessarily enjoy the flavors of *Brettanomyces*, they work in the context of some wines, and I do not instinctively find them aversive. If I were to drink that wine again, now, after having tried tens of thousands of wines in the intervening period, would I be experiencing it in the same way as I did previously? Or would my experience of it be different? And, if the former is the case, how is it that now I might like a wine that I once hated? This leads to two further questions. Can we separate liking from judgments of quality? Or is liking part of the actual perception itself?

The Function of Flavor

Perhaps the primary function of our sense of flavor is to guide us toward foods that are good to eat. Of course, smell on its own also acts as a warning signal: it can alert us to dangers such as fire, and deter us from staying in potentially disease-ridden environments, such as open latrines. And, as we discussed in chapter 2, there may be a role for smell in choosing a mate. Smell also has an essential role in assessing potential food sources for palatability—we often sniff foods, especially meats and dairy products, before using them. But the smells and flavors of foods also have a reward value. We get a lot of pleasure from eating and drinking.

The functioning of reward in flavor gets even more sophisticated when we think about our ability to modulate food intake. In Western societies many of us could easily afford to buy and eat a surfeit of food. If we misjudge our intake and undereat or overeat what our bodies require by just a small amount each day, over time we risk starvation or becoming obese. Some people do indeed end up eating far too little or far too much, but many people seem to keep their intake pretty much right. Indeed, what is remarkable is not how many obese people there are in Western society—even given that obesity is a growing health crisis—but how few, considering the supply of high-calorie, affordable foods readily available. Clearly, our sense of flavor is directing us to the

Finding food has always taken effort. It follows that, if we are to make the considerable effort (and, in the past, expose ourselves to risk) to find food, we have to be strongly motivated. The anticipation of experiencing flavor, along with the potential elimination of feelings of hunger, has driven us to make this effort. Evolution has always offered us flavor as a bribe to get us to eat, so that we survive and pass on our genes.

right foods, rewarding us when we consume them, and is also moderated by intake. This is all highly relevant for wine tasting.

To be able to acquire tastes has clear value in evolutionary terms, as does dietary adventurousness. In our evolutionary history we had to be careful to avoid poisonous foods, but we also benefited if we did not restrict our food choices too much. Many plants are poisonous, so the connection between vision, smell, memory, and emotion was highly important. We identify potential food sources visually. We smell them as we put them in our mouths. We remember how we felt when we tasted them, and shortly after. If they made us ill, this linking of the senses would help us to avoid repeating the experience. If they tasted good and did not make us ill, all was well. But what if they did not taste good, and did not make us ill? If we could acquire a taste for this sort of food, we would benefit significantly. Further, if we and our kin could accept this food while others did not, we would have more of it to ourselves. Thus, evolution has always driven us to appreciate acquired tastes. This factor applies very much in wine

Our Tastes Are Adaptable

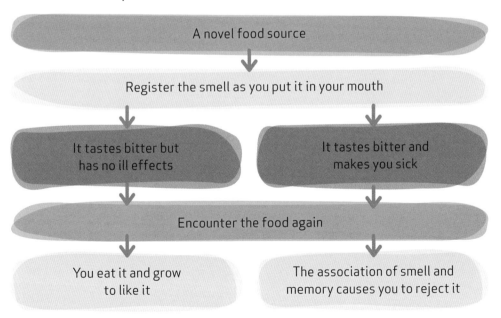

tasting, because many of the flavors in wine are initially quite aversive. With perseverance, however, we come to love them.

We have just discussed how it might be useful to be able to acquire tastes for things that we initially found unpleasant, as long as these foods and drinks were not harmful and had some nutritious content. But how exactly do we acquire tastes? Everyone seems to like some things, but other tastes take time to develop, and not everyone develops them in the same way.

Flavors that seem to be innate, and liked by everyone, tend to be overlooked. The flavors that really seem to grab people, and turn them into geeks, are often initially quite challenging and must be acquired. This is as true of wine tasting as it is of any other aspect of flavor. There are some wines that everyone seems to enjoy, the ones often described as "crowd-pleasers." Crowd-pleasing wines tend to have a little bit of sweetness, and lack edges from acidity and tannins. Their flavor is driven by sweet fruit. These are the sorts of wines that wine geeks despise, and which wine writers struggle to say anything positive about. This raises the question of acquired tastes and pleasure. Most people find the taste of cola quite appealing the first time they drink it. It is sweet, but it has acidity and bubbles to counter the sweetness, especially when it is served chilled. But very few people become obsessed by cola, or would pay a lot of money for it, or would discuss the experience of drinking it with their friends.

The first time most people try coffee, they find it quite bitter and hard to drink. I progressed from drinking instant coffee with milk and two sugars to an Americano (a long black coffee); espressos sometimes seem a little too bitter. Coffee is interesting because, beyond flavor, it has a psychological function—a coffee break helps to punctuate the day. There is more to the appreciation of food and drink than "hedonic valence" (how much we like or dislike something).

The Process of Acquiring Tastes

Now think about strongly flavored cheeses, or proper coffee, or craft beers—flavors that take some acquiring. Initially, you might not enjoy these tastes. Some people find them so objectionable on first tasting that they never go back. But once tastes are acquired, they can become the most enduring of all tastes. Fine wine fits into this category. Given the world's best wines to taste, novices often wonder what the fuss is about. Old wines have complex flavors that wine drinkers only really begin to appreciate some way into their careers. It is only when tastes are hard to acquire that connoisseurship grows around them. There are many more geeks in cheese, coffee, beer, and wine than in any readily appreciated food or drink

I asked Barry Smith, head of the Centre for the Study of the Senses at London's Institute of Philosophy, to address the question of individual tastes, and how two people can differ in their assessment. "The bad argument is that you taste the wine and I taste the same wine; you like it and I do not like it, so you say to me it cannot taste the same way to you as it does to me. If it tasted the same way, you would see it was lovely and you would like it. But why is that the case? It might taste exactly the same but you like that flavor and I do not." So there is a step missing here. Can we separate hedonics (how much we like something) from perception? "Yes, we can do that in principle," says Smith. "Philosophers might be interested in whether liking was an intrinsic part of tasting. Is it that whenever you taste something, you cannot separate how it tastes from whether you like it? That is, if you like it, it would taste different from if you did not like it. As a philosopher I am interested in that separation. If you cannot separate them, how can you acquire a taste for something?"

Obviously our tastes are not static. Hedonics is interesting, but it is not the whole story. Whether you like something or not can change with time and is not stable, but is perception stable over time? Smith continues his argument:

"Suppose I did not like something. The first time you taste alcohol or beer you do not like it. Then there is a time when you really like it. Does it taste the same to you now as it did then? Some people say, no, I did not like it then, and if I like it now it must taste different. Or, if it tastes exactly the same way before and after, what explains the change in my liking? Is it nothing to do with how it tastes? Is it just that I sort of flip? This needs to be explained. It is a little bit of a paradox."

I suspect it tastes pretty much the same, and Smith agrees, noting that he has had experience of this himself.

"When I was a novice taster, I tasted lots of great white Burgundies and thought this was the epitome of white wine. I remember reading about Condrieu as one of the world's great white wines. So I rush out, buy this expensive Condrieu, put it in the fridge, get ready: I am very excited. And I open it up and I do not really like it. I was surprised. I thought: why do people like this? I was disappointed in me as much as in anything else. Then I was talking to someone a little more experienced in wine.

The Greek philosopher Heraclitus stated that you cannot step into the same river twice. This is because the second time you do so, the river will be different, and also you will be different, because your first experience of stepping in will have changed you slightly. Any account of the acquiring of tastes must acknowledge this observation.

They said: don't you love that bitter apricot kernel flavor? Don't you like the oiliness of it? I suddenly went back in my mind and thought that is exactly what it tasted of. It was oily and fatty and had this bitter apricot character. I thought: that is right. They said: it is really good with salty seafood. I suddenly could put all those things together in my mind. Without changing how I remember it tasting, I thought: I want to try that again. Now thinking of it, with those descriptions and with that way of articulating and expecting it to be like that, I loved it. Now it is one of my favorites."

Smith's explanation for this change in liking is that the new information—what to expect in Condrieu—directed his attention when he revisited the wine. He compares it to experiencing a whole symphony versus listening to particular elements of it:

"Here is this single thing: did I like it? No. Then my attention is directed to those apricot flavors, to the slight bitterness—to the voluptuousness of it and the oiliness of it. Now that I recognize those, I am kind of understanding what the parts are and why they behave together as they do, and it completely transformed my experience of it. Does it taste the same as it did? Yes. But the way I experienced that taste is different because someone has directed my attention to it a different way."

Smith stresses the importance of separating liking and perceiving:

"Can I concentrate on how it tastes rather than whether I like it? Can I hold this aside? Some people say you cannot: tasting and liking are just one. But Edmund Rolls's work [Smith is referring to the brain imaging work of Professor Edmund Rolls at the University of Warwick, and previously at the University of Oxford] shows us that the brain processes the liking and the identification separately. The perceptions are insula, interior insula, and orbitofrontal cortex, and liking is nucleus accumbens. But he also has this nice work on sensory specific satiety. I give you a piece of chocolate and you like it. I give you another piece, you like it. Eventually you say, 'I do not want any more chocolate,' but I say the experiment must continue. You end up despising it. But if I give you a different brand of chocolate, you would notice it like that. Which means you are keeping track of the identity of the flavor, even though the hedonics are varying. I think this is a very nice result, because this shows that it is part of the brain's job to still say same or different, even when the hedonics are varying."

The Jarring Note That Piques Interest

Smith cites a paper that Rolls published with Fabian Grabenhorst about identifying odors. This compared the responses of people to natural jasmine and artificially synthesized jasmine. Artificial jasmine is much cheaper than the real thing and contains just a subset of the key volatile molecules. "[Artificial jasmine] is good enough for the brain to say, okay, I have the basic pattern, that is jasmine," says Smith. "If you give subjects artificial jasmine and natural jasmine, can they tell them apart? No, they cannot. The two odors smell the same. Now you say to them: forced choice,

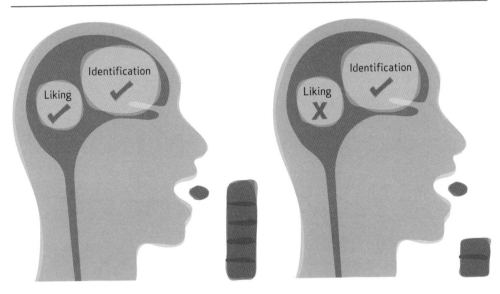

Liking and Identifying
The brain processes involved in liking and identification are separate—we continue to identify a flavor even when our liking for it alters. For example, if we eat a lot of chocolate, we may not want to eat another piece, but we are still able to identify the flavor easily.

you have got to choose one rather than the other. Which do you like better? They say, they are the same. No, just choose. They choose the natural jasmine. Why? Because natural jasmine has 2 percent indole in it." Indole on its own smells unpleasant, and 2 percent is quite enough to be aversive, so the brain is dealing with a mix of aromas that are both positive and negative. "But 2 percent of it seems to pique the interest of the other aromas. It gives a contrast effect," explains Smith. "It gives a kind of cliff for the olfactory system: here is a sudden change from one to the other, making you terribly aware of the nice properties. So a little bit of nastiness with the niceness probably piques interest." Smith applies this to wine. "Well made, smooth, completely manipulated wines are boring. You want something a little quirky. It just piques your interest to have something that is contrasting."

The Sense of Smell Is Alert for Change

Smith suspects that this might be because of the way that smell is fundamentally different from vision. He asks:

> "What is your sense of smell for? It is to notice change more than anything else. With vision you maintain a continuous perceptual scene. It is important that vision is always filling out the world for you. The sense of smell seems to turn off if nothing has changed. That is why you do not notice the smell of your own home. But if you suddenly smell garbage or smoke, your system is on to it. Your system is: just keep everything the same, and if anything new happens, let me know. I think that is true if you are having lots of wines, and then someone has put in some extra thing in there: it kind of gets you."

Our appreciation of odors can change with time. In smell there is a very interesting phenomenon known as the "mere exposure effect." This is where our liking for something increases as we are repeatedly exposed to it, and it is thought to be very important in preference acquisition. One example of mere exposure would be in interpersonal relations, where you find someone more pleasing and likable on repeated encounters. This phenomenon was first studied extensively in vision by social psychologist Robert Zajonc. He presented people with a number of novel pictures in rapid

Barry Smith asks why winemakers often blend in just a tiny proportion of another grape variety. "How can 5 percent of Cabernet Franc or Petit Verdot make any difference? If your system is geared up to recognize 100 percent Cabernet Sauvignon, it will say 'so what?' if it gets it. But if you get something that is just a little bit changed or different, I think it piques your interest. Your olfactory system says that there is something nice or interesting here. This could be a clue to why these small percentages in blends matter."

succession, showing each for only a fraction of a second. Later on, the same people were shown a range of the pictures that included those they had seen earlier, plus others that they had not seen. Because the exposure in each experiment was so short, they could not reliably say which images they had previously seen and which they had not. But when they were asked to pick their favorites, liking increased for the images that had been shown more often, even when familiarity had not increased. That is, people liked the pictures they had seen the most, even though they were unable to remember which ones that had and had not been shown. This observation suggests that sometimes we might be making decisions about liking unconsciously, without thinking about them. Then, after we have made the decision, we use our thinking to rationalize the decision we have made.

Mere exposure has also been studied for smell. Here, it is quite hard to do the experiment well because it is difficult to find odors that are entirely novel. But experiments can be devised to answer the question: do we like odors because they are familiar? One of the most interesting studies in this area was carried out by Sylvain Delplanque and colleagues in 2015. They gave participants several odors, and asked them to rate each odor's pleasantness, intensity, and familiarity. What they found is that neutral and mildly pleasant odors showed an increase in pleasantness ratings: the mere exposure effect was working with these smells. But unpleasant and very pleasant odors remained unaffected by the frequency at which they had been encountered. It seems that for very nice smells and nasty ones, mere exposure does not work. One explanation for this is that we already like nice smells, so repeated exposure cannot make us like them more, and that nasty smells are nasty because we are supposed to find them aversive. This unpleasantness has survival value, and it would be a bad thing if we grew to like, for example, the smell of human excrement.

John Prescott and colleagues have also carried out an interesting study on mere exposure for smell, which is highly relevant to wine tasting. Their hypothesis was that attention might be an important element in mere exposure for odor. In an identification task, different smells were chosen either to be targets (the team would draw the subjects' attention to them) or nontargets (the subjects' attention was not drawn to them); otherwise, all the smells were exposed to the subjects uniformly.

There is one smell that has survival value, but which can be good or bad in different contexts: the smell of smoke. We are very sensitive to it, but there is a big difference between smelling smoke in a forest, warning us that we need to leave quickly, and the smell of smoke in the cave where we are cooking and staying warm, and where we need to stay close to its source.

Liking increased only after exposure to the target odors. The team concluded that active attention could well be an important determinant of exposure effects. How does this apply to wine? If the mere exposure effect means that we like certain smells more only when we are paying attention to them, this suggests that someone looking for certain aromas in a wine—say, an expert trying to examine them analytically—will begin to like those aromas more. If Prescott and colleagues are right, people will only like more those elements of a wine's aroma that they are actively looking for. This could reinforce the importance of having a wine vocabulary. Mere exposure probably does not have any effect in people who drink wine without thinking about it.

Associative Learning

Eugenol, a smell often encountered at a dental surgery, offers an example of associative learning. In one study it was shown that eugenol induced the emotion of fear in people scared of the dentist, but not in those who were not. This could be relevant to our wine preferences. Our first encounter with a wine might have been on vacation, or on a visit to the winery. If the flavor of the wine was distinctive enough, we might be drawn repeatedly to its smell as a consequence of associative learning.

There is another interesting concept in psychology that could be relevant to wine: associative learning. This is where an event or thing becomes linked to another through experience. Associative learning plays an important role in our lives. To a degree, our liking for particular smells is a result of a learned association between that smell and the emotional context in which it was first encountered. First, we associate the emotion with the smell; later on, the smell alone can stir the emotion we felt when we first encountered the smell.

Learning is important in flavor perception. As discussed in chapter 1, we associate the taste of sweetness with corresponding aromas, to the point that the smell of strawberries is regarded as sweet, even though we cannot smell "sweet." And as well as taste-to-odor learning, odor-to-odor learning also exists. This occurs when two smells are paired together and smelled repeatedly, and one takes on the quality of the other. This learning process differs across cultures where typical diets are different, and so learned associations between tastes and smells, or smells and smells, also differ. These forms of learning are likely to play an important role in wine appreciation, where specific smells and tastes occur together in the flavors of different wines.

In chapter 3 I discussed a well-known research paper from the field of neuroeconomics, in which functional magnetic resonance imaging (fMRI) was used to show that the information people were given about a wine could change their actual perception of it, and how pleasant they found it. By manipulating the subjects' understanding of the price of the wine they were drinking, the team altered brain responses to the same wine; the parts of the brain that experience pleasure were more active when subjects thought the wine was higher priced. The price was not just affecting perceived quality—it seemed to be affecting the actual quality of the wine by changing the nature of the perceptive experience. The results showed that our expectations as we approach wine change the nature of our wine-drinking experience.

In 2003, Christelle Chrea and colleagues studied the influence of cultural factors on the connection people make between perceiving odors and categorizing them. In one experiment, French, Vietnamese, and U.S. participants rated several everyday odorants in terms of how they smelled, and then sorted them on the basis of their similarity. The three ethnic groups differed in the way they assigned these smells to each of four groups: floral, sweet, bad, and natural. But they agreed for three groups: pleasantness, edibility, and cosmetic acceptability. In a second experiment, they sorted just fruit and flower odors to see whether there is consensus at a finer level. The French and U.S. participants separated fruit from flower odors, but this separation was nonexistent for Vietnamese participants. This difference could arise from cultural differences in how odor is perceived.

A study in 1998 looked at the topic of odor categorization with Japanese and German participants. They were presented with six each of "Japanese," "European," and "international" odorants and asked to rate them on intensity, familiarity, pleasantness, and edibility. They were also asked to describe associations with these smells, and to name them. There were significant differences between the two populations on all measures, but within the groups people were quite consistent.

Across all cultures, smells are considered to be closely linked to emotion. Nice smells make people feel good and bad ones induce negative moods. Odors have a similar effect on thinking and behavior to emotional stimuli, and can even cause changes in physiological parameters, such as heart rate or skin conductance. And there is also the role in smell in awakening long forgotten memories. In 2009, Sylvain Delplanque and colleagues published a study attempting to classify the words we use for emotional effects caused by smells. Their results suggested that the feelings or experiences induced by smells are structured around a small group of six dimensions that reflect the role of olfaction in well-being, social interaction, danger prevention, arousal or relaxation sensations, and conscious recollection of emotional memories.

The media love the idea that the wine trade is an elaborate fraud, perpetuated by people who are more or less making it up when they taste wine. People outside the wine trade find the idea that experts cannot tell the difference between cheap and expensive wines quite hilarious. The vast majority of the population think that anyone who spends a small fortune on a bottle of fine wine is being had by some sort of scam. Surely the emperor has no clothes? I suspect that we find this idea somewhat reassuring, too: we think that if the experts cannot tell the difference, then neither can we, and so there is no need to be spending a lot of money on expensive bottles of wine.

And then there were Frédéric Brochet's experiments, mentioned in chapter 1, in which he got professionals to smell a white wine and then a few weeks later a white wine colored red. They described the wine completely differently, even though it would have smelled the same, just because of the color change. And people seem highly suggestible when they are tasting wine. If they are told it is more expensive, not only do they report enjoying it more, their brains seem to show activity suggesting that at a subconscious level they do enjoy it more.

Is Wine-tasting Expertise Just an Illusion?

Clearly, anyone subjecting themselves to tough blind-tasting exams, such as the Master Sommelier or Master of Wine tests, believes in wine-tasting expertise. The performances of those who pass those trials indicate that it is possible to be an expert taster to quite a high level. So what do the studies that show otherwise mean? First, I would argue that, for those of us involved professionally with wine, we need to show a little humility; if we do not, there is a good chance that humility will be forced on us when we taste blind. But I would also argue that the poor performance of a large number of tasters does not call into question the whole basis of wine tasting. It takes only a few tasters—actually, just one—to taste blind accurately in any one situation to confirm that the skill exists; their performance validates the whole process. No one would ridicule the sport of golf, for example, just on the basis that a novice performed poorly at the Augusta National.

Say, for instance, we are talking about terroir as expressed in the wines that come from two neighboring vineyards. The fact that almost no one, when tasting blind, can recognize the vineyard from the wine does not matter. If just one taster can do so, this difference is real, and therefore matters. Let us think about another scenario. In a wine store, a couple choose a bottle of fine

A few years back, Robert Hodgson—statistician, small-scale winemaker, and owner of Fieldbrook Winery in California—analyzed the results of the California State Wine Show. Surprised by the varying success of his wines in different shows, he persuaded the organizers to let him analyze the data from the judging process over four years. His conclusions were damning, indicating that the results were little different from what might be obtained by chance, and that many of the judges were reaching almost random verdicts.

Bordeaux from a good vintage. Just before they leave, they are given the same wine to taste blind, plus a much less expensive one. They cannot tell the difference, but still they buy the expensive wine. Have they wasted their money? I would argue, no. As long as there exist differences between the wines, and experts who can identify the differences, wine drinkers buy the wine in faith. In time, they may develop their own palates such that they can appreciate these differences themselves. For now, what they have purchased is an authentic product. We can have a discussion about what it is that makes one wine higher in quality than another, and who gets to decide what "fine" wine is, but for now it is safe to say that wine expertise is not illusory, even though it is complicated and difficult, and very few tasters, if any, get it right all the time.

Finally, we come to the aesthetics of wine. There are lots of very good wines in the marketplace, from many different wine-producing countries, made in a large range of different styles. Who is to say one is better than another? The decision is clearly made in the marketplace: there is a wide spread of pricing in wine. And experts often agree that some wines are fine, while others are not. The study of the aesthetics of wine is of interest for this reason, but for a long time wine drinking was not afforded the status of an aesthetic experience. In the late eighteenth century, the influential German philosopher Immanuel Kant claimed that the pleasure of wine was only personal and idiosyncratic, and that any judgments on it were simple personal preferences.

John Dilworth, Professor of Philosophy at Western Michigan University, has written on this topic. He has compared what he calls "imaginative" and "analytical" experiences of wine. Most people think of wine appreciation as an analytical activity, where experts carefully distinguish the various sensory qualities of the wine. Dilworth suggests that this quasi-scientific approach is seriously defective, and maintains that in order to appreciate wine we need imaginative as well as analytical experiences of it. He suggests that wine appreciation—unlike art appreciation, which also has an imaginative element—has an improvisatory element that is highly individual.

Originally, our sensory capabilities evolved because they helped us survive. Dilworth thinks that wine tasting has coopted these faculties in the pursuit of pleasure: "Human feelings of delight, attraction, and enjoyment initially earned their evolutionary keep

Kant argued that, because wine is ingested, observers cannot be indifferent, which is a requirement for a true aesthetic experience. He thought that the senses of taste and smell are more subjective than objective: "The idea obtained from them is more a representation of enjoyment than a cognition of the external object."

as reinforcers of survival-enhancing behaviors . . . . But once the relevant cognitive and affective mechanisms were in place, they became available for reuse in entertainment, artistic activities, and play—in recreation, in a word."

Dilworth uses the analogy of the arts. The meaning achieved by the arts is imaginative or representational rather than literal or real. The emotions we feel listening to a powerful piece of music, "have no reality independent of the immediate experience of them by a sensitive listener." It would be wrong to confuse the experience of music with the sensory configuration of the heard sounds, even though there is no obvious way of linking the two. Likewise, how do we understand abstract art, such as that of Kandinsky, or Picasso in his Cubist period? Dilworth points out that a literal account of the visual content, describing shapes, lines, and hues, does not help. The sensory qualities of the painting do not reveal its meaning. But this is exactly what we do with wine. "Exactly this kind of gross confusion, of exhaustive literal descriptions of sensory qualities with experimental meaning, constitutes the ruling orthodoxy in discussions of wine."

Wine and Imagination

Dilworth points to the role of flavors, aromas, and colors of wine in the imagination in appropriately receptive experiences of them. In wine tasting, we typically assume that a two-part process takes place. First, we have the analytical part, where we actually perceive what is there. Then we have the bit where we interpret what is there, and react to it, bringing our perceptions into the equation. Dilworth argues that this is wrong: wine tasting is a single, imaginative experience that includes all the flavors and aromas, and their enjoyment.

Alcohol plays a role in the imaginative appreciation of wine, turning a sober sensory experience into one that is less inhibited, where the cognitive system of the drinker is more suggestible, and a wider range of cognitive exploration is possible.

But we should not compare wine appreciation with art appreciation. Dilworth says that a better comparison is with improvisatory theater. Wine gives us each a sensory theme on which we can carry out artlike improvisations. In this process, we are the artists. Alcohol in the wine helps to set us free to do this.

One of the implications of this view is that we should do away with absolute ideas of wine quality. People like different wines, and some people prefer mass-produced, fruit-forward wines. If we consider wine to be the raw material for personal improvisation, this problem is removed. Dilworth states, "Those who harbor secret admiration for some wines that are out of favor with the critics need no longer feel guilty concerning their tastes."

Douglas Burnham and Ole Martin Skilleås are authors of the book *The Aesthetics of Wine* (2012), which looks in depth at this subject. They argue that wine appreciation is an aesthetic activity similar to viewing a painting or listening to music. While this may seem uncontroversial to many, in academic circles it is disputed. Typically, objects that are aesthetically appreciated fall into one of three categories: visual (such as paintings and dance); aural (music); and linguistic (literature, poetry). This classification ignores touch, smell, and taste. Traditionally, these proximal senses—we have to be in contact with the subject in some way to use them—have been regarded as too subjective to be of use in aesthetics, which is restricted to the senses that can be used at a distance. Burnham and Skilleås ask, why are there no art categories corresponding to these excluded proximal senses?

Wine tasting can only be aesthetic in the sense of aesthetic practice, taking into account the full context of those perceiving it—what they have learned, their skills, and their language for describing flavors. Wine tasting is aesthetic in an intersubjective sense: we compare our sensory impressions to arrive at our judgment. Individual tasters do not do it in isolation.

Normally, aesthetics revolves around the intention of the artist. Citing the example of a beautiful landscape, Burnham and Skilleås argue against this, saying that it is possible to regard an object aesthetically without claiming it to be a work of art. For them, aesthetics refers to the response of a group of perceivers.

Notions of Competency

To help with this discussion, Burnham and Skilleås introduce the term "competency," which refers to the knowledge and experience we bring to the appreciation of an aesthetic object. This competency can be divided into three branches: cultural, practical, and aesthetic judgment. Cultural competency is conceptual in nature: it is the knowledge of kinds and styles of wines, for example. We might ask ourselves: what is desirable in this style of wine? How should it develop in the bottle? Practical competency is the ability we possess to taste wine: to detect, dissect, and discriminate what is found in the glass. It is our sensory competence that is developed by experience. Burnham and Skilleås emphasize an important point: this all takes place in the context of "intersubjective practices." This might be the procedure and conditions for tasting, the sequence the wines are tasted in, and the serving temperature. All of these conditions help to enable the exercise of judgment. Another part of this practical competency is the experience of different styles of wines. The development of a suitable language for describing wine is also vital for discerning the characteristics of the wine. We learn about wine by tasting alongside others and developing a vocabulary for wine.

The third type of competency is "emergent perception," or "aesthetic judgment." Global descriptors used by tasters such as "balanced," "elegant," "harmonious," "complex," or "profound" are referring to properties of the wine that only exist as a combination of the various sensory attributes of the wine. They are emergent properties that are not reducible back to the component parts of the wine, so they are themselves based on aesthetic judgments. The authors comment: "Aesthetic judgments are grounded in what is present to mind there and then—the properties that have emerged within the singular act of judgment—and not in the presence or absence of objectively describable and generally desirable elements or clusters of elements."

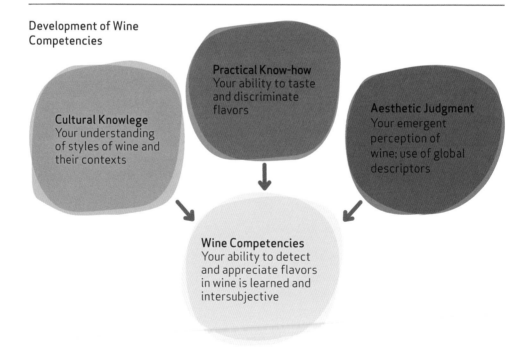

Development of Wine
Competencies

Practical Know-how
Your ability to taste
and discriminate
flavors

Cultural Knowlege
Your understanding
of styles of wine and
their contexts

Aesthetic Judgment
Your emergent
perception of
wine; use of global
descriptors

Wine Competencies
Your ability to detect
and appreciate flavors
in wine is learned and
intersubjective

So, aesthetic judgment represents the ability to move from smells or flavors to the attributions of emergent properties. To do this effectively, we need each other; we need to learn and be guided by others. This ability is acquired intersubjectively. The emergent properties are based on sensed properties of the wine, but the ability to detect and appreciate them must be learned. Aesthetic practice in wine tasting requires a "community of judgment" with broadly similar tastes and compatible sets of competencies.

Aesthetic judgments about wine present themselves as normative: if I find a wine complex or balanced, I expect you to do so, also. Burnham and Skilleås are suggesting a shift of the focus in aesthetics from the individual perceiver (which is normally the case) to communities of judgment. Fine wine, as we know it, is an aesthetic system.

Influence of the "Wine World"

If individual tasters belong to an intersubjective community of wine tasters, fine wine becomes an aesthetic system, as Skilleås says:

> "Our perspective is that wine is not something that just exists, it is something we do. Wine tasters, producers, journalists, importers, and so on form what we call "the wine world" [this is an implicit and explicit reference to Arthur Danto's essay of 1964, "The Artworld"]. To you and me, the progression of tasting, for instance, or the glasses we use, is second nature. But these too we have acquired from others—not to mention the vocabulary and the standards we set. Far from being the object without parts that critics of wine in aesthetics have maintained, wine is an object that is in part constructed by the community of wine—the wine world. The progression just mentioned is one way in which wine becomes an object that we can talk about."

In Skilleås's view, judgments of quality cannot be divorced completely from the way wine is treated as an object:

> "Unwittingly or by design, we learn to taste, talk about and judge wine from others. We call this guided perception, but we may as well have expanded this to 'guided judgement.' We think that the normativity of judgements of wine rest on

guided perception and judgement. We are, as it were, members of the wine world, and we judge on its behalf. Of course, we like to stand out and to assert our independence—sometimes to go out on a limb, maybe—but none of this would make any difference if there were not shared norms for what constitute the desirable properties of wine."

John Lambie, a former manager of the Scottish soccer club Partick Thistle, is credited with the following anecdote. On being informed by his medical team that his striker was concussed to the extent he could not remember his own name, Lambie replied, "Tell him he is [Brazilian star] Pelé and get him back on." The story raises an interesting point: to what degree does our sense of identity, and how we see ourselves in relation to the world, affect our thinking, behavior, and performance?

But what about the identity of the wine tasters themselves? Does that affect their experience of wine? Significantly, I think, because we understand the world around us in terms of stories. We have an internal narrative—a set of stories about how the world around us works—and it is through the lens of this narrative that we interpret reality. This filtering of experience, and the process of fitting it into our own internal story framework, gives each of us a unique perspective on the world. We can share our worldview with our friends and family to some degree, but many aspects of it are personal to us as individuals.

Aesthetic Systems and Notions of Wine Quality

How does that relate to wine? We interpret and understand wine in the light of our own narratives. The appreciation of wine is not just about what tastes good. For example, when is a wine a "great" wine, or a "fine" wine? The judgment of wine quality can only exist within the framework of an aesthetic system—a narrative built up on the recognition of certain features of wine as being desirable, and which also has things to say about where the wine came from and how it was produced.

In the world of wine we find different narratives or aesthetic systems that overlap to some extent, but which also differ significantly. Controversies can arise when these narratives clash. What narratives are there? First, there is the classic fine wine narrative, where great wines are produced in Bordeaux, Burgundy, and Champagne. Second, there is the U.S./Robert Parker narrative, which saw the British fine wine establishment as complacent, and British writers in bed with the trade. Parker becomes the consumer advocate with an easy-to-understand points system and fierce independence, he develops a strong following, and his taste for ripe, generous, big wines resonated with his readers. Suddenly we have a new fine wine narrative that clashes to a degree with the earlier one. Third, we have the constellation of biodynamic, authentic, and/or natural wine narratives, where power is eschewed in favor of elegance, and where a strong part of the story concerns how the wine is grown and made, with an emphasis on vineyard health and minimal manipulation in the winery. In particular, the newer natural/authentic wine narrative has clashed significantly with the U.S./Robert Parker fine wine narrative.

"We toyed with the idea of different aesthetic systems, using the established European values of wine against the Parker school," says Skilleås. "However, I think that today it is the world of natural wine that would be the hottest candidate to represent an alternative system. This is mainly because the values of the natural wine enthusiasts go well beyond the qualities of the wines, to include the way they have been made. The natural wine movement is quite happy to sacrifice aesthetic values on the altar of nature."

What all this reinforces is that we come to wine from our own perspective, and so the notion of rating or judging wine has to be seen with this taken into account. A rating cannot be a global, universal score that is a property of that wine. If you do decide to follow a critic, you need to choose one whose own narrative of wine is largely overlapping with yours; you need to adjust for differences and calibrate yourself to the critic.

If we are to interpret wines, it is helpful for us to be aware that we are doing so in light of our own wine narrative. This is why stories are so important for the appreciation of wine. "Wine needs words," said Hugh Johnson, and he was right. But even more than that, wine needs stories. It is these narratives that help us to understand wine, help us to fall in love with it, and help us progress in our journey through this most engaging and life-enhancing grape-derived phenomenon.

Very few commentators suggest that wine is an art form, but I will conclude by asking whether there is a way that wine might be considered as art. Is it so outlandish to suggest that an art gallery could have a smell exhibit? Given the appropriate technology, could an artist manipulate smells in a similar way that a sculptor works with bronze or a painter works with oils on a canvas, to create something beautiful and meaningful? If so, surely wine would be considered to be the ultimate in the art of flavor.

Constructing Reality

Dreams and hallucinations are states of mind where we experience our own reality—one that differs significantly from what is normally called "reality." Could these states reflect the ability of the brain to construct reality from limited sensory input? And is what we experience of reality actually something that we construct around a skeleton of reality that we extract from the world around us? A new theory of how the brain works that is currently causing a lot of excitement in neuroscience suggests that this may so.

Could a Zombie Be a Good Wine Taster?

Although I would not say that I was an expert on the genre, I have seen enough zombie films to know that a zombie is a human that—apart from possessing a strong desire to chomp on other humans, thus initiating what is left of them into the zombie family—acts in an entirely involuntary, unconscious manner. Zombies are not given to introspection.

Given this, would a zombie be a good wine taster? I assume that they possess a sense of flavor (they certainly enjoy live human flesh), so in practice they could sense wine if they were to drink it. But I think they would be poor at it, because a lot of the skill of wine tasting involves conscious thought, comparing what we are experiencing with past experiences of wine, interrogating the smell and flavor of the wine, searching for what is there, and then analyzing what we find.

Attentive readers of this book will know by now that when we are tasting wine, we are not acting as simple measuring devices. We are assessing, in a conscious way, a perception that has been presented to our consciousness by our brains. By this stage our brain has done a lot of work on the information that it received from our mouth, nose, and eyes, and we are not able to access these processing steps, nor are we aware of what has occurred. But it is now that we are able to use various cognitive strategies to explore the wine in the glass. This is where the zombie wine taster would struggle. They would have a taste, but likely the only judgment they could make is whether they liked or disliked it.

What sets us apart from zombies is our consciousness, the topic at the heart of this chapter. In chapter 3 we looked at how the brain processes sensory information. Now we will take this one step further, and look at consciousness itself, one of the most interesting and difficult topics in neuroscience, psychology, and philosophy. Neuroscientist Chris Frith quips that when many neuroscientists reach the age of about fifty they feel they have sufficient wisdom and expertise to set about solving the problem of consciousness. Tackling this fiendishly difficult concept is widely considered to be a massive pitfall for academics.

One of the problems in discussing this topic is that we all feel familiar with it already, and often have our own strong ideas about the subject which we know to be right, as Frith explains: "Psychology is different from other sciences in many ways, but the most important difference is that everyone has their own intuitions about psychology. This includes psychologists: we all use folk psychology all the time." Psychology is also a contentious, multidisciplinary topic. Because it is difficult to research, there are many different opinions in the literature. But the view that I present in this chapter is particularly engaging and interesting from a conceptual viewpoint, and is also the one, I think, that is gaining the broadest support.

"With disciplines like physics or molecular genetics we accept that we know little or nothing about the subject and respect the experts who do. The psychologist who makes some exciting new discovery is told either that everybody knew that already or else that it must be nonsense."

Chris Frith

Consciousness and Navigation of the World

In short, consciousness is a tool that organisms have developed in their brains during evolution to help them respond appropriately to the world around them. That is a bold claim and I shall try to support it, because many will find it quite a threatening idea. When it comes to the possession of consciousness, I do not know where the taxonomic dividing line lies. Descartes famously argued that only humans are conscious, but it seems likely that animals such as dogs, orcas, dolphins, elephants, and parrots are conscious, too. This is despite the fact that it is impossible to be certain about animal consciousness because no animal exists that can speak to us about their experience.

What is the problem that consciousness solves? We need a means of navigating through a complicated external world, responding fast enough to the varied stimuli that we face. The scale of the challenge that this presents is highlighted by the difficulties faced by those working on artificial intelligence (AI). It is only when you start to try to replicate with a computer what the brain does that you realize that the job it accomplishes seemingly effortlessly is actually fiendishly difficult.

Most people attempting to generate AI would begin by creating a device that can measure the variables in the environment and feed the data thus obtained into a large computer program for processing. For example, you might use a digital camera to collect visual data, and then use a clever algorithm to identify the important features in the images—this is something modern digital cameras do quite well, detecting faces in order to focus on them rather than the background. You might use a microphone to detect sound, and then do a similar sort of advanced processing to make sense of these data, just as the Siri program on the iPhone recognizes your voice. Very soon, though, you would be dealing with a huge amount of data, especially once you included memory (access to previously stored data) in the equation. If that were the way our brains worked, we would quickly be swamped by information, and we would be unable to process it fast enough to respond on the necessary timescale.

In the last few years a lot of progress has been made in AI by using a modified form of neural networks called deep learning, with scores of stages of feature extraction, nonlinear processing, and then passing the restricted set of information up to the next level, which is something much closer to how brains work, without getting as far as consciousness.

Before we jump straight to consciousness, let us begin by looking at the specific case of vision. We think of our visual field as complete and accurate. But really, it is something our brain has created for us out of the information taken in by our eyes. As you look around, it is only actually the very center of the visual field that is sharply in focus, although we labor under the impression that everything is in focus (it is because our eyes rapidly jump around, so whenever we look at things they always seem sharp). We are not aware of the blind spot in our vision where the optic nerve meets the retina, because the brain fills this in for us. And as you move your head around, and your eyes scan this way and that, the visual environment seems stable and constant despite the fact that the information coming into your retina is changing fast. Although we are frequently moving, we sense the visual

If we could work by means of deep learning—take in all the external data, feed in our experience (memory), and then calculate the appropriate response—the brain would have no need for consciousness. We would simply be automatons, like zombies. It seems that consciousness evolved as an elegant solution for a complex computational problem.

environment as stable. We feel we are the ones that are moving while it remains stable. But if you were to see the information that comes in through your eyes, just as if it were a feed from a TV camera, it would be unwatchable. The brain has put together this "model" of the visual environment you are in so it all seems stable and constant, and you can attend to the interesting things in it.

This is why Go-Pro footage is so unsatisfying. These small, waterproof video cameras that you can attach to your bike, surfboard, or head yield some interesting films, but fail to replicate what it is like to experience reality. For example, Go-Pro footage of a cycle route down a mountain path carries just a part of the drama of the journey, but is not totally convincing. This is because, when you are actually cycling down that path, your visual system constructs a stable image of the environment that you are moving through, even though it is not what your eyes are taking in. The Go-Pro benefits from being quite wide-angle, but our visual system does not operate in the same way that a video camera does.

Approximations of Human Experience

The same is true of first-person shooter video games, such as the immensely popular *Call of Duty* series. The graphics may be incredible, but it does not feel like being there because we cannot build up our visual model of the environment. These games would be fully convincing only if the game console could track our eye movements and then be responsive to them in real time. Good movie makers have an understanding of how vision works, whether this is intuitive or learned. Try to look at a movie from the maker's perspective, examining the techniques they use. They will typically string together short clips, cutting in close then out again, focusing on items that are of interest to the viewer from a biological point of view (what is that hand doing? what is that face?). The camera will jump around and many of the clips are very short indeed, but when this is done well and they are joined together we do not notice it, and we are drawn into the experience.

So, in vision, the brain is modeling the world around us to create a visual scene that is incomplete, but feels complete and useful and does not use up too much processing power. We recognize patterns and objects, which all jump out of an otherwise confusing and detailed scene, and we instinctively interpret what is there without

Very occasionally, the brain's system of making sense of visual input is momentarily tricked. We have probably all experienced the weird feeling that occurs when we are on a train that is stationary at a platform and we see the train on the opposite side pulling away. For a few seconds we think that it is us that are moving; it is a very powerful illusion.

Basic Requirements of Artificial Intelligence (AI)

Hearing
A microphone would pick up sound and feed it to processors, which would pull out relevant information from background noise, for example, to achieve speech recognition.

Vision
A camera would take in the visual scene. Processing here would make use of object recognition, in the way that a digital camera is programmed to focus specifically on faces.

Smell and Taste
Chemical molecules, instead of being detected by our nose and tongue, would be picked up by sensors and fed to the AI, which would recognize and identify them.

Touch
A mobile, corporeal AI would require pressure sensors to mimic those of our skin and inner body. They would help the AI to navigate its environment without self-damage.

even realizing what we are doing. This higher-order processing makes sense of what otherwise would be a confusing scene, and it does it very efficiently. We are not consciously aware of this processing; instead, we consider what we "see" to be an exact representation of what is there. Or, to put it another way, we have the illusion that we have a direct perception of the world. This is not the case, but we feel it to be the case, because we are not aware of the work our brains are doing behind the scene.

The Brain's Need for a Model

In chapter 3 we began to explore the idea that a lot of our perception is not an exact correspondence with reality. We extract from a complex mass of sensory data just those features that are most relevant. And we navigate the world by learning to recognize objects—their properties, typical behaviors, and appearances. These object representations are multimodal, combining information from a number of senses. The exact mix of the senses in the "object blend" will depend on the nature of the object, so it is impossible to say which sense is more important in its makeup.

The brain needs a model because it offers the only way of navigating reality in real time, given the level of complexity involved in the world around us. This is where we turn to the current hot topic in neuroscience: predictive coding. It is now widely thought that this is the way the brain works; it is a complex but powerful idea that has the potential to explain difficult concepts such as consciousness and perception.

Simply put, the brain acts as a predictive device. It anticipates incoming sensory data with a set of expectations (known in the trade as priors) and compares these predictions with the actual sensory data that come in. The brain is looking for "error messages," which help us to refine our model of the world outside.

There are two heroes in this new theory of the way the brain works. The first is the celebrated German scientist Hermann von Helmholtz. In 1866 he published a paper on the way that the brain makes unconscious inferences. He noted that there was a lag of some 200 milliseconds between a signal connecting with the senses and the conscious experience of this signal. His verdict was that it takes time for the brain to work because the brain is making unconscious inferences. In essence, this idea was the

If you had a map that corresponded exactly with reality, and was on the same scale as it, then the map would clearly be useless. Instead, a good map reduces reality to a more manageable scale and contains solely information that will be of use (see p.59).

beginning of what is now referred to as predictive coding. The other hero is Presbyterian minister and statistician Thomas Bayes, whose work was published in 1763, two years after his death, but was largely unappreciated until the 1950s. Addressing beliefs and probabilities, Bayes suggested that if we have a strong idea about the way the world is, we make a prediction knowing that there is a high probability that this will turn out to be true. But because the state of the world is changing, and we never know exactly what is going on out there, there is always some error in our predictions. It is this error that allows us to refine our predictions and make them better. Bayes's theory tells us just how much we need to change our predictions in order to make them more accurate.

What the brain is doing is constructing an internal sensory model. That is what we perceive: "reality" is actually something that is being created by our brains. It is a prediction of what is out there, and then we use incoming sensory information to modify the model. We are also able to operate in an almost unconscious fashion when there is no difference between what we predict and our experience. For example, if I reach out to pick up a pen, I do it almost without thinking. My brain predicts how far I will need to reach and the force I will need to use. As long as the pen weighs what I would expect it to weigh, I will accomplish this act—which seems simple but is actually quite complex—without even thinking about it. But should the pen weigh considerably more or less than I was expecting, the prediction error will cause me to take note of what I am doing. I will suddenly divert my attention to the act. This is what happens when we pick up a piece of lead or a large piece of polystyrene. When something is unexpectedly heavy or light, we tend to be surprised every time. Professor Barry Smith of the Centre for the Study of the Senses at the University of London explains more about the implications of predictive coding:

"All our perceptions are hallucinations, in the sense that they are created by our brain. However, our perceptions are hallucinations that are strongly constrained by reality. These constraints derive from the evidence provided by our senses, but also from our prior beliefs. Furthermore, in this framework, there is no essential difference between hallucinations and delusions. Both result from the assessment of evidence constrained by prior expectations."
Chris Frith

> "The old model was that information coming in from your receptors comes in through the sense modalities and gets computed; you abstract from those and make a judgment about how things are. That is not what we believe any more. We believe that the brain is making top-down predictions about what sensory information it will get. And when it gets the input, it is either correct, so you can score it off, or you get an error message: it was not correct, and you have to revise your priors."

Meeting up with Smith to discuss predictive coding, I suggest that what we are doing in perception is model the world around us. The computational problem is too hard for us to do directly, so we model reality. We play the model and then we use reality to confirm or disconfirm it. Smith agrees:

"This came from the 'forward model' about action. Suppose you were going to pick up your recorder from the table. The common sense for you is to use your eyes to guide your hand to it, but that would be too slow. By the time you have sent the information from the visual cortex, up to the sensory motor, down through the arm, it is too late. So the brain already predicts the movement and the sensations you expect at the end of your fingers, and it keeps a copy of that. When you reach out and touch, if what you get at the end of your fingers after a certain movement is what you predicted, you cancel it out. In other words, you never really pay attention to what is happening in your fingers. There is a disconnect."

How Our Brain Creates Reality

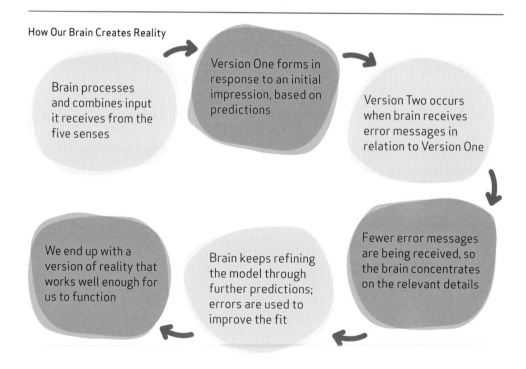

Brain processes and combines input it receives from the five senses

Version One forms in response to an initial impression, based on predictions

Version Two occurs when brain receives error messages in relation to Version One

Fewer error messages are being received, so the brain concentrates on the relevant details

Brain keeps refining the model through further predictions; errors are used to improve the fit

We end up with a version of reality that works well enough for us to function

Smith then demonstrates the "waiter's effect," a well-known phenomenon. "Hold your hand out straight, and I will place a bottle on it. When I lift off the bottle, your arm goes up a little bit. Now lift the bottle off yourself with your other hand; it does not go up. This is because you have predicted what the weight change will be and you have corrected for it, but you cannot predict my movements so you cannot do the calculation." He adds that this is why you should never take a glass off a waiter's tray when they come to the table; instead, let them do it. "So, you predict what your arm will feel like when that bottle comes off, and you change your muscle tension accordingly: that is the forward model."

Predictive Coding and Wine Tasting

How might the predictive coding theory apply in the context of a wine-tasting event? Smith explains:

"Suppose you know you are tasting New Zealand Pinot Noirs. You have done a lot of this: you look at the color, you smell, before you even get the wine to your mouth you have very strong expectations about what is going to happen. There is room for a little bit of what you do not expect, maybe a little extra acidity or sweetness, but it would be very strange if, when you got the wine to your mouth, you got the taste of a Bordeaux or a Cabernet: it would freak you. You already go looking for things that you expect to be there. If we believe the predictive coding story, you cancel sensations out: you almost do not pay attention to them. It is a bit like a checklist. Now imagine the idea that someone who is not used to tasting is expecting to get a glass of red wine, and they are predicting it is a red wine (so in some sense the brain is predicting lower acidity, fullness, a black or red fruit). Once this comes in, it cannot be paid attention to, so the most important thing for them to pay attention to is liking or disliking. It is almost as if when people are tasting wines when they are not thinking about it, they cannot remember what it tasted of—the main thing was rushing to the verdict of 'I liked it' or 'I did not like it.' What professional tasters do is one of the weirdest things we make ourselves do, which is overcome our natural ability to just discount lots of things because they are familiar. You are going to have to make

"With your senses, and for any sensory experience, the brain has a prediction about what it is going to get. When the sensations come in, if everything matches the prediction, all well and good. If you get something that is radically surprising, this creates an error message."

Barry Smith

yourself pay attention to all that information. Some of it is redundant: on a personal level you know a lot about what a New Zealand Pinot Noir should be, so you do not need to pay special attention to it, but in your job you do. You are trying to overcome the brain's ability to discount."

Dreams and Hallucinations

Evidence that the brain has the capability to create "reality" comes from the existence of experiential states that have no basis in the outside world. Drugs such as mescaline, lysergic acid diethylamide (LSD), psilocybin, and N,N-dimethyltryptamine (DMT) are known as psychedelics and cause changes to consciousness often referred to as hallucinations. Users experience an altered reality that is not subject to the usual sorts of constraints, and which may differ considerably from true reality. There has been a recent revival of interest in psychedelics as potentially useful therapeutic tools, although they remain illegal in practically all countries because of fears about their negative effects on users' mental health.

Ayahuasca is a traditional psychedelic that is used by native communities in the Amazon in religious ceremonies. It is a psychedelic tea made by mixing the ayahuasca vine, which contains DMT, with the chacruna shrub, which contains monoamine oxidase inhibitors (MAOIs). DMT is normally broken down by the stomach but the Amazonians learned that the chacruna, with its MAOI activity, blocks the breakdown of DMT, enabling it to enter the bloodstream. Together, the combination is a potent one—although at the price of enduring vomiting and diarrhoea at the same time. People taking ayahuasca under the guidance of shamans report intense spiritual revelations concerning the nature of the universe and human purpose on earth; they claim to gain access to higher spiritual dimensions where they make contact with beings who act as guides or healers. People have testified to their lifelong depression being cured through these intense psychedelic experiences.

Not everyone has tried psychoactive drugs, but we all experience the hallucinations of sleep: dreams. Researchers looking at the brain patterns of sleepers have identified one phase of sleep in which they appear to be awake, although their muscles are not

Ayahuasca is seen by many as a plant medicine rather than a drug. Celebrities such as Lindsay Lohan, Sting, and Paul Simon have all spoken of its use, and ayahuasca tourism has become big business in Peru and Colombia. In lodges all over the Amazon, resident shamans guide curious Westerners through the hallucinatory experience, but this mind-altering spiritual quest is not without risk. Some shamans are better than others, and a recent spate of deaths and rapes has cast a shadow over the drug.

responding, except for the muscles that control the eyes. This phase, known as rapid eye movement (REM) sleep, is when dreams occur. If awakened during REM sleep, the vast majority of people would report having been in a dream. But the memory of dreams is short-lived: should you wake just a few minutes after the end of REM sleep, you will not recall the dream.

In an amusing research paper from 2000, Sarah-Jayne Blakemore, Daniel Wolpert, and Chris Frith proposed an explanation of why we cannot tickle ourselves. It all relates to the work our brains do in prediction. Our motor systems have an internal forward model: they predict what is going to happen when we act. The brain commands the fingers to tickle, and at the same time generates a forward model predicting the sensory consequences of this action. The sensory consequences of the move to tickle can be accurately predicted when such a movement is self-produced, and this prediction can be used by the brain to attenuate the sensory effects of the movement. But when someone else makes a move to tickle us, there is a discrepancy between the sensory prediction we make and the sensory feedback that we receive. The bigger the discrepancy, the more we feel the tickle. The authors used functional neuroimaging to look at what is happening in the brain and found that the somatosensory cortex and anterior cingulate cortex are activated less when we try to tickle ourselves than when someone else does it, suggesting that these are responsible for the sensory attenuation. They also think that the cerebellum might be involved in generating the prediction of the sensory consequences of movement.

The few dreams we recall from REM sleep are vivid experiences very similar to those of reality itself. It is just that their content bears no relation to reality. What is going on? With both dreams and hallucinations it seems that the brain's reality-generating device (whatever that may be) is active in the absence of any input or constraint from reality. Instead, it draws from memory, producing an experience that seems very real indeed.

Consciousness and Free Will

In 1983, Benjamin Libet and colleagues published a paper that has since become famous. Its conclusions are surprising, and philosophers and neuroscientists have been debating them ever since. In this experiment, subjects had to perform a simple motor task such as moving their wrist or fingers at any time of their choosing within a window of thirty seconds. They were asked to identify when they were first aware of their decision, urge, or intention to act by indicating a time on a clock; Libet referred to this as the W time point. Next, he used an electroencephalogram to monitor their brain activity. The surprise finding was that a

preparatory brain activity called the readiness potential (RP) preceded their action by about 550 milliseconds, and there was a gap between the W and RP of some 350 milliseconds. It seems that the brain initiates the activity before we even imagine that we are making the conscious decision to act. The finding has since been replicated elsewhere. What are the implications? Many have argued that this result leaves our notion of free will stone dead. They say it proves that actions are initiated by preparatory brain activity rather than conscious decisions, and that free will cannot exist if a conscious decision is not involved.

Now, this is disturbing stuff. Not many of us are happy with the idea that we are not free to choose what we do, say, and think. The assumption that we have these freedoms is fundamental to the way society is structured. Granted, there may be genetic and environmental influences that push us one way or another in terms of the actions we take, but after those are accounted for we assume that we still have considerable scope in being able to say yes or no, and make our own choices.

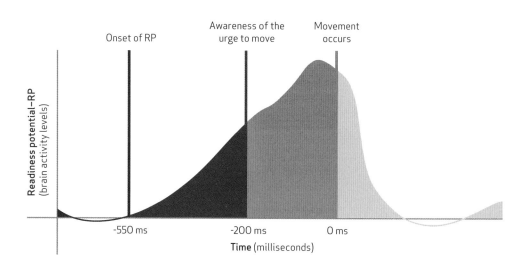

The Libet Experiment

This graph represents results from Benjamin Libet's experiment, which has been repeated many times. It shows that brain activity precedes the decision to move. Readiness potential (RP) records the cortex voltage fluctuation. The time lapse has implications for theories of free will.

Can Libet's experiments be interpreted differently? Some have argued that the actions that were studied by Libet were more automatic than willed. Many of our familiar everyday actions are performed automatically, with very little conscious deliberation. In these experiments, subjects agreed to making a movement within the next thirty seconds, and it could be argued that a conscious decision was followed by a more-or-less automatic process—the subject may have left the decision of precisely when to act within that window to the unconscious brain. But the consensus is that these actions are actually willed, so that argument fails. Another potential escape is methodological: when exactly does the point W occur? The fact that subjects are shifting their attention from their task to looking at the clock might be a problem with this experiment's design. Also, very little is riding on the choice they make, so it is one of disinterested agency.

In the interpretation of Libet's experimental results, there is one interesting observation that could save free will. Subjects reported that they had a conscious wish, but they could choose to suppress or veto it. In his experiments, sometimes Libet could see an RP which was then followed by a veto, and thus no action. It could be that our free will is akin to dining out at a restaurant, where we choose from a limited number of options, rather than cooking at home, where we have to initiate our choices from scratch.

It may be that we are presented with desires or urges by our unconscious, which we then can choose to repress or fulfill. Consciousness could therefore be, in part, a selective process. We make a decision from a raft of available possibilities proposed to us by our unconscious brain. Conscious free will may act to control which acts we choose to do, rather than initiate voluntary acts.

Sweet Anticipation

David Huron, Professor of Music at Ohio State University, is the author of an absorbing book, *Sweet Anticipation: Music and the Psychology of Expectation* (2006). Its ideas tie in very well with the concept of predictive coding as the basis for conscious perception. When we listen to music, our relationship with it changes with repeated exposure. We predict what is coming, and then there is a pleasure derived when the music matches our predictions. "Sweet anticipation" refers to these positive thoughts and feelings that come from predicting a future event and seeing it take place.

Generalizing his work from music, Huron produces a broader account of expectation that he calls the "ITPRA theory": the acronym represents five response systems: imagination, tension, prediction, reaction, and appraisal. The first two occur prior to the event, and the final three occur during or after it.

In Huron's work, the imagination response is about anticipating and evaluating possible outcomes, while tension serves to shape attention and arousal according to the nature, certainty, and importance of the potential outcomes. Then, as the event begins, prediction ascertains how well the event matches the prior expectations. Reaction is an immediate response to the event, and the conscious appraisal response is a final, more measured and thought-out assessment of what happened.

The predictions we make and the degree to which they are successful result in a reward or penalty. Successful predictions yield a positive emotional reward; unsuccessful predictions result in surprise, which, depending on the context, may or may not result in a negative emotional penalty. By attaching emotional consequences to our ITPRA processing, evolution has motivated us to improve our anticipatory skills. In turn, the skills help us to respond correctly to our highly variable environments. The pleasure we get from music is but a by-product of this capacity.

Positive Effects of Unsuccessful Predictions

We rapidly tire of music when we can tell exactly what is going to happen next, which is why music to which we have been overexposed can end up being very annoying. Conversely, we develop a relationship with interesting music. This is not simply familiarity at play; it is because the brain is being rewarded for its increasing ability to guess correctly what is coming next.

In some contexts, surprises resulting from unsuccessful predictions can lead to rewards. It can be boring if all our predictions are all fulfilled. In chapter 6 I mentioned the mere exposure effect, where we come to like smells more once we have been exposed to them a number of times, as long as they are not bad or very attractive. In his analysis of music and anticipation, Huron suggests how mere exposure might be working. According to Huron, some music manages to combine surprise with the fulfillment of predictions. One possible explanation for this is that, while a conscious expectation satisfied is rewarding, an unconscious expectation that is satisfied is more rewarding still. Thus, if we have had some subliminal exposure to a stimulus—for example, a very brief exposure, an exposure some time in the past, or when we were distracted—we might gain an unconscious expectation and be extremely satisfied when we meet the stimulus again and our unconscious predictions are met.

Huron believes that we need to expand our concept of the senses to include the sense of the future: "In many ways, expectation can be regarded as yet another sense: a sense of future. In the same way that the sense of vision provides the mind with information about upcoming events. Compared with the other senses, the sense of future is the closest biology comes to magic."

In addition to predicting the future, consciousness allows us to do something else that is of great use: interpret the intentions of others. With only limited information, we are—to a degree—able to read how others are thinking. This ability is called theory of mind. Interpreting others is a vital skill in social interactions, but most of us do it so effortlessly that we do not realize how remarkable it is.

The brain is alert to how others act and behave. In the early 1990s, Giacomo Rizzolatti and colleagues made an important discovery. Investigating monkey behavior with neuroimaging, they confirmed that neurons fired in the monkey when it performed an action, but realized also that neurons fired when the monkey saw the same action performed by another. They termed these mirror neurons. Assuming that we humans also have mirror neurons (which is hard to prove for ethical reasons), it is as if we understand what people are doing by reading their intentions. In social interactions, we understand the intentions of others not by thinking about them but by feeling them almost instinctively. Mirror neurons allow us to sense the intentions and emotions that others are experiencing even when they do not make them explicit. If we see our friend smile, our smile neurons smile too: we understand instinctively and immediately what is going on in this social interaction. Indeed, when someone smiles at you, it is hard not to smile back. If someone grimaces, you can sense they are in pain. Yawning is contagious. The existence of human mirror neurons is not proven beyond doubt, but it seems likely that they exist and help us to get along with others.

And so we arrive at the nature of conscious experience. If we consider our consciousness, the one thing that seems apparent is that it is a unity. All the various aspects of being conscious are experienced together, rather than there being separate modes of consciousness that are somehow fused together. This is a subject we will return to in the final chapter.

Our brains allow us to predict the future, and this prediction comes with emotions tied in. Generally, we are conservative—we are more alert to potential danger at some times than others, depending on how challenging we predict the situation to be. It is this ability to sense the future that makes possible the arts, and aesthetic activities such as listening to music, watching a movie, and enjoying fine wine. These are all activities that hijack the emotional rewards brought by anticipation.

The Language of Wine

One of the problems of tasting wine is how we communicate our perceptions to others. We can be quite clear about what we experience as we taste a wine, yet find it very difficult to put these perceptions into words. So, how can we meaningfully communicate our experiences of wine? How much does the language we have for taste and smells influence the perceptions themselves? Does having a developed vocabulary help anchor our perceptions as we taste wine? And do all cultures share this difficulty of translating smells and tastes to words, or could this in part be cultural?

Finding Words to Share Our Perceptions

When we share a bottle of wine around the table, we usually like to make comments on it. We might complement whoever bought the bottle on its quality, but often we will move a little beyond that and actually try to describe its properties in a bid to show our appreciation. The wine trade takes this to a whole different level.

When I first started drinking wine in the early 1990s, I tried to write tasting notes as a way of remembering the bottles I had drunk, and also as a way of learning more about wine. Of course, I had read some tasting notes from others. For example, one of the first wine books I had studied was U.S. critic Robert Parker's *Wine Buyer's Guide* (1987), a weighty doorstop of a volume. His tasting notes were enthusiastic, bold, and quite easy to understand for a novice. I was also familiar with the brief notes that newspaper columnists would use to describe their recommended wines. I was beginning to gather a set of wine words, but my first steps in writing tasting notes were faltering and brief. Here is an example:

Charles Melton Shiraz 1987
£7.49 Oddbins
Drunk 25 May 1993
Chocolaty, concentrated, full-flavored spicy Shiraz. Excellent.

Reading through the other notes I made at the time, it is clear that I had very little vocabulary for wine.

When sharing a meal, we may compliment the host: "This spaghetti bolognaise is excellent!," or "I really like this beef: did you get it from the butcher on the corner?" But comments on food are usually in nonspecific terms, and involve a broad assessment of quality, almost always positive. Our thoughts on wine are different.

We have a limited vocabulary for taste and smells, and this makes describing our perceptual experience as we drink wine quite difficult. But what is interesting is that we do it so often: in the wine trade we are always sharing our experience of wine in words. This simply does not happen with food. Restaurant reviewers do not try to describe the perceptual experience of eating steak and fries. Steak tastes of steak and it can be good or bad, and likewise fries taste of fries. But we are always talking about how wine tastes. This has interested linguists, and they have been using what they have dubbed "winespeak" to look at the ways in which words are used to describe sensory experience. More of this later.

My own experience was that as I read the work of others, I slowly began to develop a vocabulary for wine. The set of wine words that I possessed was expanding, and, armed with this growing lexicon, I began to find that the wine gave me more. The words I had for wine were acting like pegs that I could hang my perceptions on, and because I was paying more attention to certain aspects of the wine, I was seeing more. It seems that the relationship between perception and the language we use to describe it goes both ways: language affects perception as well as being used as a tool to describe that perception.

Does Language Shape What We Perceive?

Linguist Guy Deutscher, in his book *Through the Language Glass* (2010), looks at the extent to which our native language shapes our perception. Currently, the dominant, "nativist" view in linguistics is that language is an instinct: the fundamentals of language are encoded in our genes, and are universal across cultures. The nativist school holds that people are born with a linguistic toolkit, hence all languages share the same universal grammar and underlying concepts. But Deutscher, pointing to a growing body of research that suggests language affects how we perceive the world, argues that cultural differences are reflected in language in profound ways.

Deutscher cites the use of language to describe color. Colors exist in a continuum, so when does blue become green? If two people have different languages in which color description is divided up in varying ways, will they experience the world differently? The color blue is a case in point, as discussed in chapter 1. In his three-volume, 1,700-page magnum opus *Studies on Homer and the Homeric*

Age (1858), William Gladstone—later to become British prime minister—noticed the paucity of Homer's color vocabulary, and the fact that blue was almost entirely absent. Black had 200 mentions, white 100, red fewer than 15, and yellow and green fewer than 10 each. Nothing was described as blue. Was it only Homer's Greek that had this strange color bias? No. Philologist Lazarus Geiger looked at other cultures and found no reference to blue—not even in describing the sky. The only exception was Egypt, which by coincidence was the sole culture able to produce a dye colored blue.

That the relationship of language and perception can vary is known as linguistic relativity. The most famous version of linguistic relativity is the Sapir-Whorf hypothesis, named for linguist Edward Sapir and his student Benjamin Whorf. It states that the way we think is affected by the language we use, and someone with a different language will think and see the world differently. Each language represents reality differently, so we all perceive reality differently. The Prussian philosopher Wilhelm von Humboldt was perhaps the first to suggest this; his thesis was that, since language is the forming agent of thought, thinking is dependent not only on language itself, but to a certain extent on individual languages also. Whorf went further, claiming that the grammar of each language "is not merely a reproducing instrument for voicing ideas, but rather is the shaper of ideas."

An example of how language can change reality is the "turquoising" of the traffic lights in Japan. International convention stipulates that traffic lights must be red–orange–green. In Japan, the lights follow this convention, but the green is a distinctive blue-green. In the past, Japan used the word *ao*, meaning green and blue. But now, in modern Japanese, *ao* has come to mean blue, while *midori* means green. When the first traffic lights appeared in Japan in the 1930s, the go light was a regular Western green and went under the name of *ao shingoo*. But then *ao* came to mean blue in Japanese, and so a discrepancy arose between the name and the color of the go light. The solution? In 1973 the government changed the color of the go light to turquoise. It was still greenish to conform to the international convention of green for go, but the added blue reduced the confusion caused by the term *ao shingoo*, which is still in common use.

An extreme interpretation of what has become known as the Whorfian hypothesis is that language determines thought, and

Researcher Jules Davidoff traveled to Namibia to conduct an experiment with the Himba tribe, who have no word for blue and make no distinction between blue and green. He showed them a circle with eleven green squares and one blue, and they could not pick out the blue one. But the Himba have many words for green, and when Davidoff varied the shade of green in one square, they could pick it out.

our thinking is constrained by language. This idea is no longer supported. For a while, the nativist view, with the concept of "universal grammar," attributed to Noam Chomsky, stole the stage. But the pendulum has swung away from the view that language does not influence thought at all. Deutscher's argument that cultural differences are reflected in language, and that language does influence our perception of the world, seems strong. How much language mirrors culture, and how much language shapes culture, is difficult to separate. The two likely develop together.

Cultural Differences in Describing Wine

The language used to describe wine varies across cultures. The flavor references, for a start, are different. People may well be looking for different things in a particular wine, depending on their expectations and knowledge. The question we need to address is whether having a different descriptive language for wine will change the perception of the liquid in the glass. I suspect that when we smell and taste the wine, we all have a pretty much equivalent experience, at least at first. It is when we actually think about this experience, and try to verbalize it, that the language differences will come into play.

Steven Shapin, Professor of the History of Science at Harvard University, says, "The relationship of talk to the private experience of taste is and always will be problematic. We know enough about the priming effects of expectation—background knowledge—to know that the categories we use to communicate about taste may be present at a cortical level. They may be causal factors in the private experience of taste. Our descriptions of the private experiences of taste can, at least on occasion, prompt memories and frame subsequent experiences."

The way we speak about wine today is actually quite new. For a long time, people who wrote about wine tended to avoid describing its actual flavors altogether, perhaps because of the difficulty of putting flavor experiences into words. For example, Hugh Johnson, one of the greats in wine writing, has never really gone in for descriptions of actual wines. In 2014 he wrote an article in *The World of Fine Wine* magazine, tracing the evolution of the tasting note. He credits nineteenth-century author Cyrus Redding as the first wine writer to begin to describe wines,

When looking at a painting in a gallery, the first glance will be the same for all of us. Then, after a moment, how we look at the painting in more detail will be different. What details do we notice? Where do we fix our gaze? How does the painting make us feel?

noting also the work of Henry Vizetelly in the latter part of that century. André Simon took up the mantle in the twentieth century, publishing more than a hundred books on wine; he favored anthropomorphism, likening wines to types of people and even, in some cases, trees. George Saintsbury, another notable author, wrote widely about wine but did not devote much time to describing its flavor. Things began to change in the 1970s.

In 2005, in an article in London newspaper *The Times*, Jonathan Meades took a shot at the way language is used in wine descriptions. He pointed out that when Johnson's iconic *World Atlas of Wine* (1971) was first published, Johnson offered a lexicon of fewer than eighty descriptors for tasting notes. Meades clearly disapproves with the way this list has since burgeoned:

> "The globalization of wine-making and the type of people now buying it have caused that lexicon to be vastly augmented. A new, qualitatively different language has evolved. The old one, founded in the certainties of St. James's and St. Estèphe, was a code. It was as hermetically precise and exclusive as the jargon of any other self-regarding profession. This has largely disappeared, drowned by a clamorous demotic which, far from being codified, attempts to express (rather than classify) a wine's qualities and, equally, to demonstrate the verbal invention of the merchant, sommelier, writer, buff, [or] casual drinker."

In *Wine Tasting* (1968), celebrated auctioneer Michael Broadbent detailed how to taste wine and describe it. Émile Peynaud followed suit with *Le goût du vin* (1983), reaching the French-speaking audience. But the real transition happened with the advent of Robert Parker. Parker's scores, coupled with his vivid tasting notes, just seemed to work, and according to Johnson both were necessary. "His secret is the energy and commitment, the sheer joy in wine and lust for life, that make his words flow and create conversation," says Johnson. "By the 1990s, the air was thick with fruit and nuts." Johnson also mentions Ann Noble at the University of California, Davis, and her development of the Wine Aroma Wheel. This groups aromas into related categories, to allow students of wines to pick out components of a wine and describe it more accurately. The device set people free to begin to describe wines in more concrete, literal terms. Johnson wrote:

"If the older literary style of description had largely drawn on the relatively small stock of words to describe color, smell, taste, and structure, the 1980s opened up a vast new field, borrowing descriptions from the whole vegetable world and beyond."

Hugh Johnson

"We can discern many stylistic shifts in recent years. The first was an invasion of similes to supplement a limited supply of adjectives. Wines are no longer merely delicate or fine, but 'like' lemons or nettles, or indeed boysenberries or loganberries. They go further than merely resembling fruits; they 'offer' them, in confusing but perfectly categorical medleys—most categorically of all on the laminated wine cards of bars with peremptory lists of the usual suspects, each expressing to perfection the stoniness, the nettles, or tropical fruit customarily attributed to its grape or region. And above all, the minerality. Who launched this elusive (but now apparently universal) quality and descriptor? Such a thing certainly exists in wine, but nine times out of ten the writer simply means acidity, and might have said so."

Johnson also cites Jancis Robinson, who he believes has a more cerebral viewpoint than Parker; both were prominent in the same era. "She generally eschews the fruit-salad school in her crisp analysis," he says. "You sometimes feel she is marking exam papers." For him, the most important aspect of writing about wines is love for them: "Is not a writer's enthusiasm what gets readers reading?"

The Academic Perspective

Steven Shapin at Harvard University has written extensively on how our language for wine has changed over time.

Very little description of wine: Is it good or not?	André Simon & George Saintsbury: Limited wine description, usually metaphorical	Maynard Amerine & Edward Roessler: 'Modern Sensory Methods of Evaluating Wine'
Pre-20th century	Early/mid-20th century	1976
"Wine gives great pleasure, and every pleasure is of itself a good." William Makepeace Thackeray	"Food without wine is a corpse; wine without food is a ghost..." André Simon	"Terms frequently used to describe a particular aroma or bouquet are *rancio, foxy, flor-sherry*." Amerine & Roessler

"The language used to describe wine at any period from antiquity through the sixteenth and seventeenth centuries was different from present-day usages in the type and the elaborateness of its predicates. Consider this from a physician's mid-sixteenth-century survey of the wines then available in England: the tastes of wines are categorized, in Latin, as *dulcia*, *astringentia*, *austera*, and *acerba*, and 'such like as are *acria* and *acida*, for the most part wherof we have never one proper name in English.' And this broadly similar list of tastes from a seventeenth-century text titled 'The Blood of the Grape': 'There are four tastes of wine: sweet, acute, austere, and milde.' That is pretty much it: some Italian commentaries back to the Middle Ages seemed to have ranged more widely, but the four-taste list was common in the sixteenth, seventeenth, and eighteenth centuries, and it is not easy to find early modern writers reaching out much beyond that."

One of the turning points in how we talk about wine was the work done by the enology department of the University of California, Davis, in the 1970s and 1980s. In 1976, Maynard Amerine and Edward Roessler published a manual for the sensory evaluation of wines. Their goal was to replace vague and fanciful wine terms with a set of more precise words, shifting from the likes of "masculine," "naive," "harmonious," and "presumptuous" to a standardized vocabulary that was more analytic in nature.

In the early days, asserts Shapin, the main issue with wine was its soundness— is it good or not? Soundness included honesty, because many wines would have been adulterated. He refers to a phrase made famous by Shakespeare: "good wine needs no bush," meaning that good wine does not need to be advertised as such, because people recognize its soundness and are drawn to it. Further, wine was seen as healthful, and wine of good quality was highly regarded for its medicinal effect.

Ann Noble's Wine Aroma Wheel	Robert Parker: More elaborate language	Émile Peynaud: *Le goût du vin*	The rise of wine writing and criticism: Descriptive vocabulary burgeons
1980s			1990s
"Fresh: Cut Green Grass, Bell Pepper, Eucalyptus, Mint" Ann Noble	"I like white wine when it's young and vigorous." Robert Parker	"The sweet taste of alcohol counterbalances the taste of the acids." Emile Peynaud	"Are the flavors delicate or aromatic? Fresh or baked?" WSET

Ann Noble's development of the Wine Aroma Wheel was a major step forward in pushing "winespeak" in a more scientific, rigorous direction. The wheel consists of three concentric rings designating wine smells. In the center are broad olfactory categories, such as woody, earthy, floral, herbaceous. More specific subcategories lie in the middle ring, and actual smells are found on the outer ring. The aroma wheel was designed to overcome the difficulty of recognizing smells and putting them into words. Shapin describes it as an "intersubjectivity engine." The wheel equipped students of wine with a lexicon that empowered them to begin tasting in a way that seemed more objective and repeatable. Without offering full objectivity, the wheel gave the impression of objectivity.

Amerine and Roessler's work, enlarged upon by Noble and others, had a profound impact on the way the wine industry developed in the twentieth century. It encouraged abandonment of fanciful language for one that was more structured. By attempting to focus on what is actually in the wine, it laid the foundations of a more scientific approach to wine quality. The growing global popularity of wine owes much to the way that commercial wine has become more accessible, both in terms of its packaging (varietal labeling, for example) and its flavor (cleaner, with more emphasis on attractive, fruity notes). Specifically, it is interesting to consider how much this greater popularity might be due to changes in the way that the wine trade and consumers spoke about wine. However, there has been a downside. The common, shared language for wine has been so successful that it has led to a uniformity of approach that might slow further advancement.

Most people working in the wine trade undergo some kind of training, usually involving exams in which they are asked to analyze and identify wines blind. The Wine & Spirit Education Trust, for example, has a Standard Approach to Tasting (SAT) that gives students a structure to assist them in analyzing wines. This is a brilliant place to start, but should everyone approach wine tasting in the same way?

Wine Prototypes

Experienced tasters come to wine tasting with a set of prototypes. When we taste, we have a preselected set of descriptors ready. For example, we may know that the wine is Sauvignon Blanc, or we may guess from the first taste (if we are tasting blind), that it is Sauvignon Blanc. Thus, experienced tasters first ask, what sort of wine is this? Then we assemble, without realizing what we are doing, our roster of words for that wine type. For Sauvignon, my descriptors include grassy, green pepper, grapefruit, gooseberry, citrus, herb, tomato leaf, blackcurrant, and pithy. My more global terms would include sharp, fresh, vivid, precise, focused, and linear. So I taste the wine, and then subconsciously I pluck a range of these that I think most closely match what I am finding in the wine; finally, I apply them in my note.

Of course, we think that we are describing what is there. But experts rarely just smell, taste, and describe exactly what they find. Interestingly, trying to describe what is there seems to be the strategy that many novice tasters adopt. In my experience, novices find writing tasting notes extremely hard, but will occasionally identify a smell or taste that is outside the normal wine vocabulary for that type of wine, but which is certainly present in the wine, once it is pointed out. Sometimes, though, it is hard to use these untypical descriptors in my notes, because they are not words that are part of the wine trade "code" for describing wine.

In chapter 2 we saw how color can have a powerful influence on the words that experts use to describe a wine. This is known as perceptual bias, and experts are especially prone to it. Studies by Gil Morrot and Wendy Parr show that the knowledge that experts have about a wine, whether it is the color or sight of the label, causes them to override what they actually experience. Instead, experts allow their thinking (cognition) to act in a top-down way and overshadow their perception. As we taste wine we decide what it is and then our prototype for that wine guides what we look for and even influences what we experience.

A colleague of mine, Chris Losh, editor of the drinks trade magazine *Imbibe*, has some interesting things to say about how structured tasting notes are not always the best way of describing drinks. He recalls a session where he tasted whiskies with some bartenders. They had never been educated about wine tasting, and wrote very different notes to the ones Losh came up with:

> "Mine were solid, by the book—and desperately dull. Theirs were chaotic, erratic—and fizzing with inspiration. I still remember one of them describing a twelve-year-old malt as being 'like walking through a dew-covered garden on a spring morning'—a sentence that absolutely nailed the product and also, crucially, made me want to drink it. And this, I think, is where the problem lies. Our structured approach to writing tasting notes is designed to strip visceral reaction out of the process—or at least to minimize it; to render our judgments coolly analytical and free of the distorting effects of emotion."

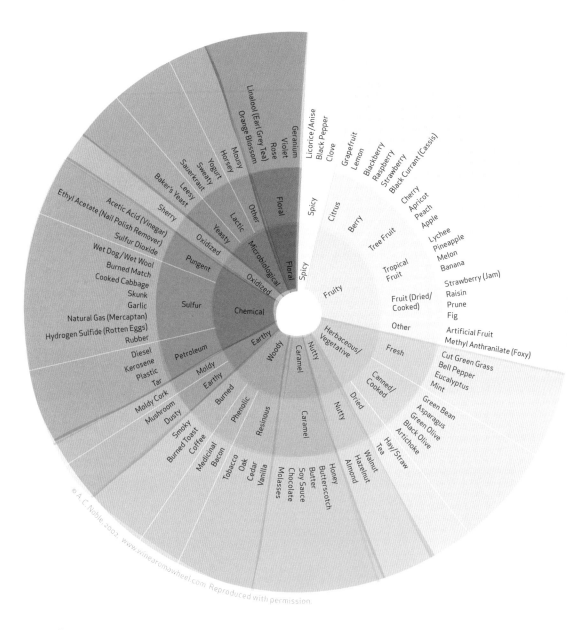

Licorice/Anise
Black Pepper
Clove
Grapefruit
Lemon
Blackberry
Raspberry
Strawberry
Black Currant (Cassis)
Cherry
Apricot
Peach
Apple
Lychee
Pineapple
Melon
Banana
Strawberry (Jam)
Raisin
Prune
Fig
Artificial Fruit
Methyl Anthranilate (Foxy)
Cut Green Grass
Bell Pepper
Eucalyptus
Mint
Green Bean
Asparagus
Green Olive
Black Olive
Artichoke
Hay/Straw
Tea
Walnut
Hazelnut
Almond
Honey
Butter
Butterscotch
Soy Sauce
Chocolate
Molasses
Vanilla
Cedar
Oak
Tobacco
Bacon
Medicinal
Coffee
Burned Toast
Smoky
Dusty
Mushroom
Moldy Cork
Tar
Plastic
Kerosene
Diesel
Rubber
Hydrogen Sulfide (Rotten Eggs)
Natural Gas (Mercaptan)
Garlic
Skunk
Cooked Cabbage
Burned Match
Wet Dog/Wet Wool
Sulfur Dioxide
Ethyl Acetate (Nail Polish Remover)
Acetic Acid (Vinegar)
Sherry
Baker's Yeast
Leesy
Sauerkraut
Sweaty
Yogurt
Horsey
Mousy
Orange Blossom
Rose
Violet
Linalool (Earl Grey Tea)
Geranium

Spicy
Citrus
Berry
Tree Fruit
Tropical Fruit
Fruit (Dried/Cooked)
Other
Fresh
Canned/Cooked
Dried
Nutty
Caramel
Resinous
Phenolic
Burned
Earthy
Moldy
Petroleum
Sulfur
Pungent
Oxidized
Lactic
Yeasty

Spicy
Fruity
Herbaceous/Vegetative
Nutty
Caramel
Woody
Earthy
Chemical
Oxidized
Microbiological
Floral

Floral
Other

© A. C. Noble 2002. www.winearomawheel.com. Reproduced with permission.

Wine Aroma Wheel

Devised by Professor Ann C. Noble, this wheel gives a set of descriptors to enable wine tasters to put their perceptions into words. To use the wheel, begin at the center, matching the general terms to the wine in question, before moving to the more specific terminology on the outer layers.

For all the progress that has been made possible by the structured approach to tasting, the mood in the wine world seems to be that we might have lost something in our shift. People are beginning to ask questions about the most effective ways of communicating our experience of wine in words. Noted U.S. wine commentator Matt Kramer published a short book—more like a manifesto or pamphlet—titled *True Taste: the Seven Essential Wine Words* (2015). In it, he prompts us to move away from our obsession with focusing on flavor identification and descriptors, to more global, thoughtful, subjective terms that capture the qualities of the wine better. He writes: "Too many tasting notes now offer little more than a string of fanciful flavor descriptors with the judgment revealed only in the score itself—a numerical 'thank you ma'am' after the more energetic 'slam, bam' of the flavor descriptors." Kramer's seven preferred terms are insight, harmony, texture, layers, finesse, surprise, and nuance.

Using Words to Share Perceptions

When we read a language, we turn letters, which are visual sensations, into words. As soon as we see words on a page, these visual sensations become loaded with meaning. Think of a love letter, a hostile tweet, or a tax demand: the visual sensations immediately stimulate an emotional response. In wine writing, the opposite happens. We begin with our conscious perception elicited by a flavor, to which we add our memory and learning, and we turn the resulting emotional response into letters on a page. We hope the letters will in some way convey our perceptions to others, who lack the same flavor stimulus. We are attempting to share, in as transparent way as possible, our private world of perception. But what are the most effective and legitimate ways of doing this? Should we enlist figurative language in descriptions of wine? This is where we turn to the field of cognitive linguistics.

Not long ago, Ernesto Suárez Toste, Rosario Caballero, and Raquel Segovia carried out a study entitled "Translating the Senses: Figurative Language in Wine Discourse." The initial stage of the project involved collecting 12,000 tasting notes, from a range of British and U.S. publications (*Wine Advocate*, *Wine Spectator*, *Wine Enthusiast*, *Wine News*, *Decanter*, and Wineanorak. com). The text was cut, pasted, and cleared of all extra information to create a data set. The types of metaphors used were tagged, and then a concordance used to track each instance of any type of metaphor of interest.

We reach for metaphors because of the impoverished language we have for describing tastes and smells. "Because there is no single lexicon with the expressive potential to cover all the range of sensorial impressions, the intellectualization of sensorial experience is inextricably linked to the figurative uses of language," explains Suárez Toste. "There is no problem with this as far as such areas of human life as poetry are concerned, but the inherent subjectivity of sensorial experience represents innumerable difficulties when technical discourse is under scrutiny."

What about the good old tasting note? "This relies heavily on a combination of terms articulating the remembrance of the taster's repository of aromas and flavors, connotations, and, above all, figurative language which, although it may be perceived by the layman as deliberate obscurity, is a valuable tool that allows the (only partially satisfactory) communication of the experience of tasting wine. The vocabulary used points to various figurative phenomena (synesthesia, metonymy, metaphor), all of which are indispensable tools for articulating what is an intrinsically sensorial experience."

Why Resort to Metaphors?

Suárez Toste and colleagues separate these metaphorical wine descriptions into various categories, such as wine as a living creature, wine as a piece of cloth, and wine as a building. Such descriptions may seem risible, but the metaphors are born of necessity. We would like to have a more exact way of sharing our experience of wine in words, but such precision is not available. Moreover, tasters who restrict themselves merely to naming aromas and flavors can easily fail to communicate some of the more important aspects of the wines' characters, such as texture, structure, balance, and elegance. Suárez Toste explains where metaphors can be particularly helpful:

> "Currently we are obsessed with structure and mouthfeel. These usually demand architecture and textile metaphors. One curiosity that our audiences enjoy is that a wine can be

"Wine folks use metaphor all the time. Aroma wheels are okay for identifying aromas, but the structure and mouthfeel almost always demand the use of figurative language. It has nothing to do—at least not necessarily—with waxing poetical about something sublime . . . . For one thing, we personify wine most of the time. Not simply by saying it has a nose instead of a smell. It has character, it is endowed with human virtues and vices. It can be generous, sexy, voluptuous, whimsical, shy, demure, bold, or aggressive. We almost cannot conceive wine without personifying it."
Ernesto Suárez Toste

described in the same tasting note as silky and velvety. Of course, the terms are for them mutually exclusive. The idea is that both are different realizations of a textile metaphor (but almost synonymous for the critic's purpose). The connotations are smooth and expensive, fresher in silk (more used for whites) and warmer in velvet (more frequent in reds), but essentially the same. And that is just the beginning. Lists of materials are boring when compared to words that unconsciously betray the textile metaphor: this wine is seamless; is bursting at the seams; the fruit is cloaked by tannin; wears its alcohol well; a core of tannin is wrapped in layers of fruit; and so on."

Others have studied the cognitive linguistics of wine. Researcher Isabel Negro has written about the use of the French language in wine tasting. She notes the heavy use of synesthetic wine descriptions in French, and suggests that this is because in France winespeak conveys a cultural view of wine tasting in which, uniquely, all the senses are used. And compared with English winespeak, French winespeak has a unique feature in that hearing is invoked. "Wine tasting is metaphorically represented as listening to a music composition, as evidenced by the metaphorical expressions notes, *registre*, *harmonie*, and *finale*, among others," says Negro. "This is a specific feature of the French discourse."

After all this discussion, what is a good tasting note, and what is a bad one? This depends to a degree on the purpose of the notes. Are they attempting to describe a wine so that someone might be able to recognize it in a lineup on the basis of the note? Or are they trying to capture something more transcendent and emotional? Wine creates an experience and emotion in us and we are trying to express this with our note rather than just trying to describe the sensory experience of the flavor molecules in the wine.

Negro tallied up the different sorts of wine metaphors used by type in French wine descriptions. The most popular metaphors were wines described in human terms (476); the second most common metaphors were synesthetic (147). Wines as food was next (70), followed by wines as clothes (45), as objects (31), and as buildings (28).

Doug Wregg, a U.K. wine buyer for importer Les Caves de Pyrene, says this about tasting notes: "Tasting notes can be the factual reconstruction of objective analysis (given the limitations of objectivity), or they can rise above that and seek to capture the spirit of the wine, and the spirit of the taster while tasting the wine," he says (we can assume that he is referring here to wines that are actually worth talking about in the first place). "The wine has to speak to the taster, there must be something of nature in it, a quality that elevates it above the commercial quotidian."

Wregg thinks of wine tasting as an experience that triggers a transcendent moment and takes us to another place. "The senses are overwhelmed by this experience; the 'spontaneous overflow of powerful feelings' leaves an individual incapable of articulating the true nature and beauty of the sensations." Borrowing his terms from Wordsworth, he likens the writing of good tasting notes to writing poetry. "It is only when this emotion is 'recollected in tranquillity' that the poet/writer can assemble words to do the moment justice. It is necessary for the poet/writer to have a certain personal distance from the event or experience being described, so that he or she can compose a poem/tasting note that conveys to the reader the same experience of sublimity. With this distance the poet can reconstruct the 'spontaneous overflow of powerful feelings' the experience caused within himself."

Wregg does not favor tastings where people plow through a hundred or more wines in a session, and rues the times he has spent sitting on tasting panels. "Invariably I end up disillusioned, feeling that wine is a mere commodity, existing to be judged rather than understood." He states his preference: "In real life, so to speak, I drink wine with friends and as an accompaniment to food. And if a bottle knocks me on my ass . . . I will simply scribble down a few words at the time to remind me to write a tasting note at a later date. And looking at those words will enable me to retrieve the experience." But Wregg acknowledges: "Of course, its original immediacy will be mediated by my ego, it will filtered through time, and ultimately coarsened by the imprecision of language. The excitement of tasting and drinking can never be truly recaptured— it is the intoxicating Dionysian moment reconfigured within a unifying Apollonian response."

Wregg concludes: "Beauty comes in myriad forms; great wines can evoke great reactions and poetic impulses, they make us explore beyond the limits of our normal responses, they induce humility and elicit generosity. When tasting it is satisfying to have a responsive palate; it is wonderful though to take the experience to the next level and give something back."

One of the issues that bedevils attempts to capture smells and flavors in words is the difficulty we have in naming them. We even find it difficult to name familiar smells. In normally functioning people, experiments have shown that only about 20 to 50 percent of common odors are correctly named (the success rate for visual

"Often I hanker after a kinesthesia that would enable my tasting impressions to be instantly transformed into music, something purer, more fluid, and more spiritual than words. Although I am dimly aware there is an underlying melody, I have not got the musical vocabulary and notation skills, so rather than tabulating it thus I try to leave myself open to sensations and jot down reactions in any order, recording the relevant—and seemingly irrelevant— words that nudge into my head."

Doug Wregg

identification is close to 100 percent). People can tell the differences between smells but they cannot match them to the right words, despite being perfectly articulate in other circumstances.

The view of Jonas Olofsson and colleagues is that we fail at olfactory naming because of a cumulative deterioration of signal quality over multiple processing stages, from odor input to verbal output. From a neurobiological viewpoint, it is the functional organization of the olfactory system that makes it hard for us to map odors to names. In one set of experiments, Olofsson and colleagues scanned the brains of subjects while they showed them olfactory and visual cues, followed by words. What they were focused upon was their response time, which is normally determined by semantic incongruency—whether or not the cue matched the word. In the event, performance was slower and less precise when people were matching a word to a smell, rather than a picture. Looking also at which brain regions were activated, they concluded that the way smells are processed and linked to words is quite distinct. Olofsson states that we find it difficult to link smells and words because of the way that the brain is structured.

Most of the odors we smell are mixtures, and, as discussed in earlier chapters, we tend to lump together patterns of different smells as one combined smell, without being able to pick individual smell features from the mix. People cannot identify more than three, or at most four, odors in a mix. Perhaps it is the way that smell objects are represented in the brain that makes this task of matching smells and words difficult.

Rich and Specialized Vocabularies for Smells

But this view has been challenged by the work of Asifa Majid, a researcher from Radboud University in The Netherlands. She has studied two groups of hunter-gatherers: the Jahai people of Malaysia and the Maniq of Thailand. These two groups have a much larger vocabulary for smells than we do in the West, and they have specific words for experiencing smells (rather than using such constructions as "it smells like . . ."). Majid and her colleague Niclas Burenhult tested ten Malaysian Jihai against ten native speakers of U.S. English. They found that the Jihai, unlike the Westerners, were as consistent in naming odors as they were colors, and they were more consistent. The English speakers used source-based descriptions rather than the abstract, basic smell terms that the Jihai favored. These basic terms were not from a single source but related to a broad class of objects; this is something we lack to a degree in English, claim the authors. "For the Jihai, a cultural preoccupation with odors aligns with a high codability of smells in language," says Majid. So would the Jahai and Maniq be better at describing wines? Majid cannot say for sure:

Asifa Majid, with her colleague Ewelina Wnuk, drew up a list of fifteen of the abstract basic smell words that the Maniq hunter-gatherers in Thailand use to describe odors. In their environment—rain forest—the sense of smell is important for interpreting environmental cues, and it makes sense that they should have a large smell vocabulary, and an enhanced ability to verbalize the smells they perceive.

"I think it is important to distinguish everyday vocabulary from specialist genres. English speakers have an everyday vocabulary for colors (red, green, blue, purple) but a visual artist will use much more specific vocabulary to talk about particular shades of color (Yves Klein's International Klein blue, for example). In the same way, although Jahai and Maniq speakers have an elaborated smell vocabulary, it is for the everyday smells they encounter. These general terms might not be subtle enough to capture all the fine nuances of a wine, just as our basic color vocabulary might not capture the fine nuances of an artist's palette. It is an empirical question: one we have not tested."

Framing and Wine Tasting: How Words Can Get in the Way

"Framing" is a social science term that refers to the background concepts and perspectives that influence how we think on certain issues. In this sense, framing is part of the narrative structure with which we see the world. U.S. author George Lakoff has popularized the term in his book *Don't Think of an Elephant* (2004), in which he looks at how certain words and ideas have framed political discourse in the United States. For example, he asserts that the term "tax relief" has a strong framing influence:

"The word 'relief' evokes a frame in which there is a blameless Afflicted Person who we identify with and who has some Affliction, some pain or harm that is imposed by some external Cause-of-pain. Relief is the taking away of the pain or harm, and it is brought about by some Reliever-of-pain. The Relief frame is an instance of a more general Rescue scenario, in which there is a Hero (the Reliever-of-pain), a Victim (the Afflicted), a Crime (the Affliction), a Villain (the Cause-of-affliction), and a Rescue (the Pain Relief). The Hero is inherently good, the Villain is evil, and the Victim after the Rescue owes gratitude to the Hero."

How does this apply to wine? The use of words is inseparable from our experience of it. Even the names of wines, or the grapes that they are made from, carry supplementary meanings—the frames—that influence our experiences. For example, I have a friend who claims to hate Gewürztraminer. For her, the word comes loaded with meaning, and to each experience of Gewürztraminer there is a framing effect that comes from the name. If she were to taste a Gewürztraminer blind and not know that it is made from this variety, there would be no such frame and she would be freer to enjoy it.

Everyone approaches wine with words, and the words influence the interpretation of the experience of wine itself. So, once we have the word "Gewürztraminer" in our minds, it is hard not to let this influence our perception of the wine in the glass. Our words can get in the way of our actual experience. This is a warning for wine experts like me, because we have template descriptions for different wine styles that we all readily rush to when we know (or think we know) what sort of wine we are tasting.

Indeed, some researchers think we move too quickly to words, rather than dwelling in the sensory experience. Melanie McBride, a doctoral researcher at York University, Toronto, has worked on intersensory learning involving smell and taste. "In cultures where smell is primary in learning and considered a critical dimension of experience, they have more language/words for it because it is a higher priority for them," she explains. "In the West, where developmental psychology theories such as Piaget's ages and stages still dominate our thinking, we see physical knowledge as a low stage we are to grow out of, and 'into' social knowledge."

Her view is that in our culture we move away from the sensory experience itself and go straight to words. For wine tasting, the implications are obvious. We jump straight to winespeak, and this distorts the experience of tasting and smelling the wine. So, next time you try a wine, pause before you allow yourself to rush and write a tasting note. Do not analyze the wine. Stop the words forming in your mind. Dwell on the actual tastes, textures, smells, and flavors. Allow the wine time to speak to you and bypass your critical faculties. Then, and only then, reach for your words. It will be a different experience, and you may well enjoy the wine more.

Melanie McBride gives the example of experiencing strawberries: "[As children] we had to stop smearing the strawberry on our face and mashing it into our mouths because this was considered a lower and more infantile way of relating with knowledge than using words, signs, and symbols. And so when the sensory stage is pathologized as being infantile, we basically stop a process of learning that should have continued."

Is Wine Tasting Subjective or Objective?

A remarkable double-think is commonly found among well-known wine critics. If they are questioned, they almost invariably affirm that wine tasting is a subjective process: your own palate should be your guide, and there is no such thing as "wrong" when it comes to tasting wine. Yet it is obvious that they believe wine tasting to be an objective process, one in which their expertise gives them an advantage over us; they are the ones with expertise, and we are expected to pay for access to it. This chapter explores the various claims for the objective and subjective nature of wine tasting.

Saying One Thing and Doing Another

Let us imagine a typical scenario. A famous wine writer is giving a talk to a group of consumers. At last the event comes to the stage where everyone gets to taste some wine. People begin to sniff and sip from their glasses. "What do you get?" she asks, but she senses that her audience is a little too nervous to say what they really think about what they are tasting. This often happens: people can be a bit scared about wine: they do not want to look silly, and they are embarrassed by their lack of knowledge. She offers reassurance: "Like what you like. It is all subjective. Don't let anyone tell you which wines you should prefer. Wine tasting is personal. There are no right and wrong answers when it comes to wine."

They all relax, and begin drinking. The conversation gets louder, more wines are poured, and by the time the evening draws to a close it is getting a bit rowdy. But just before the end, the wine writer gets up and does a sales pitch, encouraging them to buy one of her books and subscribe to her newsletter. She is in the business of selling information about wine and professional ratings of specific bottles, information that by its very nature is aimed at telling people what they should (or, in all likelihood, will) like. So is there some objectivity to wine perception after all? Many of us who write about wine say one thing—that wine appreciation is subjective—yet behave as if it were totally objective.

Professor Barry Smith at the University of London has a great interest in flavor perception: "All the great wine critics go on and on telling you things, and then they say, of course, taste is subjective and it is all a matter of individual opinions. And then they tell you which vintage is better than another, and which domaine is better. And I think, hold on, I thought it was all subjective and a matter of opinion. So is this just autobiography? If so, why should I care about your view, particularly?" Smith does not think that wine writers really believe in subjectivity in wine tasting: "I have noticed this clash between what they say—the official line—and what they actually do, which is to rate and give very normative pronouncements about which domaines are better, which châteaux are producing better wine, and which vintage is better. So they do have very clear judgments about this." Steven Shapin, Professor of the History of Science at Harvard, says:

> "In modern times, we assume that our task—the only legitimate task—is to form our own assessment of wine's goodness. That is democracy at an organoleptic level; it is subjective individualism raised to a moral principle. Even in the 1950s, the great Russo-American wine merchant Alexis Lichine—who himself contributed to a growing ornateness in wine-talk and whose palate was advertised as legendarily accurate—knew the demotic drill: 'Drink the wines you like the best. Trust your own palate, and do not listen to what anyone else tells you you ought to like.' Submitting to the taste of another would be illegitimate: why defer to anyone else's authority when you have your own capacity to judge?"

Liking Versus Flavor Perception

Barry Smith agrees. He also thinks that it is important to make a distinction between liking and perception of flavor, something not always managed successfully by wine writers. He argues that:

> "In their favor you might say that they are confusing the perception of the flavor of a wine with evaluating it purely hedonically (I like, I do not like) . . . I think when critics say it is all subjective, they are saying your preferences are subjective.

"A lot of ordinary tasters think the whole point of tasting is to come up with a verdict: thumbs-up, thumbs-down. If you give someone a wine and ask, 'What do you think of that?' they say, 'I quite like it,' or 'I do not like it.' You think: I was not asking that, I was asking what do you think of it? Not, how is it for you? But, can you tell me more about it? What do you notice? What is going on?"

Barry Smith

But there must be a difference between preferences and perception. For example, I do not see why critics could not be very good at saying that this is a very fine example of a Grüner Veltliner, or this is one of the best examples of a medium-dry Riesling, but it is not for me. Why cannot they distinguish judgments of quality from judgments of individual liking? It seems to me you could. You know what is expected of this wine and what it is trying to do: is it achieving it? Yes, but it is not to your taste."

If wine tasting is entirely subjective, then every opinion about wine has equal validity, and expertise is of little value. Everyone is their own expert, and critical recommendations are rendered so personal as to be redundant. Discussions about subjectivity and objectivity in wine tasting are not completely abstract, but why discuss subjectivity and objectivity in wine appreciation at all? I would argue that it is important that our understanding of the theoretical basis of wine assessment should be as accurate as possible, even if that makes wine seem more complicated. People are sitting exams with tasting elements to them, exams that could have an important bearing on their professional lives. The assumption of those setting the exams is clearly that wine tasting, as carried out by professionals, is an objective practice. That has implications for wine tasters of all kinds, surely?

Arguments for Subjectivity

In previous chapters we have looked at how the brain creates the perception of flavor. We have also discussed the nature of reality itself, and the theory that our view of the world around us is actually a model, informed by reality but not corresponding to it. And we discussed individual biological and cultural differences in flavor perception that might cause people to experience the same wine differently. Do all these considerations destroy the possibility of objectivity? Let us begin by looking at the position taken by neuroscientist Gordon Shepherd, in his work "Neuroenology: How the Brain Creates the Taste of Wine" (2015), in reference to food:

"Flavor is not in the food; it is created from the food by the brain. There is a clear analogy with other sensory systems. In

Consider the Earth as it would have been millions of years ago, before the evolution of animals. Chemicals that we would now call flavor chemicals existed then, but did any of them have flavor before animal life evolved? Is the flavor of salt, say, a property of salt? But salt cannot have had a flavor before animals evolved, and the sea would not have been salty. That is because saltiness is a property of human perception, not of the sea itself.

vision, for example, color is not in the wavelengths of light; color is created from the wavelengths by the neural processing circuits in the visual pathway; these include center-surround interactions for color-opponent mechanisms. Similarly, pain is not in the agents that give rise to it, such as a pin or a toxin; pain is created by the neural processing mechanisms and circuits in the pain pathway, together with central circuits for emotion."

Extrapolating from this view, the flavor of a wine is not a property of the wine itself, but rather of the interaction between the wine and the taster. The flavor does not exist except in the conscious perception of the taster, after it has undergone a lot of processing in the brain.

Living organisms evolved sensitivity to chemicals because there was utility for them in being able to respond in some way to the chemicals in their environment. Initially, bacteria developed means such as the whiplike flagellum to move toward or away from chemicals in their environment. Many millennia later, humankind and other animals developed far more sophisticated chemical

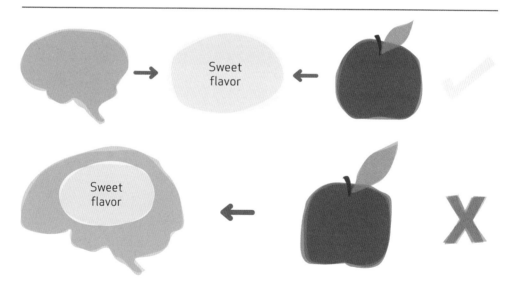

Flavor Isn't Created By the Brain

To preserve objectivity, some have suggested that we need a level between the chemistry and the perception, which is flavor. This is an objective property of the item that is perceived subjectively.

senses. Human perception of flavor is the result of evolution. For us, chemical entities smell and taste because there is selective advantage in our being able to smell and taste them. The flavor of chemicals is a property conferred on them by us.

Thus, what we experience as we taste wine is a perceptive event, created somewhere in our brains. The event is prompted by the chemical properties of the wine, but it is interpreted by our subconscious and conscious processing of the information gathered by our senses. It is impossible for two of us to have identical experiences as we taste wine together, because each of us is genetically different and has different past experiences of wine; both factors help to shape our current experience. It is from these arguments that it may be concluded that the experience of tasting wine is largely a subjective one.

Barry Smith has long considered the subject of subjectivity and objectivity in wine tasting, and he agrees that the perception of wine is subjective. "Yes, it is subjective, and it is variable," he says. "Not only across individuals, but it is variable in an individual across time, and across different conditions." However, Smith does not accept that the existence of subjectivity precludes the possibility of objectivity in wine flavors. The way he rescues the idea of objectivity is to introduce an intermediate level between the composition of wine and perception:

> "The way I like to do this is to say, here is the chemistry (the volatile and nonvolatile elements). And people often go from talking about the chemistry to talking about how amazingly varied our perceptions of wine are. They ask: how could we ever get laws that go from the chemistry to all this variation in perception? It must mean that there is no such thing as objective taste. What I say is, you need an intermediate level. We need a level in between the chemistry and the variable perceptions, and this is flavor."

Flavors: Midway Between Chemistry and Perceptions

Smith goes on to elaborate on the theory: "Flavors are emergent properties: they depend on but are not reducible to the chemistry. Then these flavors are things that our varying and variable perceptions try to latch onto. Each flavor perception is a snapshot

"As a professional taster you are taking snapshots in each of your tastings and trying to figure out what the flavor properties of that wine are that will continue to endure and alter as the wine ages. How would it taste if it were a degree or two colder or warmer? You make predictions and then you can go back and sample it later and say, I was right: I figured that it needed another hour in the glass and needed to be one degree warmer and it would change like this. The thing about which you are making the predictions is flavor. This is what depends on, but is not reducible to, chemistry."

Barry Smith

of that flavor. We do not even want to think of it as static; we want to think of a flavor profile as something that itself evolves and changes over time."

Having postulated this model of flavor as a changing entity that exists at an intermediate level—acting like an arena where data are deposited by the senses for evaluation by the perceptive systems of the brain—Smith spells out the implications of the idea:

"Now, with this intermediate level you have two tough jobs instead of one. One task is to say, what is the relationship between the chemistry and the flavors that emerge? The second task is, what is the relationship between the flavors and individual flavor perceptions? These two jobs need to be done independently, but they have to reach the same terminus. Having this intermediate level gives you the job of saying how does the chemistry give rise to flavor, and how does my individual experience as a taster lock on to flavor? Do not try going from the chemistry to perception: you need that middle level."

In the wine trade, objectivity is taken as a practical given. We take part in wine competitions, where medals or scores are awarded; we share our tasting notes, often with scores attached; we take wine exams where tasting is part of the examination; we sell our expertise; we recommend wines to others; we discuss wines that we taste together. None of this suggests belief in wine tasting being a subjective matter in any significant way.

For Smith, therefore, the perception of flavor involves interaction between three distinct states or realities. The first state consists of the chemical properties of the wine. These are objective properties: we can measure the wine's chemical composition, and when we share a bottle together, the liquid in each of our glasses will have the same chemical composition. Importantly, some of these chemicals have tastes and smells.

The second state consists of the flavor of the wine. This, too, is an objective property of the wine because the sum of the flavor-active chemicals, working together, produces the wine's flavor. Here, immediately, Smith's theory runs into controversy because not everyone agrees that the flavor of wine can be objective. Critics of the theory argue that flavor as an objective reality cannot exist without perceiving subjects, and so it is not an objective property.

The third and final state is our own perception of the flavor; this is subjective because we each have a different biology, and a different set of experiences. Flavor perception is subjective because of the way perception works, which is to model reality. Because we all model reality differently, a strictly objective perception of the taste of a wine is impossible. Our attention must then shift to the relationship between our perception and the wine's flavor.

Specifically, how closely does our subjective perception tally with the objective property of the wine's flavor?

The neat trick here is the creation of the second state—the flavor of the wine as distinct from its chemical composition. The proposal of the second state allows us to regard wine flavor as an objective property of a wine, quite apart from its perception by individuals. This addresses the fundamental contradiction touched upon earlier, that people are encouraged to trust their subjective responses to wine, yet everyone in the wine trade behaves as though wine assessment is a largely objective process.

The Search for "Objective Flavor"

What does this discussion tell us about our approach to tasting wine? I pour myself a glass and take a sniff, followed by a mouthful, and I contemplate it. I am trying to "get" the wine by interrogating it. I repeatedly come back to it, and it reveals itself to me. Some days I seem to taste with more clarity than other days, and the wine shows more of itself to me. All the while my behavior indicates that I believe the wine possesses a flavor that I am trying to assess. And all of these activities indicate that I consider the flavor of wine to be an objective property of the wine. According to Smith's three-part model, the taste is in the wine, and we try to "get" this when we taste. According to the model, only stage three, perception, is subjective, which helps us to deal with inter-individual differences in flavor perception.

It is best to remember two further considerations if we are to avoid sliding into the dead end of subjectivity when we consider wine tasting. First, our knowlege of wine influences our flavor perception. Second, our sense of taste is adaptable and able to learn to appreciate flavors that are new to it. To a large degree, we have wine knowledge in common within a shared aesthetic system. This common, intersubjective body of knowledge helps us to overcome some of the difficulties caused by the reality that we can never have exactly the same experience of flavor.

In the previous chapter we traced the way in which the language for wine has changed over time. The big leap forward came with the work of the department of enology at the University of California, Davis, in the 1970s and 1980s, and the creation of the Wine Aroma Wheel. This led to a shift from global, figurative terms, which attempted to capture the whole of the wine and its emotional impact on the taster, to a more precise language that focused on actual components in the wine. The focus shifted away from the effect of the wine on the taster and toward the chemistry of the liquid in the glass. Suddenly, wine-tasting notes had the appearance of objectivity. A shift had been made from the merely subjective to a much more scientific and precise-sounding language. This continued with the rise of the wine critic, and the development of the 100-point scale for assessing wine quality. A score out of 100 promises to be much more precise—and objective—than a five-star rating system, for example. In his article, "The Tastes of Wine: Towards a Cultural History" (2012), Steven Shapin has more to say on this subject:

> "The idea and aura of objectivity—if not its actual attainment—are crucial to modern descriptive wine language. Many wine drinkers are now evidently drawn to language that picks out real constituents, substances that are thought of as the scientifically warranted material causes of subjective experiences. The complexity of subjective experience is then treated as the aggregate of its taste—and smell—relevant constituents, and it is those constituents that we think, or hope, to pick out by descriptors such as asparagus, fig paste, or peach skin. We may understand that there are problems in concluding that we have thereby achieved objectivity, but there is something about the idea of objectivity that is central to the historical appearance, and the cultural role, of this way of talking about wine tastes and smells."

Education by the Wine Community

As wine drinkers, we learn to write tasting notes by reading those of others, and discussing wine with others more experienced than ourselves. We begin to develop a language for wine: a cohort of descriptors that we can marshal in our attempts to describe our sensations, and which undoubtedly act as hooks on which we can hang our perceptions. We taste wines considered to be fine by others, and thus develop sensibilities for what constitutes fineness in wine. This shared aesthetic system of wine is not subject to the problems of subjectivity that bedevil actual perception of flavor.

In conclusion, each person's biology, knowledge, and prior experience are important factors in shaping their perception of flavor, suggesting that there is a strong subjective element in the activity. But we also understand that wine tasting involves shared knowledge (an aesthetic system of fine wine appreciation) and shared experience (what we call our "taste" is not static but changes with experience, and we learn to like new wines that are highly regarded by experts). These factors help to offset differences in perception that would otherwise make wine tasting and assessment a lonely, isolated practice.

Not everyone, though, would agree with Smith's three-part thesis of flavor perception. The New Zealander cognitive scientist Wendy Parr has this to say:

"A consensus model of taster behavior is inappropriate for most sensory analysis of the complex beverage known as wine. Demonstrated differences amongst wine tasters, reflecting each individual's physiology, experience, and knowledge, limit the usefulness of consensus models. Further, research demonstrates that perception involving taste and smell, important to wine tasting, is much more diverse amongst people than is perception involving vision, hearing, and trigeminal stimulation."

This perspective, coming from an expert who frequently works with sensory panels and has firsthand experiences of the individual differences of the participants, is one that we cannot ignore. It is a reminder that, while there is a surprising amount of agreement on the taste of wine—much more than we might expect when we consider the biological differences and the different experience and context of different tasters, there is still a degree to which consensus is just not possible. On a purely practical level, being able to assume a large degree of shared objectivity in our communications about wine brings enormous benefits. But whether we will ever be able to compensate for our individual, subjective differences sufficiently to share our perceptions of wine in a way that is absolutely, 100 percent meaningful is unknown.

The language we currently use for wine could be conferring an aura of objectivity on our experience of wine, when expressed in words. Indeed, changes in how we communicate about wine—not only in what we say but also in how often we say it (there are now far more words written about the taste of wine than formerly)—could themselves be helping us move toward a common, shared experience. Our intersubjective discussions do much to shape how we experience wine.

10

A New Approach to Wine Tasting

Those of us concerned with wine need to take a fresh look at the way wine tasting is currently practiced. In particular, we need to revisit the role of the critic, and think afresh about the concepts used in wine flavor chemistry. Is a reductionist approach to wine tasting still justifiable? And how should we think about communicating about wine, and the use of tasting notes? A more informed and realistic theoretical basis to wine tasting could eliminate some of the anomalies and conflicts found in the wine world. This chapter brings together our new understanding of flavor and the way the brain works, integrating this information with new ideas about wine flavor chemistry to come up with a fresh synthesis on the taste of wine.

Do We Have Many Senses, or Just One?

How many senses do we have? One of the conclusions that might be drawn from the different topics brought together in this book is quite radical: sensation is a unity. We should move away from thinking that we have five separate senses to seeing all sensation—and all perception—as just one sense. This is because consciousness is a unity, not subdivided but a single sensation combining many elements. Yes, you can focus on a particular part of your conscious field at any one time, but all your perceptions, your knowledge of yourself, and your thoughts, memories, and emotions are experienced at the same time. As I sit and write, I am aware of what is going on in my environment, in my body, and in my mind. My internal landscape is a seamless, single consciousness, yet I am able to set aside almost all of the signals I am aware of as I work. As we saw in chapter 7, the brain is good at predicting, and as long as its predictions are matched by external reality it can ignore the signals and concentrate on the important stuff: items that do not match the brain's predictions.

Consider the following scenario. Walking in the street, you are suddenly bundled into the trunk of a car by three strangers, and

In almost everyone, all the aspects of consciousness are unified into one. Interestingly, people with severe epilepsy who have had surgery to separate the hemispheres of the brain sometimes experience two simultaneous states of consciousness.

rushed to their hideout. You end up tied to a chair, gagged with a bag over your head. The moment they remove it, you are terrified but your brain springs into action, making predictions and quickly mapping your environment and your kidnappers. Everything is registered: the location's sights and smells, the taste of the gag, the men's appearance and mood, your own fear. Your thoughts, emotions, and perceptions are held together in one conscious field, and information from all the senses is brought together seamlessly into a whole experience. The terror you feel is fueled by your anticipation of what might happen—your brain predicts from the context and the flow of events what might be coming next, and tries to work out how to respond. From the information you receive, and from your understanding of how the world works, you anticipate injury and even death. But then someone realizes that you are not their target and you are let go. What your ordeal has shown you is that, while scientists like to separate out the different senses to study them, that is not how we experience them. This realization has profound implications in wine tasting.

Different Ways to Taste Wine

It is wrong to think that there is just one ideal way of approaching wine. Wine can be tasted, and tasting notes can be written, in different ways, so it is a question of matching the approach to the task. In the wine trade, we tend to focus on analytical tasting, where we are attempting to grapple with the identity of the wine, and capture its qualities in the form of words. This is a challenge: it is almost as if we have to unlearn what comes naturally. In the normal way of flavor perception, the brain processes a lot of the sensory information before we are even aware of it.

As professional wine tasters, we interrogate the wine. As we pay attention to its various attributes and look for things that we think might be there, we are likely to see details that other people, simply drinking the wine, might miss. This is where our previous experience is so important in what we do.

Tasting analytically is like trying to get behind a movie set to see all the workings that are going on—assuming those workings are accessible to us at all. As wine tasters we learn about the characteristics of different types of wine and form prototypes of them, which we then use as a guide when we taste. In chapter 3 we saw how we develop smell and flavor "objects" in our brains. This seems to be how we understand the world around us: we manipulate objects that we recognize and confer specific properties on them. If we see a car, we immediately recognize what it is, and as long as it behaves as we would expect we feel free to take no more notice of it. The "objects" in our brains might be sights, or smells (for example, "coffee" is a complex smell mixture that varies, but we immediately recognize it as coffee), or the result of a combination of senses (for example, the shape, color, smell, texture, and taste of an orange). From a very early age we begin to identify and learn about different objects, and we retain the ability to form new objects when presented with novel stimuli in adulthood. We store representations of these objects and, as we model the world around us, we access them and manipulate them. Objects give us a rapid way of understanding all the sensory input that we encounter. Wine professionals probably have encoded various smell objects—or even wine-type objects—in their brains. When we taste, we often recognize the wine straight away by using one of these objects, and later on we fill in the details. For example, we might have a representation of Sauvignon Blanc that is cognitively accessible, and which we retrieve when we taste a wine that we think is, or know to be, a Sauvignon Blanc. Wine tasting, for experts, is prototypical.

To taste analytically, the environment should be controlled. We discussed how important the context and the setting are in terms of shaping our perception. For analytical tasting, these factors have to be controlled as much as possible, and the environment should be as neutral as possible. But only up to a point. Evidence shows that if we try to assess a wine free of the influence of color, eliminating visual cues by using black glasses, for example, the quality of our judgments is likely to suffer.

A study from Dominique Valentin and colleagues at the University of Burgundy looked at the effect of color on judgments of quality in wine professionals. Twenty-three French and twenty-three New Zealand professionals tasted Pinot Noir wines from France and New Zealand. Surprisingly, they found that for professional tasters wine color was not a major factor, though it was a little more important to the French judges than the New Zealanders. Judgment of quality was largely shared across the two cultures. Interestingly, the black glasses were a problem: they muted or attenuated the judges' verdicts on the wines. Professionals rarely if ever judge wine without sight cues, which may be why the tasters struggled to taste with the same discriminatory range from the black glasses. Thus, analytical tasting depends on screening out all the extrinsic influences that

Whether we like it or not, the context of the wine-drinking experience changes the nature of our perception. It is no different from how our enjoyment of food in a restaurant is influenced by whether the restaurant itself is welcoming or bleak.

Perception of Wine Is Influenced by the Tasting Environment

Wine tasting is affected by environmental factors that distract the senses: food smells, music, and colored lights are just some examples. The best environments for wine tasting lack all of these.

can affect our perception of wine, while keeping wine tasting within the bounds of a naturalistic setting. Incongruency is bad: we have an accepted way of tasting wine, and we are comfortable with it, and as far as we can we should stick to it. Analytic tasting is best in a clean, well-lit environment, without any competing smells in the background. The wine should be served in a suitable glass, at the right temperature for the wine style. Most would agree that music should not be playing, and the environment should be as free of other distractions as possible.

The London-based Wine & Spirit Education Trust (WSET) is one of the world's leading providers of wine education. WSET teaches a structured approach to tasting that is helpful because, when you first start tasting wine and thinking about what you are tasting, it is very difficult to be able to put the sensations into words. The structured, checklist approach helps to focus attention on different aspects of the wine in order to capture the wine in tasting notes (see p.200). The notes do not make for good reading, but they are a good place to begin. WSET also publishes a lexicon of words for use in notes. This sort of training is valuable at the beginning stage, but it does present a simplistic view of the perception of wine. After all, one person's "medium acidity" is another person's "high acidity," and it is hard to rule on emergent properties of wines such as harmony, elegance, and balance. It reflects a fundamentally reductionist view of wine, isolating and identifying individual components one by one. Such an approach results in a description of the wine, but it fails to capture its essence, because the wine is a whole. As tasters learn their craft, they recognize the limitations of structured tasting notes and progress to a more mature view of how to record the essence of the wine as a whole.

Writing a tasting note for a wine is a bit like trying to describe the features of a thief or assailant to the police. It is a very difficult thing to do because that is not how we see people, or how our brains work. The way we model the world, creating a "reality" in our brains that is subsequently informed by what is actually out there, makes us all potentially unreliable witnesses.

Tasting for Enjoyment

If we are primarily seeking pleasure from our wine-drinking experience, we need to take an almost opposite approach to that of analytical tasting. In this book we have discussed how much our perception is influenced by factors other than wine chemistry. For pleasure, instead of neutralizing the environment and reducing all the variables to get the best out of wine, we need to use the environment to our advantage. Stripped of context, the wine in the glass only delivers a portion of what it is able to. We need to

WSET Diploma Systematic Approach to Tasting Wine®

APPEARANCE

Clarity/brightness		clear – hazy / bright – dull (faulty?)
Intensity		pale – medium – deep
Color	White	lemon-green – lemon – gold – amber – brown
	Rosé	pink – salmon – orange – onion skin
	Red	purple – ruby – garnet – tawny – brown
Other observations		e.g. legs/tears, deposit, petillance, bubbles

NOSE

Condition	clean – unclean (faulty?)
Intensity	light – medium(-) – medium – medium(+) – pronounced
Aroma characteristics	e.g. fruits, flowers, spices, vegetables, oak aromas, other
Development	youthful – developing – fully developed – tired/past its best

PALATE

Sweetness		dry – off-dry – medium-dry – medium-sweet – sweet – luscious
Acidity		low – medium(-) – medium – medium(+) – high
Tannin	level	low – medium(-) – medium – medium(+) – high
	nature	e.g. ripe/soft vs unripe/green/stalky, coarse vs fine-grained
Alcohol		low – medium(-) – medium – medium(+) – high
		fortified wines: low – medium – high
Body		light – medium(-) – medium – medium(+) – full
Flavor intensity		light – medium(-) – medium – medium(+) – pronounced
Flavor characteristics		e.g. fruits, flowers, spices, vegetables, oak flavors, other
Other observations		e.g. texture, balance, other
		sparkling wines (mousse): delicate – creamy – aggressive
Finish		short – medium(-) – medium – medium(+) – long

CONCLUSION   ASSESSMENT OF QUALITY

Quality level	faulty – poor – acceptable – good – very good – outstanding
Reasons for assessment	e.g. structure, balance, concentration, complexity, length, typicity

Assessment of readiness for drinking / potential for aging

Level of readiness for drinking/ potential for aging	too young – can drink now, but has potential for aging – drink now: not suitable for aging or further aging – too old
Reasons for assessment	Reasons for assessment e.g. structure, balance, concentration, complexity, length, typicity

The wine in context

Origins / variety /theme	for example: location (country or region), grape variety or varieties, production methods, climatic influences
Price category	inexpensive – mid-priced – high-priced – premium – super-premium
Age in years	answer with a number not a range or a vintage

Notes for students: For lines where the entries are separated by hyphens—students must select one and only one of these options. For lines starting with "e.g." where the entries are separated with commas—the list of options are examples of what students might wish to comment on. Students may not need to comment on each option for every wine.

WSET Diploma Wine-Lexicon: supporting the WSET Diploma Systematic Approach to Tasting Wine®

DESCRIBING FLAVORS
Be accurate: think in terms of clusters
Be complete: don't just rely on lists of descriptive words; aim to describe the quality and nature of the flavors too

Primary aroma/flavor clusters: the flavors of the grape

Key Questions	Descriptive Words	
Are the flavors delicate or aromatic? simple/neutral or complex? generic or well-defined? fresh or cooked/baked? underripe or ripe or overripe?	Floral	acacia, honeysuckle, chamomile, elderflower, geranium, blossom, rose, violet, iris
	Green fruit	green apple, red apple, gooseberry, pear, peardrop, custard apple, quince, grape
	Citrus fruit	grapefruit, lemon, lime, (juice or zest?), orange peel, lemon peel
	Stone fruit	peach, apricot, nectarine
	Tropical fruit	banana, lychee, mango, melon, passion fruit, pineapple
	Red fruit	redcurrant, cranberry, raspberry, strawberry, red cherry, red plum
	Black fruit	blackcurrant, blackberry, bramble, blueberry, black cherry, black plum
	Dried fruit	fig, prune, raisin, sultana, kirsch, preserved fruits
	Herbaceous	green bell pepper (capsicum), grass, tomato leaf, asparagus, black currant leaf
	Herbal	eucalyptus, mint, medicinal, lavender, fennel, dill
	Pungent spice	black/white pepper, licorice, juniper

Secondary aroma/flavor clusters: the flavors of winemaking

Are the flavors from yeast, MLF, oak or other?	Yeast (lees, autolysis, flor)	biscuit, bread, toast, pastry, brioche, bread dough, cheese, yogurt
	MLF	butter, cheese, cream, yogurt
	Oak	vanilla, cloves, nutmeg, coconut, butterscotch, toast, cedar, charred wood, smoke, resinous
	Other	smoke, coffee, flint, wet stones, wet wool, rubber

Tertiary aroma/flavor clusters: the flavors of time

Do the flavors show deliberate oxidation, fruit development or bottle age?	Deliberate oxidation	almond, marzipan, coconut, hazelnut, walnut, chocolate, coffee, toffee, caramel
	Fruit development (white)	dried apricot, marmalade, dried apple, dried banana, etc.
	Fruit development (red)	fig, prune, tar, cooked blackberry, cooked black cherry, cooked strawberry, etc.
	Bottle age (white)	petrol, kerosene, cinnamon, ginger, nutmeg, toast, nutty, cereal, mushroom, hay, honey
	Bottle age (red)	leather, forest floor, earth, mushroom, game, cedar, tobacco, vegetal, wet leaves, savory, meaty, farmyard

Other observations: sweetness, acid, tannin, alcohol and texture

Use sparingly to create a more complete description do not use instead of low – medium – high etc.	Sweetness	austere, thin, drying, unctuous, cloying, sticky
	Acidity	tart, green, sour, refreshing, zesty, flabby
	Alcohol	delicate, light, thin, warm, hot, spirity, burning
	Tannin	ripe, soft, unripe, green, stalky, coarse, chalky, grippy, fine-grained, silky
	Texture	stony, steely, mineral, oily, creamy, mouthcoating

CONCLUSION ASSESSMENT OF QUALITY
Use evidence: don't just give an opinion, every comment must be backed up with evidence
Be comprehensive: comment on all of the key elements that contribute to quality

Note to students: in certain papers the examiners ask for other concluding remarks too. Read the Candidate Assessment Guide for details.

Primary aroma/flavor clusters: the flavors of the grape

How well balanced are the components of the wine?	Structural balance	acid, alcohol, tannin vs. flavor, sugar	
	Other	• intensity, length of finish	• expressiveness
		• complexity, purity	• potential to age

Note to students: The WSET Level 4 Wine-Lexicon is designed to be a prompt and a guide for students. It does not attempt to be comprehensive and it does not need to be memorized or slavishly adhered to.

add to the wine-drinking experience all the contextual cues that can help make the experience even better.

There are two core skills in being a critic. First there is the ability to taste accurately and describe what is there. Then there is the ability to appraise the wine critically: this is "taste" in the sense of having good or bad taste in appraising wine.

This is where we can be creative. It is as if the choices we make about how and where we serve the wine are part of the drinking process. We acknowledge that we have a part to play in enjoying wine. For example, we might decant the wine, not only because it may change the wine's characteristics in a positive way, but also because the process builds anticipation and expectation. In this context we might choose lighting and music that help to create a positive atmosphere, and ideally we would choose to drink the wine in good company, with good food. For analytical tasting, the presence of food, with the attendant smells, would be a disaster, but for enjoying wine it can be a real positive. We may choose the wine to match the appropriate food and occasion, or even vice versa. This is integrating wine into its context, and making use of our knowledge of the multisensory nature of flavor in a creative way. Philosopher John Dilworth suggests that wine tasting is akin to improvisatory theater, and that we have a creative role to play in the process. It is up to us to make the experience as pleasurable as possible. Alcohol itself helps to release our natural inhibitions and give us greater freedom to do this.

The third possibility is to taste wine as a critic. This is a little different to analytical tasting, even though it also has scrutiny and analysis at its core. For critics to be useful, they have to bear in mind that their readers are not going to be looking at wines analytically: they are drinking for pleasure. Yet critics often have to taste large flights of similar wines and require some sort of analytical approach to discern the differences between them, and assign quality ratings. A good critic will learn to extrapolate from the artificial setting of analytic tasting (with spitting, of course) to the naturalistic setting in which their readers will be consuming wine, at home or in a restaurant.

How Can We Become Better Tasters?

In chapter 6 we looked at whether some people are naturally gifted at tasting wine, and so at an advantage, or whether wine tasting is a skill that can be improved and refined. The tentative conclusions are that as long as you have a normally operating sense of smell and taste, you have the potential to become an expert wine taster.

There is evidence that our senses can be sharpened with practice, partly because of increased sensitivity and partly because of better cognitive abilities that help us make sense of what we are experiencing. There is evidence that with practice we can also become better at recognizing smells, although many studies suggest that experts are no better at naming odors than novices. Developing an improved language for wine not only allows us to capture and share our experiences more effectively, but also changes what we perceive. The sorts of templates we have stored in our brains for different wine types can help us structure our approach to tasting, and focus on what is in the glass.

I am a firm believer in interrogating the wine: and, like a journalist or chat-show host conducting an interview, the better the questions, the more revealing and interesting the responses. A novice taster and a wine expert sharing the same glass together, even if they possess equally keen senses, will experience the wine quite differently. Experts will find a lot more in the wine, and will articulate their perceptions more clearly. Experts have learned how to interrogate and interpret the liquid in the glass, and they have the ability to add to the sensations they experience, using their own knowledge of tasting similar kinds of wines.

The achievements of professional wine tasters are evidence that the diminished role that smell plays in the West is a cultural phenomenon rather than a universal biological diminution of olfaction in humans. The traditional idea that humans are poor at olfactory discernment relative to animals is being supplanted by the realization that we are actually very good at it: it is just that we use it for different purposes. The facts suggest that the more we emphasize smell, the more attention we pay to it, and the more we develop our smell language, the better we will get at it. Olfaction is a neglected sense, but it should not and need not be so.

What kind of training could make us better tasters? Despite the multimodal nature of wine perception, smell is giving us most of the information, so smell is worth focusing upon. To train ourselves, we should smell as many things as possible, and obtain a pack of various wine-related smells to improve our smell memory. Ann Noble, inventor of the Wine Aroma Wheel, has published a set of "standards," examples of the various odors in the aroma wheel, that can be prepared at home. Active, directed training like this, smelling the environment around is, will reap rewards. And,

For the purposes of wine criticism, the two key questions are as follows. First, is there a standard of taste in wine? That is, can there be a broad, universal agreement about which wines are the best? And second, are there wine critics who fulfill the role as ideal critics?

of course, we should taste lots of wines, write notes on them, and actively seek to develop our vocabulary for wine. It is useful to taste with others, discuss the wines with them, and study their tasting notes. Which notes do you think capture the wine most effectively? When others describe elements of a wine that you have in front of you, how well do they do it? What do you get in the wine yourself? Taste blind, for sure, but also taste sighted. Sometimes tasting the same wine first blind and then sighted is a very effective strategy. By all means have your own template and apply it to the wine you are tasting, but make sure you actually taste the wine in front of you and give it a chance to speak. A good interviewer is mostly a listener rather than a talker. With wine, you ask good questions, and give the wine the time it needs to answer.

What Is an Ideal Wine Critic? Do They Even Exist?

We have seen that wine may be analyzed, or drunk for pleasure, but what of the wine critic who claims the authority to inform and

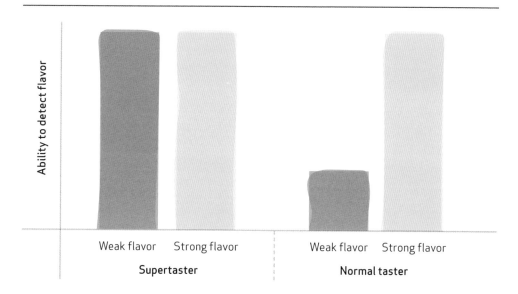

Supertaster Versus Normal Taster

This stylized diagram shows how supertasters and normal tasters differ in their experience of flavor.

Supertasters experience flavors so intensely that they are not necessarily ideal as critics.

persuade others of the qualities of wines? Do wine critics have anything in common with critics of paintings, sculpture, and other arts? And can a common standard be applied to them all?

In the eighteenth century, the British philosopher David Hume, trying to solve the problem of how to define standards in aesthetics, asked: Is there such a thing as true beauty, and how do we separate good taste from bad? In his influential work, *Of the Standard of Taste* (1757), Hume was the first to outline what he believed to be a true standard of taste and beauty, that is, agreement among what he called "ideal critics." He then spelled out that in such a critic five factors should coexist: "strong sense, united to delicate sentiment, improved by practice, perfected by comparison, and cleared of all prejudice." For the wine-tasting critic, the one attribute that stands out here is "delicacy of sentiment" (or taste), which occurs when "the organs are so fine, as to allow nothing to escape them; and at the same time so exact as to perceive every ingredient in the composition."

Hume developed the idea of the "ideal critic," illustrating his idea of "delicacy of taste" with the example of wine tasting:

"One obvious cause, why many feel not the proper sentiment of beauty, is the want of that delicacy of imagination, which is requisite to convey a sensibility of those finer emotions. This delicacy everyone pretends to: Everyone talks of it; and would reduce every kind of taste or sentiment to its standard. But as our intention in this essay is to mingle some light of the understanding with the feelings of sentiment, it will be proper to give a more accurate definition of delicacy, than has hitherto been attempted. And not to draw our philosophy from too profound a source, we shall have recourse to a noted story in Don Quixote. It is with good reason, says Sancho to the squire with the great nose, that I pretend to have a judgment in wine: this is a quality hereditary in our family. Two of my kinsmen were once called to give their opinion of a hogshead, which was supposed to be excellent, being old and of a good vintage. One of them tastes it; considers it; and after mature reflection pronounces the wine to be good, were it not for a small taste of leather, which he perceived in it. The other, after using the same precautions, gives also his verdict in favour of the wine; but with the reserve of a taste of iron, which he could easily distinguish. You cannot imagine how much they were both ridiculed for their judgment. But who laughed in the end? On emptying the hogshead, there was found at the bottom, an old key with a leathern thong tied to it."

Hume argues that the ability to discern elusive elements, such as (in this case) iron and leather, is a key requirement in the ideal critic, and is the foundation of taste in the cerebral sense:

"The great resemblance between mental and bodily taste will easily teach us to apply this story. Though it be certain, that beauty and deformity, more than sweet and bitter, are not qualities in objects, but belong entirely to the sentiment, internal or external; it must be allowed, that there are certain qualities in objects, which are fitted by nature to produce those particular feelings. Now as these qualities may be found in a smaller degree, or may be mixed and confounded with each other, it often happens, that the taste is not affected with such minute qualities, or is not able to distinguish all the particular flavors, amidst the disorder, in which they are presented. Where the organs are so fine, as to allow nothing to escape them; and

Changing Tastes: How a Palate Might Evolve

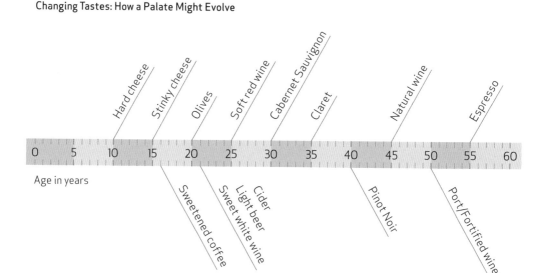

at the same time so exact as to perceive every ingredient in the composition: This we call delicacy of taste, whether we employ these terms in the literal or metaphorical sense. Here, then, the general rules of beauty are of use; being drawn from established models, and from the observation of what pleases or displeases, when presented singly and in a high degree: And if the same qualities, in a continued composition and in a small degree, affect not the organs with a sensible delight or uneasiness, we exclude the person from all pretensions to this delicacy."

Thus, in being able to distinguish nuances of flavor and interpret them in the context of good winemaking, a good wine critic resembles a good art critic who is sensitive to particulars of established principles of beauty. But what sets out the ideal wine critic from the rest of us, in this view? While we want our wine critics to possess qualities such as refined taste, good knowledge, and freedom from bias, it is not clear that we can consider a critic's rating to be a property of a wine. This is because we all bring something to the wine-tasting process. Even critics who are attempting to be impartial, and set their preferences to one side, will not be immune to a degree of "autobiography" in their ratings.

The Problem of Changing Personal Responses

Hume suggests that aesthetics is a matter of discerning objective facts, but that is not necessarily so. Matthew Kieran, Professor of Philosophy and the Arts at the University of Leeds, points out that small shifts in our responses can have very telling results:

> "Small refinements in the same discriminatory capacities and responses can radically affect our experience and appreciation of art works [and wine, equally] in ways we are all familiar with. I once thought of the work of Mondrian's late to middle period as good graphic design, nice but flat arrangements of line and color, and was puzzled as to why people thought his work particularly valuable as art. Yet once I was able to see some of these pictures as representing abstracted projections of pictorial space the structure of my experience was transformed and my evaluation inverted radically from thinking them no good to rating them pretty highly."

The verdicts of ideal wine critics, in Hume's sense, will stand the test of time: the wines they recognize as great will also be acknowledged as great by their peers, and by the majority of those who follow them. If we accept the ideal critic thesis as applied to wine, then this suggests that the top wine critics have especially refined powers, and that their judgments are pretty much objective statements of fact.

Kieran argues that the concept of the ideal critic is challenged by the problem of ideal critics not being able to agree closely enough to establish interpersonal standards of taste. He also makes an intrapersonal case against the ideal critic, referring to how we all change our views over time. "When our capacity for imaginative sympathy is extended with respect to types of people, social or ethnic groups we may previously have found it hard to be sympathetic towards, this can radically affect our experience with and evaluation of works that manifest attitudes towards them."

He argues that not only do our aesthetic sensibilities change with time, we also go through "phases" in our appreciation of things. This fluid nature of artistic appraisal on the part of the individual casts doubts on whether we can find an ideal critic.

If we go through shifts and phases in our appreciation of things, who is to say that the critic is not also on some sort of journey? We all have changing tastes in literature and music, and often developing a taste for one genre lessens our interest in another.

The same is likely to be true for wine. As we progress in our journey with wine, our tastes change; at different times we develop relationships with different wines. It can be like a doomed love affair. When you first discover Alsace Gewürztraminer, for example, you might find it amazingly exotic and exciting. Then you have a discovery phase where you find out all about it, and your relationship deepens and broadens. But one day you find yourself developing a taste for Riesling, and as you drink more of it the lure of Gewürztraminer slowly fades. One day you break up, thinking "I'm sorry, Gewürz, it's not you, it's me. I have changed."

Our propensity to change throws into doubt the notion of the ideal wine critic making normative judgments of wine from a position of superior aesthetic sensibility. It reduces the scope of the role of the critic, but I think this is quite desirable. Yes, we find critics useful as guides, particularly when we share their aesthetic system, and their preferences and style judgments align with ours. But we cannot expect them to deliver absolute, objective verdicts on the wines they are tasting.

Kieran postulates that our experience and appreciation of works (whether they be literature, music, or wine) can be affected by the way our aesthetic character has developed. When it comes to wine, liking some wines will preclude us from liking others. He suggests that shifts and radical breaks often occur in the development of our aesthetic character, and suddenly being able to appreciate certain kinds of works will make it harder to appreciate others. Emotional and personal history is involved in the development of aesthetic character. "Thus the way we appreciate a work can be as revealing about ourselves as much as it is about the work. This has implications not just for criticism as such, because a kind of impersonal appreciation and evaluation is shown to be a myth, but for a standard picture of fixing artistic value. If appreciation cannot but be personal in this way, then the notion of an ideal appreciator divested of personal idiosyncrasies fixing the relative ordering merits of artworks is useless."

Hume himself recognized how people's tastes differ, and also change with time, and how our preferences can get in the way of our attempts to criticize in a universal, even-handed way:

"One person is more pleased with the sublime; another with the tender; a third with raillery. One has a strong sensibility to blemishes, and is extremely studious of correctness: Another has a more lively feeling of beauties, and pardons twenty absurdities and defects for one elevated or pathetic stroke. The ear of this man is entirely turned towards conciseness and energy; that man is delighted with a copious, rich, and harmonious expression . . . Comedy, tragedy, satire, odes, have each its partisans, who prefer that particular species of writing to all others. It is plainly an

I might encounter a group of Cabernet Sauvignons from the Napa Valley, made from grapes harvested very late; they may have sweet, overripe, jammy flavors, with 15.5 percent alcohol or more, pronounced acidification, and evidence of aging in 100 percent new oak for too long. Is it down to personal preference if I give them low scores? Or is it part of a critic's job to offer an opinion on the style, and on how successful the wine is in that style? Are some wine styles illegitimate?

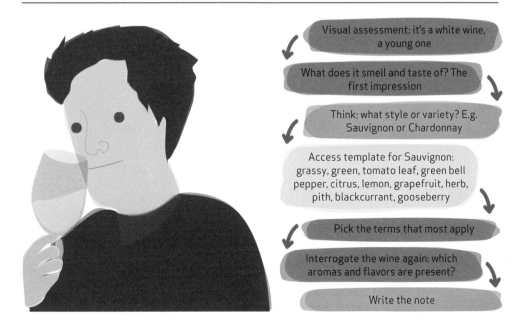

Visual assessment: it's a white wine, a young one

What does it smell and taste of? The first impression

Think: what style or variety? E.g. Sauvignon or Chardonnay

Access template for Sauvignon: grassy, green, tomato leaf, green bell pepper, citrus, lemon, grapefruit, herb, pith, blackcurrant, gooseberry

Pick the terms that most apply

Interrogate the wine again: which aromas and flavors are present?

Write the note

error in a critic, to confine his approbation to one species or style of writing, and condemn all the rest. But it is almost impossible not to feel a predilection for that which suits our particular turn and disposition. Such preferences are innocent and unavoidable, and can never reasonably be the object of dispute, because there is no standard, by which they can be decided."

In an article in the journal *Contemporary Aesthetics* (2005), Francis Raven asked whether supertasters would make good candidates as ideal critics in Hume's sense. Supertasters almost certainly have greater sensitivity to tastes, but does this actually make them poor "ideal" tasters in that they do not appreciate strong flavors, and will naturally be disinclined to praise some elements of wine, such as tannins?

Raven argues that with appropriate "gustatory education," the supertaster can overcome their personal, biological prejudices and consequently become an ideal critic. But if their critical ability is reducible to their personal tastes, then the supertaster's enhanced abilities are as much of a burden as an asset. The question is, can anyone criticize something fairly if they do not enjoy it? Is it possible for critics to somehow separate their personal tastes from their critical ones, and learn to evaluate things they do not enjoy in a robust, fair way? The fact that wine appreciation is a learned taste that must be acquired brings education into the equation. With education it is possible that, despite our biological leanings, we can acquire the ability to taste critically in a way that stretches beyond personal preferences. If this is the case, then a supertaster with superior taste buds may be at a small advantage, as long as it is possible for them to separate their personal and critical tastes.

How Do We Decide What Is Good?

There comes a point where even the most open-minded wine critic is obliged to make a judgment based on a style. Some argue that it is possible to distinguish the good from the bad within each genre of wine, even though you may not care for that style. So, I might not like oaky Rioja all that much, but if I were asked to judge a flight of Rioja, I hope I would be able to grade them in a professional manner. In other instances there will be wines disliked by me but liked by others, and which I may find very difficult to judge in this way.

Wine is not easy to pigeonhole. However, I find that with my colleagues there is a fairly close agreement about which wines are good and which are not. Certainly, for standard, commercial wines, gradations of quality seem to be relatively easy to determine. But once you get to the realm of fine wine—wines worth talking about, to use Hugh Johnson's definition—it all becomes a lot more complicated. Here we are entering into the territory of aesthetic systems, and it is probably best to see these as overlapping circles, like Venn diagrams.

If there is anything that can save objectivity in wine perception, it is that wine appreciation is largely learned, rather than innate. As professionals we usually do not embark on our journey into wine tasting alone. Instead we drink with others, we are helped into the wines at tastings, and we read what others think about the wines we are drinking. Of course, for most people, wine is just wine, and admittedly there is little to be said about commodity or commercial wines. That is not to criticize the genre of commodity wine or its professionals, but rather to suggest that it is necessary to segment the market place in our discussions of wine.

So, different rules apply to different segments of the wine market, but once it comes to fine wine, their overlapping aesthetic systems can cause problems. For example, the average European palate and the average North American palate are very different. Although this is inevitably a generalization, the preference in the United States is for red wines that have a sweeter fruit profile, that offer ripe fruit and smoothness of structure. Europeans prefer their wines a little less sweet, with more freshness and less alcohol, and a savory twist. When professionals from both sides of the Atlantic taste the same wines together, there is usually a clearly divergent group preference beyond individual likings.

For example, in May of 2006, simultaneous tastings were held in London and the Napa Valley, California, to celebrate the thirtieth anniversary of the ground-breaking Judgment of Paris event in which, in 1976, Californian wines were put on the map when French judges rated them higher than Bordeaux and Burgundy, tasted blind. In the reenactment, intended to be a celebration rather than a competition, the U.S. judges favored riper, sweeter wines than did the European judges. Also, whenever I have tasted

with my U.S. counterparts, I have often found that our palates diverge over the issue of ripeness in red wines. That is now changing, as wine culture becomes more global and less insular. These days, everyone travels more, and certainly for the younger generation (which in wine terms means anyone under fifty) there is more of a shared, international culture of fine wine. But it must be emphasized that this is in reference to fine wine; in commodity wine the rules are quite different.

Taste is inextricably linked with culture. For sure, there are biological differences between peoples, and these are important. But more important is that flavor perception is learned. Human brains perceive objects in the environment that they can manipulate, and this makes sensory processing much faster and efficient. In this way, some of the biological differences between peoples are overridden during the intersubjective process of learning about wine. For example, some 7 percent of males of Northern European ancestry are red-green colorblind. Yet this does not seem to cause them much difficulty, mainly because, from baby stage onward, they learn by recognizing objects in the environment. As we have seen, humans are not simply measuring devices, and the processing of our sensory systems includes many steps at which we can compensate for anomalies at the receptor level. For a "normal" adult, suddenly to lose this color discrimination would be very disorienting. But anyone who has never had it would not notice the loss in the same way.

We must also consider the broader notion of cultural taste, which is not a static thing. Just as with art and music, fashionable taste in wines changes over time. It is the role of the critic to arbitrate on matters of taste; if they get it right, people will follow them, but if they are out of step with the culture's broader sense of taste, people will not. It is also true that some critics will appeal to particular groups of wine enthusiasts, while the writings of others will be followed by different groups.

How Should Wine Tasting and Communication Change?

Having considered all the aspects of wine tasting covered in this book, what are the implications? What changes are necessary in the practice of wine appreciation and the ways in which we communicate about wine? These are some suggestions.

First, we need to acknowledge the importance of words, and also be wary of the impact that words have on the experience of wine. We have seen the importance of language in shaping experience, and noted how cognitive approaches, including the use of words, influence expert assessment of wine by defining and shaping their experience. Words help us to understand wine better, but they can also get in the way of and distort our actual experience of wine if we begin to use them too quickly.

Second, we need to recognize the extent of interindividual differences in flavor perception, but at the same time not make too much of them. The differences do matter, but education and participation in the shared community of wine help to overcome them to a degree. If we ignore the differences in perception altogether, we will have problems communicating about wine. Wine education, certainly, should do more to take the differences into account. There is already recognition of this factor in wine marketing, but exploitation of its potential is incomplete.

We also need to recognize that as well as interindividual differences in flavor perception, there are differences within individuals. Our tastes change over time as we learn more about wine and have greater exposure to specific wines. This is a very important point that is often missed. Then there is the importance of context: the impact on the perception of wine of all that is going on around wine. We might think that as professionals we will not be influenced by the environment in which the tasting takes place, but we are, in quite significant ways; we are simply unable to filter out these factors.

Finally, we need to recognize that reality as we experience it is something that we create ourselves. This is a rather startling and unsettling idea, but we each create our own realities, and this applies to flavor as well. We are not simple measuring devices. We bring a lot to the wine-tasting process, and enjoying or assessing a wine is a partnership in which we play an active role. Wine tasting is not as simple as we might have thought it was, but with this complexity comes an extra layer of richness.

Pleasure and Communication

Evelyn Waugh's novel *Brideshead Revisited* (1945), which is set in the 1930s, contains a lovely passage about the enjoyment of wine

and making attempts to turn its taste into words. Charles Ryder, the narrator, is recalling an idyllic summer he spent with his friend Sebastian Flyte, at the latter's family home, Brideshead, during which they discovered wine together. Surely, this is the way to write about experiencing the flavors of wine:

> "We had bottles brought up from every bin and it was during those tranquil evenings with Sebastian that I first made a serious acquaintance with wine and sowed the seed of that rich harvest which was to be my stay in many barren years. We would sit, he and I, in the Painted Parlour with three bottles open on the table and three glasses before each of us; Sebastian had found a book on wine-tasting, and we followed its instructions in detail. We warmed the glass slightly at a candle, filled it a third high, swirled the wine round, nursed it in our hands, held it to the light, breathed it, sipped it, filled our mouths with it and rolled it over the tongue, ringing it on the palate like a coin on a counter, tilted our heads back and let it trickle down the throat. Then we talked of it and nibbled Bath Oliver biscuits and passed on to another wine; then back to the first, then on to another, until all three were in circulation and the order of the glasses got confused, and we fell out over which was which, and we passed the glasses to and fro between us until there were six glasses, some of them with mixed wines in them which we had filled from the wrong bottle, till we were obliged to start again with three clean glasses each, and the bottles were empty and our praise of them wilder and more exotic.
>   '. . . It is a little, shy wine like a gazelle.'
>   'Like a leprechaun.'
>   'Dappled, in a tapestry window.'
>   'Like a flute by still water.'
>   '. . . And this is a wise old wine.'
>   'A prophet in a cave.'
>   '. . . And this is a necklace of pearls on a white neck.'
>   'Like a swan.'
>   'Like the last unicorn.'"

Wine. That beautiful liquid, rich in culture and interest, with its own transformative powers that set us free to enjoy it, interrogate it, and explore its many dimensions. We try to capture and tame it, but it resists. Our attempts to reduce it and control it, and create an impression of objectivity through the use of scientific-sounding descriptions, inevitably end up dashed against the rocks.

Our senses of taste, smell, and touch—the derided proximal senses—are fighting back. It used to be thought that they are incapable of true aesthetic appreciation, but we are now realizing our error. In time wine may come to be regarded as the archetypal proximal-sense art object. In our brave attempts to understand wine, let us not limit it and try to put it into a box.

Most importantly, though, the study of wine tasting, with its large intersubjective component (we all love to talk about our experience with wine) has helped to change the understanding of perception itself. Which, ultimately, is what this book is all about.

Glossary

Acidity

A major component of wine, made up of volatile and nonvolatile acids. The main acids in wine are tartaric and citric, with the former commonly being added during winemaking when there is not enough naturally present in the grapes. One volatile acid, acetic acid, is regarded as a fault if its levels get too high. At lower levels acetic acid can add aromatic interest and a sweet smell to a wine. Acid is perceived as sharpness in the mouth; too little of it and a wine can seem flabby, too much and it seems tart.

Aesthetics

The study of beauty, and of good and bad taste. There is some debate about whether or not wine qualifies as an aesthetic object.

Anosmia

The inability to smell. It is surprisingly disabling, and people who have lost their sense of smell often become depressed.

Astringent

The sensation of drying or puckering in the mouth caused by compounds such as tannins.

Autolysis

The decomposition of dead yeast cells, which releases flavor components into wine. Autolysis is important during the production of sparkling wines made by the Champagne method, in which the yeast cells involved in the second fermentation of the wine remain in the bottle for an extended period. It results in biscuity, bready, and toasty flavors.

Barrel aging

Wines are often aged in a barrel. This has two effects. First, there are flavor compounds from the barrel that can end up in the wine, such as lactone, which smells of vanilla, and guaiacol, which has a spicy, smoky flavor. Second, barrel aging allows a low level of oxygen exposure, which can have beneficial effects on the wine. Fermentation of white wines is often done in barrels because this seems to improve the integration of the wood flavors. Barrel fermentation can be done with reds also, but it is more tricky because of the presence of skins.

Bitterness

Wines can have bitter flavors, and these are desirable in the right context. Perception of tannin is often thought to be of bitterness.

Blind tasting

Tasting wine without knowing what it is. "Single blind" means that you know the wines in a tasting but not the order in which they are poured. "Double blind" means that you have no prior information about the wines.

Brettanomyces (Brett)

A yeast species that often grows in red wines after fermentation has finished, creating aromas and flavors of farmyards. In low doses it is not unappealing in certain wines, but at higher doses it makes all wines that have it taste the same. It is a big problem for winemakers, and is especially a risk where the pH is high or no sulfur dioxide is used during maturation.

Cognitive

The mental processes involved in how we think, perceive, judge, and reason, as opposed to reacting on an emotional level.

Dosage

A sugar solution added to a sparkling wine after *dégorgement* (disgorgement, when dead yeast cells from the second fermentation are removed as a plug) that acts to determine the final sweetness. The solution used in Champagne may be wine with sugar added, or barrel-fermented wine or brandy.

Elegant

An elegant wine is one where flavors are understated and where they merge together to create a wine that is subtle and refined. Many attain this status through aging.

Extraction

The process by which compounds are extracted from grape skins to impart tannin, color, and various flavor components.

Flavor

The perceived qualities of a food or drink. Flavor consists of input from taste, smell, touch, vision, and even hearing. These elements combine to create a perception.

Flor

A yeast that forms a thick film on the surface of a wine, especially in the production of Fino and Manzanilla sherries. It is made up of strains of the wine yeast *Saccharomyces cerevisiae*, which feeds off components of the wine and creates the nutty, appley, salty flavors that are typical of these sherries.

Harmonious

A harmonious wine is one where all the elements work together seamlessly.

Hedonic

Relating to pleasure.

Higher-order processing

The way the brain processes sensory information obtained by our sense organs, extracting only the most useful bits of information to inform what we experience.

Lactic acid bacteria

The bacteria responsible for the second (malolactic) fermentation that takes place in most red and many white wines. The bacteria have significant effect on the flavor of wine.

Lees stirring

The process of stirring dead yeast cells (lees) at the bottom of a barrel or tank. This creates flavor and texture through the release of compounds such as mannoproteins, and also scavenges oxygen. However, the process of opening a barrel and stirring wine can also add oxygen, so sometimes barrels are rolled without opening them to get the beneficial effects without oxygen being added.

Length

The time for which a wine's flavor persists in the mouth after it has been swallowed or spat out. It is generally a good thing that a wine is "long," unless it also tastes bad. "Short" is a perjorative term for a wine whose flavor stops abruptly. Wine writers often add these terms to tasting notes when they have nothing left to say.

Maceration

The process by which flavor compounds and their precursors are extracted from grape skins either before, during, or after fermentation. All red wines have some contact between the skins and flesh or they would not be colored. The length of contact, and also the presence or absence of physical processes such as pumping wine onto the skins, influences how much color and tannin will be extracted into the wine.

Malolactic fermentation

Bacterial fermentation that changes malic acid into lactic acid. This has the effect of reducing the perception of acidity. In addition, the bacterial fermentation can also have a sensory impact. For example, it can produce diacetyl, which has a buttery flavor that is not always desirable.

Almost all red wines have a malolactic fermentation, and some whites also.

Nose

A term used to describe the smell of a wine.

Objective

Wine tasting is objective when the result (or perception) is directly linked to properties of the object (the wine). It is independent of the perceiver, but would be shared by a group of tasters. *See also* Subjective.

Odorant

The term for a molecule that can be smelled.

Olfactory receptors

Proteins present in the membranes of nerve cells located in the nose. They recognize—by an as yet unknown mechanism—features of smell molecules and then create an electrical signal that is transmitted and processed by the brain to create the perception of smell.

Oxidation

A wine fault caused by excessive exposure to oxygen during winemaking, or by a wine closure that allows too much oxygen transmission after bottling. Oxidation can manifest itself as an appley character, associated with a change in color (whites get darker, reds take on a brick-red or brown hue), and also aromas of nuts and caramel.

Palate

Term for the way we experience wine when it is in our mouths.

Perception

The processing of information from our sensory organs in order to form a mental representation of the environment.

Pheromone

A smell molecule that causes a behavioral response. They are common in animals but their presence in humans is disputed because we lack the vomeronasal organ.

Plonk

An informal term for inexpensive commodity wine.

Precise

A precise wine is one where all elements are defined with tight parameters in the flavor space.

Reduction

A wine fault caused by above-threshold levels of smelly volatile sulfur compounds. This is one of the most complex of all wine faults because the compounds can have positive attributes in the right wines at the right levels. Reduced wines can smell of rotten eggs, matchsticks, garlic, or roast coffee.

Satiety

When we have had enough of something, we are satiated. This is specific to the substance in question. For example, we may have had our fill of steak, but still have an appetite for chocolate.

Smashable

An informal term used to describe a wine that is very easy to drink.

Spoofulated

An informal term to describe a wine that is affected by overripeness, too much new oak, and too much of everything generally, so that any sense of place it had has been lost. Often abbreviated as "spoofy."

Staves

Planks of oak used instead of barrels to impart oaky flavor. They are often placed in tanks where the use of barrels would be too expensive. Staves often produce disappointing results, giving a hard, angular clove and cedar edge to the wine.

Structure

Refers to the backbone of the flavor of a wine. A red wine has structure from tannins and acidity, while a white wine has structure from acidity alone. Young wines destined for long aging are typically well structured.

Subjective

Influenced by personal beliefs and opinions. A perception is subjective if it based on the perceiver's own viewpoint, rather than being based on the object of the perception. Wine tasting is widely seen as subjective rather than objective: it depends on our own viewpoint, which we might not expect to be shared by others. *See also* Objective.

Sulfides

Volatile sulfur compounds can be smelly and contribute to the wine fault known as reduction. Sometimes "sulfides" is used as a catch-all term to refer to volatile sulfur compounds generally.

Sulfites

These are added to wine as sulfur dioxide (SO2), which prevents oxidation, but some are generated by yeasts during fermentation. Most wines have SO2 added, especially at the bottling stage, but some are made without added sulfites. These are fragile and must be handled carefully, but they can be wonderful in flavor.

Supertaster

A person with an enhanced ability to taste bitter compounds such as propylthiouracil and phenyl-thiocarbamide is described as a supertaster. About 25 percent of people fall into this group, however, they might not make the best wine critics as they are very sensitive to components such as tannins.

Sweetness

Many wines contain residual sugar. This adds sweetness, but the degree to which the sweetness is perceived depends on the acidity. For example, "brut" Champagne with very high acidity and a sugar level of around 10 grams per liter can taste quite dry, while a still red wine with the same sugar level (usually added as grape juice concentrate) will have a distinct sweetness to it.

Tannin

A catch-all term to describe plant compounds that have the ability to bind proteins. These compounds, found in the skins of grapes, display complex behaviors in wine. Tannins are perceived as astringent and also slightly bitter—causing a drying sensation in the mouth. White wines are rarely tannic unless they have been fermented with the skins, which occurs very rarely. It is important that red wines should not have excessive tannin, as then they will be unbalanced.

Tastant

The term for a molecule that we can taste.

Terroir

A French term referring to how a place can express itself in a wine. This is usually a result of the effect of the vineyard's environment (soil, mesoclimate, microclimate) on the way that grapes are grown. Given sympathetic winemaking, these differences are expressed in the wine, but such terroir can be easily lost.

Texture

The way wine feels in the mouth—richly textured, smoothly textured, silky, or layered, for example.

2, 4, 6-trichloroanisole (TCA)

A chemical compound largely responsible for the fault of "cork taint." It makes wine smell musty, like damp cardboard or old cellars.

Umami

The taste of pleasant savoriness imparted by an amino acid, glutamate.

References

Books

Allhoff, F. ed., 2009. *Wine and Philosophy: A symposium on thinking and drinking.* John Wiley & Sons.

Burnham, D. and Skilleås, O. M., 2012. *The Aesthetics of Wine.* John Wiley & Sons.

Burr, C., 2004. *The Emperor of Scent: A true story of perfume and obsession.* Random House Incorporated.

Classen, C., Howes, D., and Synnott, A., 1994. *Aroma: The cultural history of smell.* Taylor & Francis.

Cytowic, R. E., 1993. *The Man Who Tasted Shapes.* Jeremy P. Tarcher

Frith, C., 2013. *Making Up the Mind: How the brain creates our mental world.* John Wiley & Sons.

Huron, D. B., 2006. *Sweet Anticipation: Music and the psychology of expectation.* MIT Press.

Sacks, O., 1998. *The Man Who Mistook His Wife for a Hat: And other clinical tales.* Simon & Schuster.

Shepherd, G. M., 2013. *Neurogastronomy: How the brain creates flavor and why it matters.* Columbia University Press.

Smith, B. C. ed., 2007. *Questions of Taste: The philosophy of wine.* Oxford University Press, Inc.

Spence, C. and Piqueras-Fiszman, B., 2014. *The Perfect Meal: The multisensory science of food and dining.* John Wiley & Sons.

Stoddart, D. M., 1990. *The Scented Ape: The biology and culture of human odour.* Cambridge University Press.

Journal articles – Chapter 1

Beeli, G., Esslen, M., and Jäncke, L., 2005. Synaesthesia: When coloured sounds taste sweet. *Nature*, 434(7029), pp.3838.

Bor, D., Rothen, N., Schwartzman, D.J., Clayton, S., and Seth, A. K., 2014. Adults can be trained to acquire synesthetic experiences. *Scientific Reports*, 4.

Colizoli, O., Murre, J. M., and Rouw, R., 2012. Pseudo-synesthesia through reading books with colored letters. *PLOS One*, 7(6), p.e39799.

Dael, N., Perseguers, M. N., Marchand, C., Antonietti, J. P., and Mohr, C., 2006. Put on that colour, it fits your emotion: Colour appropriateness as a function of expressed emotion. *Quarterly Journal of Experimental Psychology*, 69, pp.1–32.

Demattè, M. L., Sanabria D., and Spence, C., 2006. Cross-modal associations between odors and colors. *Chemical Senses*, 31(6), pp.531–538.

Deroy, O. and Spence, C., 2013. Why we are not all synesthetes (not even weakly so). *Psychonomic Bulletin & Review*, 20(4), pp.643–664.

Gilbert, A. N., Martin, R., and Kemp, S. E., 1996. Cross-modal correspondence between vision and olfaction: The color of smells. *The American Journal of Psychology*, pp.335–351.

Gottfried, J. A. and Dolan, R. J., 2003. The nose smells what the eye sees: Crossmodal visual facilitation of human olfactory perception. *Neuron*, 39(2), pp.375–386.

Levitan, C. A., Ren, J., Woods, A. T., Boesveldt, S., Chan, J. S., McKenzie, K. J., et al, 2014. Cross-cultural color-odor associations. *PLOS ONE*, 9e101651.

Maric, Y. and Jacquot, M., 2013. Contribution to understanding odour–colour associations. *Food Quality and Preference*, 27(2), pp.191–195.

Morrot, G., Brochet, F., and Dubourdieu, D., 2001. The color of odors. *Brain and Language*, 79(2), pp.309–320.

Palmer, S. E., Schloss, K. B., Xu, Z., and Prado-Leon, L., 2013. Music-color associations are mediated by emotion. *Proceedings of the National Academy of Sciences*. 110, pp.8836–8841.

Parr, W. V., White, G. K., and Heatherbell, D. A., 2003. The nose knows: Influence of colour on perception of wine aroma. *Journal of Wine Research*, 14(2–3), pp.79–101.

Schifferstein, H. N. and Tanudjaja, I., 2004. Visualising fragrances through colours: The mediating role of emotions. *Perception*, 33(10), pp.1249–1266.

Spence, C., Richards, L., Kjellin, E., Huhnt, A. M., Daskal, V., Scheybeler, A., Velasco, C., and Deroy, O., 2013. Looking for crossmodal correspondences between classical music and fine wine. *Flavour*, 2(1), pp.1–13.

Watson, M. R., Akins, K. A., Spiker, C., Crawford, L., and Enns, J., 2014. Synesthesia and learning: a critical review and novel theory. *Hum Neurosci.* 2014 Feb 28; 8:98.

Chapter 2

Buck, L. and Axel, R., 1991. A novel multigene family may encode odorant receptors: A molecular basis for odor recognition. *Cell*, 65(1), pp.175–187.

Bushdid, C., Magnasco, M. O., Vosshall, L. B., and Keller, A., 2014. Humans can discriminate more than 1 trillion olfactory stimuli. *Science*, 343(6177), pp.1370–1372.

Chaput, M. A., El Mountassir, F., Atanasova, B., Thomas-Danguin, T., Le Bon, A. M., Perrut, A., Ferry, B., and Duchamp-Viret, P., 2012. Interactions of odorants with olfactory receptors and receptor neurons match the perceptual dynamics observed for woody and fruity odorant mixtures. *European Journal of Neuroscience*, 35(4), pp.584–597.

Chrea, C., Grandjean, D., Delplanque, S.,

Cayeux, I., Le Calvé, B., Aymard, L., Velazco, M. I., Sander, D., and Scherer, K. R., 2009. Mapping the semantic space for the subjective experience of emotional responses to odors. *Chemical Senses*, 34(1), pp.49–62.

Gangestad, S. W. and Thornhill, R., 1998. Menstrual cycle variation in women's preferences for the scent of symmetrical men. *Proceedings of the Royal Society of London B: Biological Sciences*, 265(1399), pp.927–933.

Garver-Apgar, C. E., Gangestad, S. W., Thornhill, R., Miller, R. D., and Olp, J. J., 2006. Major histocompatibility complex alleles, sexual responsivity, and unfaithfulness in romantic couples. *Psychological Science*, 17(10), pp.830–835.

Gilad, Y., Wiebe, V., Przeworski, M., Lancet, D., and Pääbo, S., 2004. Loss of olfactory receptor genes coincides with the acquisition of full trichromatic vision in primates. *PLOS Biol*, 2(1), p.e5.

Matsui, A., Go, Y., and Niimura, Y., 2010. Degeneration of olfactory receptor gene repertoires in primates: No direct link to full trichromatic vision. *Molecular Biology and Evolution*, 27(5), pp.1192–1200.

Meister, M., 2015. On the dimensionality of odor space. *Elife*, 4, p.e07865.

Running, C. A., Craig, B. A., and Mattes, R. D., 2015. Oleogustus: The unique taste of fat. *Chemical Senses*, p.bjv036.

Wedekind, C., Seebeck, T., Bettens, F., and Paepke, A. J., 1995. MHC-dependent mate preferences in humans. *Proceedings of the Royal Society of London B: Biological Sciences*, 260(1359), pp.245–249.

Chapter 3

Brochet, F. and Dubourdieu, D., 2001. Wine descriptive language supports cognitive specificity of chemical senses. *Brain and Language*, 77(2), pp.187–196.

Castriota-Scanderbeg, A., Hagberg, G. E., Cerasa, A., Committeri, G., Galati, G., Patria, F., Pitzalis, S., Caltagirone, C., and Frackowiak, R., 2005. The appreciation of wine by sommeliers: A functional magnetic resonance study of sensory integration. *Neuroimage*, 25(2), pp.570–578.

O'Doherty, J., Rolls, E. T., Francis, S., Bowtell, R., McGlone, F., Kobal, G., Renner, B., and Ahne, G., 2000. Sensory-specific satiety-related olfactory activation of the human orbitofrontal cortex. *Neuroreport*, 11(4), pp.893–897.

Pazart, L., Comte, A., Magnin, E., Millot, J. L., and Moulin, T., 2014. An fMRI study on the influence of sommeliers' expertise on the integration of flavor. *Frontiers in Behavioral Neuroscience*, 8(358).

Plassmann, H., O'Doherty, J., Shiv, B., and Rangel, A., 2008. Marketing actions can modulate neural representations of experienced pleasantness. *Proceedings of the National Academy of Sciences*, 105(3), pp.1050–1054.

Polak, E. H., 1973. Multiple profile-multiple receptor site model for vertebrate olfaction. *Journal of Theoretical Biology*, 40(3), pp.469–484.

Spence, C., Velasco, C., and Knoeferle, K., 2014. A large sample study on the influence of the multisensory environment on the wine drinking experience. *Flavour*, 3(8), pp.1–12.

Stevenson, R. J. and Wilson, D. A., 2007. Odour perception: An object-recognition approach. *Perception*, 36(12), pp.1821–1833.

Weiskrantz, L., Warrington, E. K., Sanders, M. D., and Marshall, J., 1974. Visual capacity in the hemianopic field following a restricted occipital ablation. *Brain*, 97(1), pp.709–728.

Chapter 4

Benkwitz, F., Nicolau, L., Beresford, M., Wohlers, M., Lund, C., and Kilmartin, P. A., 2012. Evaluation of key odorants in Sauvignon blanc wines using three different methodologies. *Journal of Agricultural and Food Chemistry*, 60(25), pp.6293–6302.

Benkwitz, F., Tominaga, T., Kilmartin, P. A., Lund, C., Wohlers, M., and Nicolau, L., 2011. Identifying the chemical composition related to the distinct flavor characteristics of New Zealand Sauvignon blanc wines. *American Journal of Enology and Viticulture*, pp.ajev–2011.

Escudero, A., Campo, E., Fariña, L., Cacho, J., and Ferreira, V., 2007. Analytical characterization of the aroma of five premium red wines. Insights into the role of odor families and the concept of fruitiness of wines. *Journal of Agricultural and Food Chemistry*, 55(11), pp.4501–4510.

King, E. S., Dunn, R. L., and Heymann, H., 2013. The influence of alcohol on the sensory perception of red wines. *Food Quality and Preference*, 28, pp.235–243.

Meillon, S., Dugas, V., Urbano, C., and Schlich, P., 2010. Preference and acceptability of partially dealcoholized white and red wines by consumers and professionals. *American Journal of Enology and Viticulture*, 61, pp.42–52.

Sáenz-Navajas, M. P., Campo, E., Culleré, L., Fernández-Zurbano, P., Valentin, D., and Ferreira, V., 2010. Effects of the nonvolatile matrix on the aroma perception of wine. *Journal of Agricultural and Food Chemistry*, 58(9), pp.5574–5585.

Whiton, R. S., and Zoecklein, B. W., 2000. Optimization of headspace solid-phase microextraction for analysis of wine aroma

compounds. *American Journal of Enology and Viticulture*, 51, pp.379–382.

Chapter 5

Bajec, M. R. and Pickering, G. J., 2008. Thermal taste, PROP responsiveness, and perception of oral sensations. *Physiology & Behavior*, 95(4), pp.581–590.

Ballester, J., Patris, B., Symoneaux, R., and Valentin, D., 2008. Conceptual vs. perceptual wine spaces: Does expertise matter? *Food Quality and Preference*, 19(3), pp.267–276.

Bartoshuk, L. M., 2000. Comparing sensory experiences across individuals: Recent psychophysical advances illuminate genetic variation in taste perception. *Chemical Senses*, 25(4), pp.447–460.

Ericsson, K. A., Krampe, R. T., and Tesch-Römer, C., 1993. The role of deliberate practice in the acquisition of expert performance. *Psychological Review*, 100(3), p.363.

Hayes, J.E., Bartoshuk, L. M., Kidd, J. R., and Duffy, V. B., 2008. Supertasting and PROP bitterness depends on more than the TAS2R38 gene. *Chemical Senses*, 33(3), pp.255–265.

Hoover, K. C., Gokcumen, O., Qureshy, Z., Bruguera, E., Savangsuksa, A., Cobb, M., and Matsunami, H., 2015. Global survey of variation in a human olfactory receptor gene reveals signatures of non-neutral evolution. *Chemical Senses*, 40, pp.481–488.

Logan, D. W., 2014. Do you smell what I smell? Genetic variation in olfactory perception. *Biochemical Society Transactions*, 42(4), pp.861–865.

Macnamara, B. N., Hambrick, D. Z., and Oswald, F. L., 2014. Deliberate practice and performance in music, games, sports, education, and professions: A meta-analysis. *Psychological Science*, 25(8), pp.1608–1618.

Mauer, L., 2011. Genetic determinants of cilantro preference. (Doctoral dissertation.)

Parr, W. V., Green, J. A., White, K. G., and Sherlock, R. R., 2007. The distinctive flavour of New Zealand Sauvignon blanc: Sensory characterisation by wine professionals. *Food Quality and Preference*, 18(6), pp.849–861.

Pickering, G. J., Simunkova, K., and DiBattista, D., 2004. Intensity of taste and astringency sensations elicited by red wines is associated with sensitivity to PROP (6-n-propylthiouracil). *Food Quality and Preference*, 15(2), pp.147–154.

Sáenz-Navajas, M. P., Ballester, J., Pêcher, C., Peyron, D., and Valentin, D., 2013. Sensory drivers of intrinsic quality of red wines: Effect of culture and level of expertise. *Food Research International*, 54(2), pp.1506–1518.

Tempere, S., Cuzange, E., Malak, J.,

Bougeant, J. C., de Revel, G., and Sicard, G., 2011. The training level of experts influences their detection thresholds for key wine compounds. *Chemosensory Perception*, 4(3), pp.99–115.

Wysocki, C. J., Dorries, K. M., and Beauchamp, G. K., 1989. Ability to perceive androstenone can be acquired by ostensibly anosmic people. *Proceedings of the National Academy of Sciences*, 86(20), pp.7976–7978.

Chapter 6

Chrea, C., Valentin, D., Sulmont-Rossé, C., Nguyen, D. H., and Abdi, H., 2005. Semantic, typicality, and odor representation: A cross-cultural study. *Chemical Senses*, 30(1), pp.37–49.

Delplanque, S., Coppin, G., Bloesch, L., Cayeux, I., and Sander, D., 2015. The mere exposure effect depends on an odor's initial pleasantness. *Frontiers in Psychology*, 6.

Dilworth, J., 2008. Mmmm... not aha! Imaginative vs. analytical experiences of wine. *Wine and Philosophy*, Allhoff, F. ed., 2009, pp.81–94.

Grabenhorst, F., Rolls, E. T., Margot, C., da Silva, M. A., and Velazco, M. I., 2007. How pleasant and unpleasant stimuli combine in different brain regions: Odor mixtures. *The Journal of Neuroscience*, 27(49), pp.13532–13540.

Hodgson, R. T., 2008. An examination of judge reliability at a major US wine competition. *Journal of Wine Economics*, 3(02), pp.105–113.

Prescott, J., Kim, H., and Kim, K. O., 2008. Cognitive mediation of hedonic changes to odors following exposure. *Chemosensory Perception*, 1(1), pp.2–8.

Chapter 7

Blakemore, S. J., Wolpert, D., and Frith, C., 2000. Why can't you tickle yourself? *Neuroreport*, 11(11), pp.R11–R16.

Libet, B., Gleason, C. A., Wright, E. W., and Pearl, D. K., 1983. Time of conscious intention to act in relation to onset of cerebral activity (readiness-potential). *Brain*, 106(3), pp.623–642.

Saygin, A. P., Chaminade, T., Ishiguro, H., Driver, J., and Frith, C., 2012. The thing that should not be: predictive coding and the uncanny valley in perceiving human and humanoid robot actions. *Social Cognitive and Affective Neuroscience*, 7(4), pp.413–422.

Chapter 8

Caballero, R., 2009. Cutting across the senses: Imagery in winespeak and audiovisual promotion. *Multimodal Metaphor*, 11, p.73.

Lehrer, K. and Lehrer, A., 2008. Winespeak or critical communication? Why people talk about wine. *Wine and Philosophy*, Allhoff, F. ed., 2009, pp.111–122.

Majid, A. and Burenhult, N., 2014. Odors are expressible in language, as long as you speak the right language. *Cognition*, 130(2), pp.266–270.

Negro, I., 2012. Wine discourse in the French language. *RAEL: revista electrónica de lingüística aplicada*, 11, pp.1–12.

Olofsson, J. K. and Gottfried, J. A., 2015. The muted sense: Neurocognitive limitations of olfactory language. *Trends in Cognitive Sciences*, 19(6), pp.314–321.

Olofsson, J. K., Hurley, R. S., Bowman, N. E., Bao, X., Mesulam, M. M., and Gottfried, J. A., 2014. A designated odor–language integration system in the human brain. *The Journal of Neuroscience*, 34(45), pp.14864–14873.

Suárez Toste, E., 2007. Metaphor inside the wine cellar: On the ubiquity of personification schemas in winespeak. *Metaphorik. de*, 12(1), pp.53–64.

Wnuk, E. and Majid, A., 2014. Revisiting the limits of language: The odor lexicon of Maniq. *Cognition*, 131(1), pp.125–138.

Chapter 9

Shapin, S., 2012. The tastes of wine: Towards a cultural history. *Rivista di estetica*, 51(3), pp.49–94.

Shepherd, G. M., 2015. Neuroenology: How the brain creates the taste of wine. *Flavour*, 4(19).

Smith, B., 2012. Perspective: Complexities of flavour. *Nature*, 486(7403), pp.S6–S6.

Chapter 10

Kieran, M., 2008. Why ideal critics are not ideal: Aesthetic character, motivation, and value. *The British Journal of Aesthetics*, 48(3), pp.278–294.

Raven, F., 2005. Are supertasters good candidates for being Humean ideal critics? *Contemporary Aesthetics*, 3.

Valentin, D., Parr, W. V., Peyron, D., Grose, C., and Ballester, J., 2016. Colour as a driver of Pinor noir wine quality judgments: An investigation involving French and New Zealand wine professionals. *Food Quality Preference*, 48, pp. 251–261.

Index

Acknowledgments

Books like this are the fruit of many years of discovery and exploration, and the discussion of ideas with numerous colleagues. If I were to name all those who've contributed to this book, it would be a huge list, and it's inevitable that I'd forget some people. So this is a general acknowledgment of all of the scientists, winegrowers, commissioning editors, wine trade people, and wine writing peers who have shared ideas with me, listened to my rather crazy ideas, and who have been patient enough to respond to phone calls and emails with a generous, sharing spirit. Specifically, I'd like to thank Hilary Lumsden for helping to get this book commissioned, and also for starting the ball rolling when she was working with Mitchell Beazley by suggesting I write my first book on wine science (more than a decade ago now). Thanks to my

PhD supervisor, Dr. Tony Stead, for giving me the chance to experience science first hand for three years working in a lab, and to my colleagues at the Ciba (latterly Novartis) Foundation, where I worked as an editor for fifteen years, mixing with high-caliber scientists from around the world. Many of the ideas presented in this book began at this time: the chance to listen in on top scientists discussing their work sowed many seeds. Of the many people I've cited in this book, I'd specifically like to thank two, who both went out of their way to help more than they strictly needed to: Professors Barry Smith and Ole Martin Skilleås. Thanks also to the team at Quintessence, and especially Sophie Blackman, who has project managed this book very efficiently. And special thanks to HH. This book is dedicated to Danny and Louis.